1995

INCREMENTALISM
AND PUBLIC POLICY

INCREMENTALISM AND PUBLIC POLICY

MICHAEL T. HAYES

Colgate University

Longman
New York & London

Incrementalism and Public Policy

Longman, 95 Church Street, White Plains, N.Y. 10601

Associated companies:
Longman Group Ltd., London
Longman Cheshire Pty., Melbourne
Longman Paul Pty., Auckland
Copp Clark Pitman, Toronto

Senior editor: David J. Estrin
Production editor: Victoria Mifsud
Cover design: Susan J. Moore
Text art: Pencil Point Studio
Production supervisor: Richard C. Bretan

Library of Congress Cataloging-in-Publication Data

Hayes, Michael T., 1949–
      Incrementalism and public policy / Michael T. Hayes.
      p.   cm.
      Includes indexes.
      ISBN 0-8013-0576-4
      1. Political planning—United States.   2. United States—Politics
and government.   I. Title.
JK271.H498   1991
353.07′2—dc20   91-8863
                                                                      CIP

1 2 3 4 5 6 7 8 9 10-MA-9594939291

Contents

Preface

This book was originally conceived as an introduction to what I saw as the five most useful models for understanding policy-making in the United States—those reviewed in Chapters 2 through 6 of this volume. However, various readers of an earlier draft of this manuscript questioned the inclusion of these models and the exclusion of others. In responding to their comments, I realized once again just how strongly I believed in the value of the models I had selected for inclusion; these were precisely the models I wanted to cover in a text for upper-level undergraduates and beginning graduate students. Nevertheless, I was forced to examine why I believed these five models to be especially valuable in understanding contemporary American policy-making.

One answer is that they focus on institutions and actors traditionally thought to be important by students of American politics: interest groups, political parties, big business, the effects of the Constitution on policy-making, and so on. In this sense, the book is very much within the mainstream of American political science and might just as well be entitled *Great Theories of American Politics*.

In addition, the use of models to analyze the effects of various institutions and actors on policy-making highlights the ways in which different factors interact to influence outcomes—for example, the tendency under our system for corporate power to be maximized at the implementation stage by the effects of federalism. In this vein, these five models each have something different (and significant) to tell us about agenda setting, policy formulation, policy implementation, and policy change. Thus this book should be of value to courses focusing on the stages of the policy process as well as to courses emphasizing models of policy-making. In my courses, students are usually assigned a series of research papers in which they analyze a policy of their choice from the perspective of two or three of the models. If comments on teaching evaluations are a reliable guide, this seems to be a valuable teaching tool.

Beyond this, however, I have long had a scholarly interest in the limits on rational decision making and the consequent tendency to make policy by bargaining and compromising among a multiplicity of contending interests, usually resulting in incremental outcomes. The five models reviewed in Part I are thus significant precisely because they identify constraints that operate to preclude major policy change under normal circumstances. The analysis in Part II goes one step further to examine the conditions under which nonincremental change can occur within the American political system.

This book has taken several years to write. In the course of its development, it has changed enormously, profiting from the reactions of students in various courses over the years, both at Colgate and at Rutgers, as well as the comments of various anonymous outside reviewers. In addition, the manuscript was read in whole or in part by Allan J. Cigler, Ted Harpham, Roby Harrington, Dale Krane, Charles E. Lindblom, Robert Rothstein, and Joe Wagner, all of whom gave me invaluable advice.

I am particularly indebted to David Estrin at Longman, both for understanding immediately what I was trying to accomplish with the book and for providing excellent and timely advice at various stages along the way. Likewise, Victoria Mifsud of Longman has helped guide me through the production stages of the project.

I also want to express my appreciation to Cindy Terrier and Thelma Mayer here at Colgate, for typing and printing off countless drafts of book chapters over the past several years. I am also grateful to Colgate for two different one-semester leaves and for a matching grant to acquire a personal computer, which greatly facilitated the completion of the manuscript.

Finally, I would like to dedicate this book to my wife, Candace, who bore much of the burden of my near-obsession with perfecting this book over the past couple of years, and to our two sons, Timothy and Terry, for being such irrepressible sources of amusement and sheer joy.

INCREMENTALISM
AND PUBLIC POLICY

CHAPTER 1

Models of Policy Change

'

Public policy affects all of us. Governmental decisions influence how much we will pay in taxes, the kinds of weapons we acquire, the quality of our air and water, and the condition of our roads and bridges. At a less visible level, various public policies help to determine how much we will pay for heating oil, a loaf of bread, or a bag of sugar. They also affect the safety of air travel, the quality of automobile bumpers, the range of companies competing for our long distance telephone business, and the number of stations available on our television sets. In short, it is becoming increasingly difficult to think of an area of our lives that remains entirely untouched by government, even in the wake of the Reagan "revolution."

Understanding how and why policies are made is no simple matter. Policy-making at the national level is complex, and many policies involve the interaction of federal, state, and local govenments. As a consequence, the study of public policy differs from conventional approaches to American politics. Most specialists in the study of American politics focus narrowly on individual actors or institutions, such as Congress, the presidency, the courts, public opinion, or political parties. It is common to specialize even more narrowly within these subject areas, emphasizing the study of congressional committees, presidential staffing styles, or party leaderships in Congress, for example. While all this information is invaluable to an understanding of American politics, the student is left to pull these various strands together into a larger and more coherent picture of how policy is made.

By contrast, this book will focus on how a variety of actors and institutions interact to shape policy outcomes. In large part, this breadth of focus is necessitated by the fact that the framers of the Constitution gave us a system in which independent institutions are forced to share the fundamental powers of government; as a result, many institutions and actors are typically involved in an ongoing struggle over policy at any given point in time.

Beyond this, it must be recognized that policy-making is not simply a legislative or lawmaking activity. Following David Easton, we may define politics as the authoritative

1

allocation of values for society.[1] Policy outcomes are thus allocations of value for society inasmuch as they are binding on all citizens. They are authoritative (in a way that private corporate decisions, even where they affect large numbers of people, are not) because the state is recognized as the sole legitimate organ within society for making such binding allocations. Put another way, the state has a monopoly on the legitimate use of coercion to achieve its ends.

THE POLICY PROCESS

If policy-making involves the authoritative allocation of values for society, the study of public policy must look wherever this important activity takes place. In this vein, political scientists early in this century tried to draw a clear distinction between "politics" and "administration." It is now universally recognized that policy implementation and the writing of regulations are every bit as political an activity as lawmaking.[2] It follows that a focus on policy-making forces us to look not only at a multiplicity of actors and institutions but also at how issues flow over time through a more or less predictable series of stages or phases.

Various scholars have attempted to identify the stages involved in the policy process.[3] While their terminology differs, chiefly in where they choose to draw the line between one stage and another along the way, all are ultimately pointing to the same activities. For the purposes of this volume, we can identify three critical stages through which all policies must pass sooner or later: (1) problem identification and agenda setting, (2) policy adoption, and (3) policy implementation.

Problem Identification and Agenda Setting

Here the basic question has to do with how issues are selected for government attention and potential action. Why do issues arise when they do? Why not sooner? Or later? Why are some issues taken up while others are ignored? Who is involved in bringing problems to government for resolution?

The identification of public problems is anything but automatic. Problems must first be perceived and accurately defined before they can be solved. Unfortunately, many serious problems are neglected until they reach crisis proportions, and once perceived they may well be defined in various ways by different actors with sharply divergent self-interests. There is typically a struggle, in fact, as to how an issue should be defined and whether it is serious enough to warrant action.[4]

On this point, policy makers possess only a finite amount of time and attention. There are always many more problems pressing for attention than there is space on the agenda. The agenda-setting stage is thus a gateway for all the later stages. Important values are allocated for society at this stage in the sense that authoritative decisions must be made as to which issues will receive serious consideration, and which will not.

A useful terminological distinction may be drawn here between the "systemic" agenda and the "institutional" agenda. At any given time, the systemic agenda consists of all those issues advanced by one group or another for potential consideration by policy makers; the institutional agenda consists of the short list of items up for immediate and serious consideration within a particular institution (e.g., Congress). Insofar as many groups approach government seeking attention to their problems, lots of issues attain systemic agenda status; the institutional agenda is obviously a much shorter list. Given the need to pass through a number of institutional decision points under the American system (see Chapter 3), an issue must typically reach several institutional agendas to have a realistic chance of enactment. Thus the list of items with a serious chance to become law is shorter still.[5]

Policy Adoption

This stage involves the development of potential solutions to problems reaching the institutional agenda and the mobilization of support behind a preferred alternative. This is typically a legislative activity: the passage of a statute stating national policy on a given subject and the creation of new institutions where necessary to deal with a problem. As noted earlier, however, the authoritative allocation of values for society is not always completed within the passage of legislation. Ambiguous statutory mandates often give rise to new rounds of conflict in bureaucratic or judicial arenas; in a very real sense, then, policies are often formulated by the courts or administrative agencies.[6]

For the sake of clarity, in this book policy adoption will consistently refer to the struggle within Congress over the passage of a law. Failure to resolve all important issues at this stage will thus be said to create a subsequent struggle over policy implementation, to be discussed below. In any case, a multiplicity of actors will typically be involved in the policy adoption stage (as in all stages under the American system of checks and balances)—not just legislators, but also various representatives of the administration and the executive branch, interest groups, and so on.

Policy Implementation

As noted above, this is what happens after Congress passes a law. It consists primarily of the execution of policy, or the carrying out of the legislative intent of a statute (to the extent that there is a clear legislative intent). Often, this stage also involves the creation and mobilization of brand new institutions (cabinet departments, executive agencies or bureaus, or independent commissions) charged with this responsibility. Under our system, it also typically involves the participation of state and local governments, both in funding and administering programs.

Policy-making typically spills over into this stage. Clear and directive policy mandates leaving no room for administrative discretion are the exception rather than the rule. Even where the law is clear, as in the case of the 55 mile per hour speed limit enacted in 1973, local officials typically have a lot of latitude in enforcement. The operative speed limit (which *is* policy in this example in an important sense) is somewhere above 60 miles per hour and varies considerably from one place to another. Much the same thing could be said for most federal policies, ranging from the war on poverty to air pollution regulations:

effective policy diverges from the written law and varies from place to place. Thus administration is inevitably political, making the bureaucracy (and operatives in the field) extremely important political actors.

Increasingly in recent years, the federal courts have also become heavily involved in this stage of the policy process. A wide range of new interests have been granted standing to bring suits in federal courts over the past twenty-five years. The mobilization of a plethora of new citizens' groups representing consumers, environmentalists, the aged, and others over this same period has made for a dramatic increase in litigation in many policy areas, as groups with a stake in a given issue challenge particular actions by federal agencies or seek to prod these same agencies into undertaking new activities consistent with their legislative mandates.[7]

INCREMENTALISM AND POLICY CHANGE

Textbooks on the policy process typically include a subsequent stage here, focusing on policy evaluation and policy modification or termination. While such terminology seems to suggest a process of rational comparison of the costs and benefits of established policies (and many books have been written setting forth ostensibly objective criteria and methods for policy evaluation),[8] in reality this stage is no more systematically analytical than the preceding stages. Rather, it typically takes place through subsequent policy "cycles."[9] The failure of policies to completely solve problems, or the generation of unforeseen (and often unwanted) consequences, are simply dealt with in later years as new problems. It follows that a multiplicity of actors will be involved in this process of policy evaluation qua problem identification and that they will not necessarily agree on the effects of the policy any more than they agreed initially on objectives and problem definition.

The capacity of the political system to respond to pressing public problems with significant policy change (e.g., new policy initiatives or major modifications in existing policies) is so important as to merit extended treatment throughout this volume. A fundamental question here concerns the extent to which policy makers are ever really free to make major changes in past policies. At least one theorist, Charles Lindblom, has suggested that significant policy departures will typically be precluded by limits on available information and by the necessity to bargain and compromise in order to achieve political support for new initiatives. At best, he says, policy will change through a succession of small steps that may add up to a significant difference over a number of policy cycles.[10]

Whether this method of "disjointed incrementalism" is both inevitable and desirable will be the central focus of Chapter 2 and the recurring theme of the rest of the book. The drawbacks of incrementalism are nowhere better illustrated than in the nation's response to the energy crisis of the 1970s. A stable and dependable supply of energy is critically important to every American who drives a car, heats a home, turns on the lights at night, or watches television. Despite the importance of the issue and a wealth of indicators pointing to our steadily increasing dependence on imported oil, the energy crisis became salient only with the Arab oil embargo of 1973. Energy remained on the agenda under three different presidents as policy makers grappled with complex issues of oil and gas pricing, the environmental effects of increased reliance on coal, and the increasingly visible hazards of nuclear power. By 1980, after seven years of struggling with the issue, the nation still lacked any clear alternative to petroleum as a primary energy source, with the exhaustion of domestic oil supplies expected sometime in the 1990s. Although at least the beginning of a comprehensive energy policy was in place by the end of 1980, with the creation of a cabinet-level department of energy and various programs enacted to encourage conservation and subsidize the development of promising new energy technologies, during President Reagan's two terms in office, virtually all of the programs enacted during the 1970s were dismantled, and the energy issue receded from the institutional agenda. The Iraqi invasion of Kuwait in 1990 found the United States more dependent on foreign oil than ever before.[11]

Public policy regarding air pollution provides another example. Responding both to the mobilization of the environmental movement and a mass public suddenly aroused by the pollution issue, Congress passed legislation in 1970 that significantly expanded the federal government's role in pollution regulation and set technology-forcing standards for emissions with strict timetables for compliance. Almost twenty years later, however, improvements in air quality have been disappointing. With the onset of the energy crisis in the mid-1970s, automakers and smokestack industries were encouraged to seek extensions to the deadlines specified in the act. Performance standards applying only to newly constructed plants left older factories and utilities free to continue emitting dangerous levels of pollutants. Many major cities have failed to meet the mandated deadlines for compliance with ambient air quality standards, and for some (like Los Angeles) the prospects for ever satisfying the clean air standards are negligible. Environmentalists can point to incremental progress in cleaning up the nation's air, but recent scientific research identifying steadily worsening holes in the ozone layer, gradual global warming due to an alleged "greenhouse effect," and damage to forests and lakes in the northeast due to acid rain all suggest that incremental gains may no longer be sufficient.[12]

Our failure to deal more effectively with such problems also provides ammunition to critics of the Constitution, who charge that our system of checks and balances precludes a timely and coherent response to pressing social and economic problems. When President Carter left office in January 1981, scholars of the presidency and the American political system questioned whether increasing institutional fragmentation, the decline of our political parties, and the rise of special interest groups had combined to make it impossible to govern effectively, necessitating major structural reforms to meet the new conditions.[13] Certainly policy makers had failed to develop coherent and workable solutions to a wide range of problems plaguing the nation during that period: spiraling health care costs, energy, civil rights, welfare reform, and perhaps most important of all, high levels of inflation, unemployment, and interest rates.

In the wake of President Reagan's striking record of legislative successes and enduring personal popularity, few would now go so far as to suggest that the system is no longer governable. This may be the most important long-term legacy of his presidency. However, President Reagan also left a number of major problems for his successor, many of which are complex and vexing enough to tax the capacities of an ideal system to respond. The early legislative victories on tax cut and budget cut legislation have given rise to unprecedented budget and trade deficits that threaten the long-term health of the economy. Years of neglect of nuclear weapons plants have forced the closing of facilities producing tritium, without which our nuclear weapons are rendered harmless. The insolvency of increasing numbers of savings and loans seems likely to produce a federal bailout of perhaps one hundred billion dollars or more at a time when persistent federal deficits have already forced draconian cuts in many social programs. And the effects of industrial and automotive pollution, steadily accumulating for decades, cannot wait much longer for a solution. For most of these problem areas, incremental tinkering with existing policies would appear to be insufficient.

Clearly, we still need to do some hard thinking about how we formulate and implement public policies. Why are incremental policy outcomes so prevalent? Under what circumstances does our system tend to permit, or even facilitate, large change? What can be done, if anything, to enhance the capacity of the system to respond coherently and effectively to serious problems? Or is policy better made through a succession of small steps, as Lindblom suggests?

UNDERSTANDING AND EVALUATING THE POLICY PROCESS THROUGH MODELS

Understanding and evaluation of the policy process are inextricably interrelated because institutional arrangements can never be neutral; as E. E. Schattschneider observed, "organization is the mobilization of bias."[14] They remain nevertheless distinct tasks because we cannot intelligently evaluate the effects of alternative institutional arrangements—and their impact on various participants—until we understand fully how the system works.

The primary tool employed by political scientists to understand and evaluate the policy process is the conceptual model. A model is simply an attempt to represent reality by abstracting out of a confusing welter of events and observations the essential elements of an object or situation: to make some preliminary guesses as to what is relevant and what is not, and how things fit together.

Unfortunately, developing workable models of reality is extremely difficult, for the essential elements of any subject are not usually obvious but rather must be uncovered by the investigator. For example, an electric train is a scale model of its full-sized counterpart, complete with a locomotive, coal car, passenger compartment, and caboose. We all know what a train is and thus can readily recognize each of these elements and explain how they go together to make up a train. To a man from Mars observing a train for the first time, however, just what a train does and what is essential to it are not clear. Smudges of dirt and grease on the side of the boiler are potentially as vital as the coal in the coal car. The same might be said for a cow caught on the cowcatcher or for decorative markings on the sides of the cars.

When we try to interpret political events, we are all too often reduced to the state of our hypothetical man from Mars. Nothing ever takes place in a vacuum. We are typically confronted with a mass of information, much of which is irrelevant or only indirectly related to a proper understanding of the subject under investigation. Cause-and-effect relationships among the variables under examination are almost impossible to isolate, as these variables are typically related to a variety of other variables that may also be undergoing significant change. For example, was the sharp drop in inflation in the early 1980s a product of President Reagan's economic program, as the administration claimed, or was it really the result of the Federal Reserve Board's contractionary monetary policies? How much of this reduction was due to the failure of the OPEC cartel to maintain high oil prices during the same period? Similarly, are recent improvements in air quality primarily a function of effective antipollution laws or the economic recessions of the late 1970s and early 1980s, which closed many factories and lowered output in many others, thus reducing smokestack emissions? Should we attribute the sharp reduction in highway fatalities in recent years to laws mandating better safety equipment on new cars, the 55 mile per hour speed limit, or the increase in the legal drinking age in many states?

Because reality is so complex (and often subject to change), all models are subject to revision or replacement in light of experience and hard evidence. Faulty models are discarded. Promising but incomplete models are modified. Only to the extent that a model continues to "work" (i.e., helps you to deal purposefully and effectively with some aspect of reality) is it retained. Even within the so-called "hard sciences," much of what we take for granted as hard knowlege (for example, modern atomic theory) really consists of conceptual models that continue to be accurate and useful for the intellectual tasks currently at hand.[15]

Political science lags far behind the natural sciences in the development of such models. Our models are not very sophisticated, and there is little agreement on what our fundamental variables are or how they fit together. Rather, political scientists have developed a wide variety of competing models purporting to explain the policy process. None of these models, by itself, is sufficient to account for all cases of policy-making, or even all aspects of a single case. However, each of them has something to contribute to our understanding, and taken together they can teach us a great deal.

THE SOURCES OF INCREMENTALISM

This book will be primarily concerned with two questions, and thus the analysis naturally divides itself into two distinct parts. The first part of the book (Chapters 2 through 8) will be concerned with the sources contributing to incrementalism in policy-making under normal circumstances. The various models examined in these chapters all point to factors that normally operate to preclude large change. The second part (Chapters 9 through 12) will attempt to identify the factors giving rise, at least occasionally, to major policy departures.

We will limit our focus to a few models in Part I. This volume is not intended to be a comprehensive introduction to modeling within political science (or, more specifically, the field of public policy). Rather, it is primarily concerned with the prevalence and desirability of incrementalism in policy-making. The goal is to understand why major policy change is so difficult to attain and whether the political system can be changed to make it more adaptive.

We will begin in Chapter 2 with Charles Lindblom's influential theory of disjointed incrementalism. We start here because Lindblom asserts that inherent limitations on rationality and the inevitable need for bargaining and compromise among different interests preclude major policy departures for the most part within any political system. Institutional arrangements have nothing to do with Lindblom's argument; in his view, the prevalence of incrementalism is rooted in the breakdown of rationality, which is universal. For this reason, he also contends that incrementalism is a superior way to formulate policies—an argument that will be addressed throughout the rest of the book. We will see that Lindblom's theory explains much, but not all, of the incrementalism we observe in the policy process. We will be forced to look at additional models to complete our explanation of the extraordinary predominance of incremental policy outcomes.

In Chapter 3 we turn our attention to the effects of institutional arrangements on policy-making. More specifically, we will examine how the Consititution shapes policy-making in the United States. The classical model, set forth in *The Federalist Papers*,[16] provides a coherent theory of a "compound republic" based on underlying principles of checks and balances and federalism. We will see how this classical model shapes the stages of the process discussed earlier in this chapter, and how it further reinforces the tendencies toward incrementalism that would have been operative (according to Lindblom) under any institutional arrangements.

In Chapter 4 we will examine group theory, which served as the dominant paradigm within the field of American politics from the late 1940s to the mid-1960s and has undergone a renaissance in recent years.[17] The group theorists treat politics as a struggle among contending groups; policy is defined as the equilibrium emerging at any point in time among these contending interests. While such a conception of policy-making has much in common with Lindblom's theory of incrementalism, it nevertheless points our attention to some important issues underemphasized, although not entirely ignored, by Lindblom. Where the theory of incrementalism tends to treat the interaction among groups as a process of "mutual adjustment" leading to superior decisions under conditions of disagreement and limited rationality, group theory emphasizes the struggle for advantage. In short, it calls our attention to the problem of power and forces us to think more explicitly about the consequences of political inequality among contending interests. With regard to the prevalence of incremental policy outcomes, the central lesson of this chapter is that a significant part of the inertia we observe in policy-making stems from the political weakness of some groups within society (e.g., their failure to mobilize or lack of resources) that would otherwise exert pressure for significant policy change.

In Chapter 5 we will continue our focus on political inequality while shifting our attention to the special problem of the "privileged position" of business within capitalistic societies. This argument, advanced by Charles Lindblom and Ralph Miliband, holds in brief that policy makers are precluded from advocating public policies seriously threatening to corporate interests in view of the need to maintain economic prosperity, which only business can provide.[18] To some critics, Lindblom's current emphasis on corporate power seems at odds with his earlier theory of incrementalism, which stressed the interaction of a multiplicity of more or less equal actors in shaping policy outcomes. Properly understood, however, Lindblom's recent work identifies yet another factor contributing to incrementalism in the United States and other Western democracies: the inability of policy makers even to consider fundamental policy changes that could undermine capitalist interests.[19]

In Chapter 6 we will examine an alternative model that would be at once more responsive to majority sentiments and more likely to permit nonincremental change. Where the first four models covered in this volume all treat the policy process as some form of group struggle, the responsible parties model would make elections the pivot point of the policy process and thus make public policy accountable to rank-and-file voters rather than organized interest groups. Under such a system, political parties would compete for votes by taking clear and distinct positions on the issues of the day. Voters would thus control public policy by choosing one party (and its platform) over the other. While the development of responsible parties would make for a more responsive political system and doubtless facilitate nonincremental policy change, Chapter 6 suggests that it is another thing altogether to generate large change that is both intelligently formulated and sustainable over time. A good deal of incrementalism is inevitable within any political system due to inherent limitations on rational decision making that are universal.

Chapter 7 will trace the evolution of the 1977 federal law to regulate strip mining, the Surface Mining Control and Reclamation Act. This issue illustrates how the various constraints identified by the five models interact to prevent nonincremental change under normal circumstances. In particular, the surface mining case illustrates how major legislative initiatives can be eroded, not just in the policy adoption stage but also through intergovernmental policy implementation and subsequent policy cycles. Chapter 8 goes on to derive a series of generalizations from these models regarding the agenda-setting, policy adoption, and policy implementation stages, which are applied to the strip mining case study.

THE SOURCES OF POLICY CHANGE

Part II consists of four chapters devoted to identifying the circumstances under which nonincremental changes in policy do occur—at least occasionally—within our political system. Chapter 9 will explore the extent to which the requirements for rational-comprehensive decision making are essential preconditions for nonincremental change as well. Chapter 10 will identify four distinct categories of policy change and demonstrate that major policy change tends to take very different forms for familiar and unfamiliar issues. Chapter 11 employs the various lessons from Chapters 9 and 10, as well as the five models in Part I, to analyze efforts by presidents Nixon and Carter in the 1970s to effect a nonincremental change in the nation's welfare system. Chapter 12 will conclude the volume by deriving a series of generalizations regarding the sources of nonincremental change.

Ultimately, the central purpose of this book is to promote realistic expectations regarding the various sources of incrementalism and the prospects for large changes in policy. In effect, this is a book about constraints and possibilities in policy-making. We turn our attention in Part I to the constraints normally operating to preclude nonincremental policy change.

NOTES

1. David Easton, *A Systems Analysis of Political Life* (New York: Wiley, 1965), p. 21.
2. Paul H. Appleby, *Policy and Administration* (University: University of Alabama Press, 1949).
3. The major texts here are Charles O. Jones, *An Introduction to the Study of Public Policy,* 3d ed. (Belmont, Calif.: Wadsworth, 1984); James E. Anderson, *Public Policy-Making,* 3d ed. (New York: Holt, Rinehart, and Winston, 1984); and Garry D. Brewer and Peter DeLeon, *Foundations of Policy Analysis* (Homewood, Ill.: Dorsey, 1983).
4. See E. E. Schattschneider, *The Semi-Sovereign People* (New York: Holt, Rinehart, and Winston, 1960).
5. See Roger W. Cobb and Charles W. Elder, *Participation in American Politics* (Baltimore: Johns Hopkins University Press, 1975), pp. 82–93. See also John W. Kingdon, *Agendas, Alternatives, and Public Policies* (Boston: Little, Brown, 1984).
6. Theodore J. Lowi, *The End of Liberalism* (New York: Norton, 1969).
7. Karen Orren, "Standing to Sue: Interest Group Conflict in the Federal Courts," *American Political Science Review,* 70 (September 1976), pp. 723–741.
8. See, for example, E. S. Quade, *Analysis for Public Decisions* (New York: American Elsevier, 1975); Robert H. Haveman and Julius Margolis (eds.), *Public Expenditure and Policy Analysis,* 2d ed. (Chicago: Rand McNally, 1977); David Nachmias (ed.), *The Practice of Policy Evaluation* (New York: St. Martin's, 1980); and David L. Weimer and Aidan R. Vining, *Policy Analysis* (Englewood Cliffs, N.J.: Prentice-Hall, 1989).
9. See Jones, *Introduction to the Study of Public Policy,* pp. 214–218.
10. See Charles E. Lindblom, "The Science of 'Muddling Through,' " *Public Administration Review,* 19 (Spring 1959), pp. 79–88, and various other works cited in Chapter 2 of this volume.
11. On the energy issue, see Craufurd D. Goodwin (ed.), *Energy Policy in Perspective* (Washington, D.C.: Brookings Institution, 1981); Don E. Kash and Robert W. Rycroft, "Energy Policy: How Failure Was Snatched from the Jaws of Success," Paper delivered at the 1983 annual meeting of the American Political Science Association, Chicago, Illinois, September 1–4, 1983; and Franklin Tugwell, *The Energy Crisis and the American Political Economy* (Stanford, Calif.: Stanford University Press, 1988).
12. Walter A. Rosenbaum, *Environmental Politics and Policy* (Washington, D.C.: Congressional Quarterly Press, 1985).
13. See Hugh Heclo, "Issue Networks and the Executive Establishment," in Anthony King (ed.), *The New American Political System* (Washington, D.C.: American Enterprise Institute, 1978), pp. 87–124.
14. E. E. Schattschneider, *The Semi-Sovereign People,* p. 71.
15. Thomas S. Kuhn, *The Structure of Scientific Revolutions,* 2d ed. (Chicago: University of Chicago Press, 1970).
16. Alexander Hamilton, James Madison, and John Jay, *The Federalist Papers,* Clinton Rossiter, ed. (New York: New American Library, Mentor Books, 1961).
17. The foundations of group theory are set forth in Arthur F. Bentley, *The Process of Government* (Chicago: University of Chicago Press, 1908); David B. Truman, *The Governmental Process* (New York: Knopf, 1951); and Earl Latham, *The Group Basis of Politics* (Ithaca, N.Y.: Cornell University Press, 1952).
18. Charles E. Lindblom, *Politics and Markets* (New York: Basic Books, 1977); and Ralph Miliband, *The State in Capitalist Society* (New York: Basic Books/Harper Colophon Books, 1969).
19. See Charles E. Lindblom, *Democracy and Market Systems* (Oslo: Norwegian University Press, 1988), Introduction.

PART I

The Sources
of Incrementalism

CHAPTER 2

Incrementalism and the Limits of Rationality

According to Charles Lindblom, incrementalism in policy-making stems, first and foremost, from inherent limitations on human rationality. Where rational decision making requires a process of calculated choice among alternatives, policy-making is typically a process of mutual adjustment among a multiplicity of actors having different self-interests and divergent conceptions of the public interest. Agreement on objectives is impossible because the participants hold different conceptions of the problem at hand and adhere to different values. Moreover, limits on human cognitive capacities and the costs of acquiring reliable information force policy makers to operate with incomplete knowledge at best. Time constraints limit attention to politically feasible alternatives differing only marginally from previous policies. Given a lack of consensus on ends or means, outcomes will represent little more than lowest common denominators acceptable to a sufficient number to permit action. Thus large policy changes will occur gradually, if at all, through a process of feedback, or "successive approximations," as experience with minor policy changes gives rise to new demands for modification or expansion, setting off a new policy cycle.[1]

Lindblom advanced this model, which he termed "disjointed incrementalism," as an alternative to the rational-comprehensive ideal. Incrementalism explains the vast majority of cases of real world policy-making because this method of decision making consistently produces better outcomes than could be obtained through any misguided attempt at comprehensive rationality. Departures from the model are acknowledged but seen as occurring only under very special circumstances.[2]

A variety of scholars have followed Lindblom in characterizing policy-making as normally a process of decision making under severe constraints on information and consensus, giving rise to incremental outcomes.[3] Some researchers have identified instances of nonincremental policy departures, suggesting that exceptions to the model may occur under a wider range of circumstances than was previously thought.[4] None of these scholars would suggest that nonincremental policy-making is the norm, however, and certainly none would suggest that policy-making bears any resemblance to the rational ideal under normal circumstances.

THE RATIONAL-COMPREHENSIVE IDEAL

In an ideal world, policies would result from a process of comprehensive analysis. A conscious, value-maximizing *choice* would be made after a thorough examination of all relevant alternatives. Although an unattainable ideal in many cases, the rational-comprehensive method of decision nevertheless holds great appeal for students of the policy process, as it forces policy makers to specify objectives and engage in a rigorous analysis of options before proceeding.

The rational model begins by assuming that public problems will be perceived and accurately defined by decision makers. To the extent that resources are limited, it further assumes that problems will be ranked in order of priority, with the most serious reaching the agenda first.

Further, value-maximizing decisions require consensus, both on the definition of the problem and on national objectives. This means not only that policy makers share the same goals, but also that they share the same priorities. Often, important values are in conflict—as, for example, with the environmental problems raised by various forms of energy production. Policy makers must agree on how to trade off one value against another: for example, exactly how much environmental damage they are willing to accept in order to attain higher levels of energy production.

Finally, policy makers must review all possible alternatives and correctly identify the consequences associated with each. This requires a comprehensive understanding of how the world works—a "model" of reality, as discussed in Chapter 1—at least for the policy area under discussion. Without such an understanding of relevant cause-and-effect relationships, the consequences of various alternatives cannot be accurately specified.

Once a decision is made, policy implementation consists of a process of value-free execution. Put another way, there is a clear division between politics and administration. Implementors are professional managers, not politicians, trained in the "science" of administration to get the most out of agency resources. Organization is hierarchical, with managers controlling the behavior of subordinates, and elected officials in turn controllng the managers.[5]

As circumstances change, or new knowledge comes to light, policies may be adjusted as necessary but always through a process of rational analysis. Major policy departures may or may not be required by changing conditions or the identification of new problems, but in any case nonincremental change is in no way precluded by limitations on the knowledge base or human analytical capabilities.

THE LIMITS OF RATIONALITY

Unfortunately, comprehensive rationality remains a utopian ideal for most policy areas. The model is extremely demanding, as it requires high levels of consensus and knowledge base unlikely to be attained very often. For example, the model requires initially that decision makers agree on the precise nature of the problem they face. There is no guarantee, however, that a particular problem will be perceived at all, or that all actors will necessarily define it in the same way. There are no commonly accepted criteria for distinguishing legitmately public problems from private concerns.

Air pollution provides a good illustration here. To the economist, air pollution constitutes a classic example of an "externality," or third-party effect. Externalities occur where market transactions are not purely private, as parties not involved in an exchange are affected by it, whether for good or ill. In the case of acid rain, for example, utilities in the Midwest sell electricity to local consumers—ostensibly a private transaction. However, sulfur dioxide emissions from the coal burned to generate the electricity increase the acidity of rainfall in areas hundreds of miles away.[6]

To the economist, this is a clear-cut public problem providing ample grounds for government intervention in the market. Somehow the state must act to make the polluter pay (to "internalize" the externality), whether through a tax on emissions, a requirement that utilities install expensive scrubblers on smokestacks to reduce sulfur dioxide emissions, a mandate that low-sulfur coal be used exclusively, or some other method. Whatever the remedy, costs of production will go up for the plants in question, with probable effects on the rates paid by Midwestern consumers. However, as parties to the original transaction, both the utilities and local consumers should properly bear the costs of the externality.

In practice, however, the situation is seldom so clear cut. Midwestern utilities and their customers will not passively accept higher costs simply because air pollution constitutes an externality in economists' terms. Rather, they will likely exploit any limits on available knowledge to avoid internalizing the externality, arguing that the source of acid rain has not been firmly established, or that its effects have been exaggerated by environmental extremists.

Similarly, rational choice requires agreement on objectives, including agreement on the trade-offs among conflicting values. In the acid rain case, Midwestern utilities and their customers can appeal to at least two values as potentially overriding environmental concerns. One is the need to generate energy somehow in a world of dwindling oil supplies. Reliance on coal is almost dictated by its abundant domestic supplies and the high costs and/or risks associated with viable alternative sources such as nuclear power. A related value is full employment. With Midwestern states already hit hard by plant closings and layoffs in a variety of industries, any action likely to raise the costs of production for Midwestern industries (and thus make the region even less competitive) will be undertaken only reluctantly, if at all.

Finally, the rational model presumes a capacity to estimate accurately the consequences of all relevant alternatives that is often beyond the reach of policy makers. Here again, air pollution provides a good case in point. The effects of various industrial emissions on human beings, wildlife, and plants are not always easy to identify. Complete knowlege requires an understanding of the effects of exposure at different levels and over long periods of time that cannot be acquired without time-consuming and expensive studies. To make matters worse, industrial and automotive emissions recombine with gases in the earth's atmosphere to produce new chemical compounds with potentially serious effects that must be estimated. Finally, at least some of the consequences of air pollution (for example, the so-called greenhouse effect) will show up only in the distant future, and then with effects that are subject to dispute (e.g., major climatic changes, flooding of coastal areas). By contrast, the effects of pollution control on energy prices, employment, and plant location will be both immediate and readily identifiable.[7]

The problem of inadequate knowledge base is not limited to problems involving highly technical or scientific issues. Public policies often change the structure of incentives facing individual citizens. To the extent that people are self-interested and act rationally, new public policies can generate a wide variety of unanticipated consequences. Examples abound. The passage of Medicare in 1965 greatly expanded access to health care among individuals over sixty-five but also contributed to spiraling health care costs by increasing the demand for such care and by affecting the reimbursement formulas employed by private insurers. Recent deregulation of airlines has led to a more efficient rate structure, as expected, but it has also produced a plethora of new competitors on many routes, making for more flights than overworked air traffic controllers can safely monitor at many airports. Regulation of natural gas prices, intended to benefit consumers in frost belt states, instead generated a glut of gas in Sunbelt states as producers sold as much gas as possible in unregulated intrastate markets. The list of examples could be extended indefinitely.[8]

INCREMENTALISM AS AN ALTERNATIVE
TO RATIONALITY

Lindblom advanced his theory of incrementalism as an alternative to the rational-comprehensive method, which he characterized as an unattainable ideal in practice. Conflicts over problem definition and trade-offs among important values render the rational ideal impotent in selecting among alternatives: "Agreement on objectives failing, there is no standard of 'correctness.' "[9] Similarly, time constraints and limited information preclude a comprehensive analysis of alternatives. Policy makers must typically act with incomplete knowledge of the consequences of the alternatives being considered.

Incrementalism departs from the rational method on all points. It is much less demanding than the rational method, requiring neither comprehensive information nor agreement among policy makers on objectives. Consequently, incrementalism permits action where the rational ideal is paralyzed, often yielding no guidance whatever to policy makers.

Agenda Setting

The incremental method of decision making begins by identifying problems to be solved. This starting point is not as straightforward as it appears, however. In its pure form, the rational ideal begins by identifying a mix of positive values to be attained (what economists term a social welfare function). Analysis of alternatives culminates in a value-maximizing choice. According to Lindblom, however, such utopian ambitions are typically too abstract to guide policy makers, representing at best glittering generalities. Moreover, it is virtually imposssible to secure agreement on the proper trade-offs among such ideals in the abstract.

Rather, the process is typically *remedial*. It focuses on concrete problems to be alleviated (e.g., unemployment) rather than on abstract ideals to be attained (a self-actualized citizenry). The process moves away from problems rather than toward ideals, which cannot be specified with sufficient precision.

Problems are brought to government by affected publics rather than through a rational analysis of the decision makers' environment. This is what Lindblom terms *the social fragmentation of analysis*. No single actor needs to possess comprehensive information. Rather, each actor brings important knowledge to bear in analyzing the problem. Likewise, it is no longer necessary for all actors to define the problem in the same way. Disagreements can be accommodated through bargaining and compromise, and problems may be acted upon without ever being fully defined.

According to Lindblom, policy makers are not typically faced with a "given" problem.[10] That is to say, problems do not emerge, fully defined, for policy makers to solve but must rather be actively perceived and defined—a process that is far from automatic. On the whole, however, Lindblom is optimistic that most important problems will find their way onto the agenda. This stems from his assumption that almost all interests affected by any given issue will be represented in the decision process:

> In a society like that of the United States in which individuals are free to combine to pursue almost any possible common interest they might have and in which government agencies are sensitive to the pressures of these groups, the system described is approximated. Almost every interest has its watchdog. Without claiming that every interest has a sufficiently powerful watchdog, it can be argued that our system often can assure a more comprehensive regard for the values of the whole society than any attempt at intellectual comprehensiveness.[11]

One final point needs to be made before leaving the agenda-setting stage. Constraints on time and information preclude a comprehensive examination of all alternative solutions. Policy makers must somehow limit their attention to a manageable number of options, and do so in a way that screens out alternatives unlikely to be adopted. In practice, they accomplish this by *limiting their focus to incremental alternatives* differing only marginally from existing policies.

Restricting attention to small changes in policy can be justified on several grounds. The first is sunk costs. Just as most college students do not begin each day with an analysis of whether they should transfer to another school (or whether they should stay in school at all), policy makers do not often give consideration to scrapping a wide range of policies and beginning again from the ground up. Existing policies constitute a response to real public problems, and the decision to undertake them in the first place was not made casually.

Moreover, policy makers will have acquired a good deal of experience with these policies over time, building up a reservoir of knowledge they will be reluctant to throw away by moving in an entirely different direction. For this reason, it will be much easier to estimate the consequences of relatively small policy changes.

Finally, major policy departures are not usually feasible politically. Change fosters uncertainty, creating doubts even in the minds of potential beneficiaries. Moreover, most established policies will have acquired powerful supportive constituencies opposed to any significant changes in policy. In any case, the need to make numerous concessions in order to build a winning coalition (see below) almost guarantees that outcomes will ultimately be incremental. Thus prolonged consideration of nonincremental policy proposals is likely to be a waste of time.

Policy Adoption

Here again incrementalism departs from the rational method on all points. Rationality presumes a value-maximizing choice after a comprehensive analysis of alternatives. As we have already seen, the incremental model predicts that policy makers will limit their attention to incremental policy changes.

So, too, they will compare alternatives by focusing on the increments by which various proposals differ from each other and from past policies. Lindblom terms this process *margin-dependent choice*. For example, in the budgetary process, legislators normally make no attempt to comprehensively evaluate the performance of the vast range of federal policies. Rather, they focus on the increments by which spending will go up or down for various programs under different proposals. Focusing on the margins is thus an aid to calculation, permitting an intelligent comparison of proposals where a comprehensive analysis would be virtually impossible.[12]

In comparing incremental alternatives, policy makers make no attempt to identify all the potential consequences associated with each alternative. This is because the policy process is *serial*, or repetitive. (See the section below on policy change.) Adjustments can be made in subsequent policy cycles—spending a little more or a little less, modifying the legislative mandate if necessary, or giving administrators new statutory powers. Unanticipated consequences are not a serious problem for incrementalism; they merely generate new problems to be dealt with in future deliberations.

An additional aid to calculation is provided by *the adjustment of objectives to policies*. The rational method begins with a specification of objectives, followed by a rigorous comparison of alternatives and a value-maximizing choice. We have already seen the difficulty of securing agreement on trade-offs among objectives in the abstract. In part this difficulty is circumvented by focusing on concrete problems to be ameliorated. It is further simplified by considering means and ends together.

For example, the abortion issue poses difficult trade-offs between important rights: the right of pregnant women to make decisions affecting their own bodies, and the right of fetuses (which are, at a minimum, *potential* human lives) to protection in the course of their development. While activists on both sides of this controversy treat the issue as one sided, policy makers do not have this luxury. Confronted with intense and highly vocal groups on both sides of the issue, they are forced to make some kind of trade-off between these conflicting values.

It is almost impossible to do this in the abstract, however. Instead, policy makers look at a series of concrete alternatives: permitting abortions to save the life of the mother, in cases of rape and incest, or in cases where the mother's psychological health is likely to be damaged, and so on. Each of these concrete alternatives carries with it an implicit trade-off between the abstract rights of fetuses and those of pregnant women. While different policy makers make this trade-off in different ways, they all tend to do so by examining concrete alternatives, with their implicit trade-offs, rather than beginning with a resolution of these value conflicts and then moving on to specifics. Indeed, it is virtually impossible to visualize these trade-offs without first considering the practical alternatives.

Perhaps the most fundamental way in which incrementalism departs from the rational-comprehensive ideal lies in its *rejection of the idea of policy as a decision*. According to Lindblom, policies are not the product of conscious choice but rather the political resultants of interaction among various actors possessing different information and adhering to different values. The need to make concessions in order to gain adherents reinforces the incrementalism already present in the tendency to focus on alternatives differing only peripherally from the status quo. This process of mutual anticipation and adaptation, which Lindblom terms "partisan mutual adjustment," virtually guarantees incremental policy outcomes.

Policy Implementation

The near inevitability of bargaining and compromise in the formulation of policy makes for watered-down policy outcomes. In the context of administration, incrementalism often means not just a small policy change but also inadequate statutory powers and limited appropriations for most agencies, making implementation difficult. To make matters worse, the legislative mandate will typically fail to resolve all conflicts, leaving important terms undefined and passing controversial questions on to administrators for resolution. For example, what is "a reasonable length of time" in which to report a rape in order to qualify for a federally funded abortion? Under what circumstances should the Environmental Protection Agency relax deadlines or permit the substitution of "best available technology" to meet air pollution objectives?

At the same time, however, building on past policies permits administrators to learn through experience. Thus, at least one scholar has criticized the Clean Air Act of 1970 for moving too far too fast ("legislating beyond capability") when a better approach would have been to make only incremental adjustments in the expiring Air Quality Act of 1967, which administrators had barely begun to implement.[13]

POLICY CHANGE UNDER
THE INCREMENTAL MODEL

As noted earlier, a central characteristic of incrementalism is *seriality*. That is, the policy process is never ending, as the failure of a given policy to completely solve a problem merely gives rise to subsequent rounds of policy-making. In contrast with the rational model, it is not necessary to make a single comprehensive decision that will solve a problem once and for all. To the contrary, policies can be modified as necessary in subsequent iterations of the policy cycle: "Policy-making is a process of successive approximation to some desired objectives in which what is desired itself continues to change under reconsideration."[14]

This is not to say that major policy changes cannot occur under incrementalism. However, significant change will tend to occur gradually, through the accumulation of a series of incremental policy shifts. The Vietnam War constitutes a good case in point, moving from a limited program of military aid to the French in the late 1940s to a large-scale American involvement by the late 1960s, with each step along the way representing only an incremental change in posture.

Inasmuch as policy change under this model takes place through a series of subsequent policy cycles, it goes without saying that this process conforms to the tenets of disjointed incrementalism in all respects. To put it another way, the same actors who disagreed over values, trade-offs, and even problem definition initially will be the central participants in the process of policy evaluation and change. Thus policy change is not a straightforward process of learning through trial and error, but rather a political process, characterized by fragmentation, conflict, and imperfect knowledge.

The process does not just go endlessly around in circles, however, as it well might. Lindblom emphasizes the tendency to converge on a solution through a long series of iterations, in which policy makers of varying views gain valuable knowledge through experience with the policy, thus narrowing their differences. In this way, policy evaluation is characterized by social fragmentation of analysis. That is, problems are considered unsolved as long as some publics continue to express dissatisfaction with existing policies. By the same token, a problem may be regarded as solved when it finally disappears from the agenda, crowded off by other problems now considered more pressing.[15]

Conditions for Nonincremental Change

In this regard, Lindblom has suggested that departures from this pattern will occur only under very special circumstances. He categorizes problems as falling along two continuous dimensions: the first represents the degree to which decision makers understand the nature of the problem at hand while the second measures the degree of proposed change from previous policy (see Figure 2.1).[16]

According to Lindblom, rational decision making is confined to relatively minor technical problems of execution, typically made by professionals in the middle levels of the bureaucracy. Large-scale departures do occur occasionally (e.g., the New Deal or the Reagan revolution). However, lacking solid understanding of the problem at hand, such

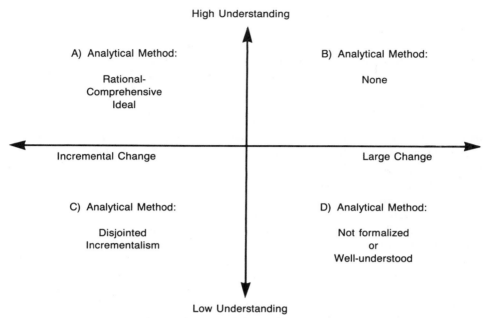

High Understanding

A) Analytical Method:

Rational-
Comprehensive
Ideal

B) Analytical Method:

None

Incremental Change

Large Change

C) Analytical Method:

Disjointed
Incrementalism

D) Analytical Method:

Not formalized
or
Well-understood

Low Understanding

Figure 2.1 Lindblom's Typology of Decision Methods

actions will fall into quadrant D, thus failing to conform to the rational-comprehensive method. The realm of large change coupled with high understanding (quadrant B) is for all practical purposes an empty cell: "The information and comprehension requirements of synoptic problem solving simply cannot be met for large-scale social change."[17]

Most policies represent small departures from existing policy, and the policy process is more often characterized by disagreement and conflict than by consensus. A significant portion of political behavior fails to conform to the incremental model, however. Contrary to Lindblom's expectations, proposals for major policy departures are surprisingly common. Proposals for a comprehensive reform of the nation's welfare system have been advanced by two different presidents. Similarly, proposals for a system of national health insurance have been seriously considered, off and on, for decades. President Carter pushed hard for a series of sweeping proposals to deal with the energy crisis of the 1970s.

If the above examples seem to suggest that such sweeping reform proposals are typically mere bargaining chips, useful for discussion but standing little realistic chance of passage, a variety of nonincremental policy enactments pose more serious problems for Lindblom's analysis. In 1970, for example, a dramatic increase in public awareness of the air pollution problem, coupled with the rise of the environmental movement, forced Congress to respond boldly, producing a significant expansion of federal regulatory authority and the creation of new line and staff agencies to deal with the problem.[18] More recently, President Carter secured passage of legislation deregulating the airline industry and abolishing the Civil Aeronautics Board—a victory made all the more striking by the CAB's well-earned reputation as a captive of its airline clientele.[19] In 1981, President Reagan obtained passage of major income tax cuts, followed by a sweeping series of draconian budget cuts, to the point of eliminating many programs altogether.[20] In 1986, the president called for the elimination of the current income tax code, to be replaced by a much simpler and broader based scheme having only three tax brackets and a much lower top rate of taxation. While the final legislation differed in many minor respects from his initial program, there is no question that the 1986 tax reform legislation began and ended as a nonincremental policy departure.[21] These examples suggest that policy makers periodically find existing policies so fundamentally ill-conceived that incremental tinkering is inappropriate. Under such circumstances, seriality can produce not "successive approximations" but rather a sharp turn in policy.

Even if Lindblom is right in arguing that most policy outcomes are incremental, it is nevertheless clear that we need to look beyond an alleged tendency to focus exclusively on marginal policy changes as an explanation. Major policy departures receive consideration too often, even where they do not pass; a convincing theory of incrementalism will have to look elsewhere for support. Subsequent chapters will demonstrate that much of the incrementalism we commonly observe in American politics can instead be attributed to three factors: the effects of the Constitution on policy-making, inherent inequalities among groups seeking to influence policy, and the privileged position of business in capitalistic societies.

IS INCREMENTALISM DESIRABLE?

As we have seen, Lindblom's case for incrementalism is rooted in the inherent shortcomings of the rational-comprehensive ideal. In contrast to the rational method, which is paralyzed by any breakdown in consensus, incrementalism does not require all participants to agree on problem definition or objectives. Differences can readily be accommodated through mutual adjustment, and different groups can support the same policy for a variety of different reasons. Similarly, incrementalism avoids reliance on comprehensive information through a variety of aids to calculation. Problems are identified in a disjointed fashion by affected publics. Analysis is limited to "realistic" proposals differing only marginally from existing policy, and attention is confined to the increments by which these proposals differ from one another and from past policy. The entire process is iterative, permitting policy makers to acquire knowledge over time and thus to converge gradually on a solution through accumulated experience.[22]

Incrementalism as a Political Market Model

Inasmuch as policies represent an equilibrium of contending forces rather than a process of conscious decision, incrementalism can be viewed as a kind of political market. (That

Lindblom should produce such a conception of politics is not surprising, as he began his academic career as an economist.) Economic markets are highly decentralized mechanisms in which innumerable individuals bargain with each other and strike the best deals they can for themselves. Where certain underlying assumptions are met (perfect competition, perfect information, and so on), the sum of these millions of individual transactions will be an efficient outcome in the public interest, superior to the results to be expected from any effort to centrally direct behavior through economic planning.[23]

In the same way, Lindblom argues, rationality is an unattainable ideal in the political marketplace as well. A highly decentralized process of bargaining among self-interested individuals—"partisan mutual adjustment"—will once again yield results superior to those produced by efforts at comprehensive rationality. Seen in this light, incrementalism is the political analogue to the efficient and self-correcting market mechanism.[24]

Political Market Failure

Unfortunately, as any economist can attest, markets all too often fail. The ideal of the self-correcting market, like that of comprehensive rationality, remains utopian at best. And political markets are no less subject to efficiency conditions than are economic markets. For the political equilibrium to yield efficient outcomes, two fundamental assumptions must be met. First, all interests with a stake in the issue at hand must be effectively represented. As we have already seen, Lindblom assumed this difficulty away by asserting that almost every important interest would have its watchdog. Unfortunately, as will be shown in Chapter 4, there is little basis in theory or empirical fact for such an assumption. To the contrary, there are systematic biases to the group universe, leaving a wide variety of interests unmobilized.

Second, and equally important, there must be a rough balance of power among contending interests, so that no one actor exerts disproportionate influence over the final outcome. Put more precisely in the language of economics, competition must be "atomistic," with so many individuals involved that no one group can wield the political analogue of market power. Here too there are ample grounds for pessimism, as political resources are unevenly distributed, permitting some groups to exercise excessive power on at least some issues. In recent years, Lindblom has acknowledged this, arguing now that business occupies a "privileged position" in capitalistic societies (see Chapter 5).[25]

Economic markets function to yield efficient outcomes at best; they are simply not equipped to deal with considerations of equity. Given an initial distribution of income among consumers, a perfectly functioning economic market will operate to yield an efficient mix of goods and services. Given a different distribution of income, an entirely different mix of goods and services will result from the free operation of the market, because different people have different tastes, and a change in income distribution increases the capacity of some consumers to satisfy their preferences at the expense of others. The second mix is also efficient, however; in fact, nothing can be deduced from the whole field of welfare economics to say whether the second is superior to the first, or vice versa. One can say only that a nation's "production possibility frontier" defines the set of efficient (e.g., maximum attainable) outcomes. The market, operating ideally, will take you to a point on that frontier corresponding to a given distribution of income. It cannot tell you where on the frontier society should operate. To do that requires a value judgment as to the proper distribution of income—a judgment that the market is not equipped to make.[26]

In the same way, incrementalism (operating as a political market) may be thought of as yielding an infinite set of efficient outcomes, each associated with a different initial distribution of power. Change the distribution of power within society and you get a different outcome—albeit one that is still arguably efficient. To say that incrementalism automatically yields desirable policies, as Lindblom does, is to leave out this critical issue of the distribution of power. On this point, the breakdown of the rational model makes it impossible to verify Lindblom's claim in any truly meaningful sense; lacking a benchmark conception of the public interest, one can never be certain the model is producing desirable outcomes.

From observation, it is plain that incrementalism cannot always be relied upon to yield good public policies. The Vietnam War is again a good case in point. It would be hard to find a better example of incremental decision making, yet policy makers over four presidential administrations moved inexorably (albeit gradually) toward disaster, piling one incremental escalation in commitment atop another until our involvement was just short of full-scale war. At no point did decision makers face up to the fundamental underlying issues: Just what was the problem we were trying to solve? What were our objectives? Could they be achieved at a reasonable cost?[27] To say that rationality is at times a utopian ideal is not to say that we can close our eyes to its imperatives.

Much the same thing might be said of America's current energy policies. A rational analysis would point to declining oil reserves combined with continuing exponential growth in consumption, a pattern that will leave the United States vulnerable to another round of Arab oil shocks within the next decade. Nor are world supplies infinite; some alternatives to oil will have to be found by the first part of the next century. Long-term planning is needed to avoid either major disruptions in our supply of energy or a drift into a reliance on coal that can have only serious long-term consequences for the environment. The longer we delay, the more options are foreclosed, making the eventual adjustment increasingly difficult.[28] In the face of this growing problem, the system seems to be responding with classic incrementalism: disagreement over the definition and seriousness of the problem, vexing conflicts over trade-offs (especially over the environmental costs of various energy alternatives), fragmented institutions, delay, and slow progress at best. The question is whether an incremental response will be sufficient under the circumstances.

Before we reject the incremental model as fatally flawed, however, it is worth recalling that Lindblom never asserts that large change is impossible; rather, it is his contention that such departures from incrementalism will be inefficient and potentially dangerous. His admonition that the informational and cognitive requirements for rational choice are incompatible with large-scale social change is sobering. Lindblom's warning is echoed in David Stockman's guilt-ridden postmortem on the legacy of the 1981 tax cuts. An ardent supply-sider, Stockman had helped push through the president's tax and budget cuts as director of the Office of Management and Budget. Charged with the responsibility for making economic projections, Stockman realized sooner than most that the numbers didn't add up. A highly ideological program had been pushed too far too fast, necessitating a search for massive budget savings that would quickly overwhelm the system's capacity for rational evaluation of ongoing policies. When it proved impossible to cut expenditures enough to offset the massive revenue losses resulting from the tax cut, the result was an unprecedented structural budget deficit stretching out for the indefinite future. Throughout Stockman's account, the lament is repeated that the changes produced by the Reagan program were so massive that no one involved fully understood the implications.[29]

To conclude, if it is true that the vast majority of policy outcomes represent at best incremental change from previous policies, it is nonetheless clear that policy makers are not afraid to consider major policy departures. We will have to look to additional models to complete our explanation of the prevalence of incrementalism in policy-making. At the same time, it would be a mistake to ignore the strengths of the strategy in compensating for constraints on information and agreement. If this method of decision making cannot be relied upon to yield good public policies—and the Vietnam and energy examples, among others, suggest that it cannot—it is not clear that any alternative method would produce better policies where the real problem is an inadequate knowledge base or an irreconcilable conflict over values. To the extent that incrementalism is rooted in the breakdown of the rational ideal, as Lindblom suggests, it may be largely unavoidable.

NOTES

1. Among the various works by Lindblom, see especially "The Science of Muddling Through," *Public Administration Review,* 19 (Spring 1959), pp. 79–88; *The Intelligence of Democracy* (New York: Free Press, 1965); and *The Policy-Making Process,* 2d ed. (Englewood Cliffs, N.J.: Prentice-Hall, 1980). A particularly clear statement of the theory can be found in David Braybrooke and Charles E. Lindblom, *A Strategy of Decision* (New York: Free Press of Glencoe, 1963).
2. See Braybrooke and Lindblom, pp. 61–79, for the only real discussion Lindblom provides of the circumstances giving rise to departures from normal incrementalism.
3. For an influential public policy text with clear roots in Lindblom, see Charles O. Jones, *An Introduction to the Study of Public Policy,* 3d ed. rev. (Monterey, Calif.: Brooks/Cole, 1984). See also Ira Sharkansky, *The Routines of Politics* (New York: Van Nostrad Reinhold, 1970). For an argument that the budgetary process is typically incremental, see Aaron B. Wildavsky, *The Politics of the Budgetary Process,* 4th ed. (Boston: Little, Brown, 1984). Lindblom's theory has been applied to making foreign policy by Roger Hilsman in a variety of works; see especially *To Move a Nation* (New York: Delta Books, 1967).
4. Charles O. Jones, *Clean Air* (Pittsburgh: University of Pittsburgh Press, 1975); Charles O. Jones, "Speculative Augmentation in Federal Air Pollution Policy-Making," *Journal of Politics,* 36 (May 1974), pp. 438–464; Paul R. Schulman, "Nonincremental Policy-Making: Notes Toward an Alternative Paradigm," *American Political Science Review,* 69 (December 1975), pp. 1354–1370; Ian Lustick, "Explaining the Variable Utility of Disjointed Incrementalism: Four Propositions," *American Political Science Review,* 74 (June 1980), pp. 342–353; and Michael T. Hayes, "Incrementalism as Dramaturgy: The Case of the Nuclear Freeze," *Polity,* 19 (Spring 1987), pp. 443–463.
5. Robert T. Nakamura and Frank Smallwood, *The Politics of Policy Implementation* (New York:

St. Martin's, 1980), pp. 7–12. For a concise statement of the classical theory, see Max Weber, "Essay on Bureaucracy," in Francis E. Rourke (ed.), *Bureaucratic Power in National Politics,* 3d ed. (Boston: Little, Brown, 1978), pp. 85–86.

6. On externalities, see Robert H. Haveman, *The Economics of the Public Sector,* 2d ed. (New York: Wiley, 1976), pp. 32–40. See also Joseph E. Stiglitz, *Economics of the Public Sector* (New York: Norton, 1986), pp. 178–198.

7. Walter A. Rosenbaum, *Environmental Politics and Policy* (Washington, D.C.: Congressional Quarterly Press, 1985).

8. On the general problem of unanticipated consequences, see Robert K. Merton, "The Unanticipated Consequences of Purposive Social Action," *American Sociological Review,* 1 (1936), pp. 894–904; and Lewis Anthony Dexter, "Undesigned Consequences of Purposive Legislative Action: Alternatives to Implementation," *Journal of Public Policy,* 1 (October 1981), pp. 413–431.

9. Lindblom, "Science of Muddling Through," p. 83. This section is drawn largely from Braybrooke and Lindblom, Chapter 5, pp. 81–110.

10. Lindblom, *Policy-Making Process,* p. 24.

11. Lindblom, "Science of Muddling Through," p. 85.

12. Wildavsky, pp. 13–15.

13. Jones, *Clean Air,* pp. 211–311.

14. Lindblom, "Science of Muddling Through," p. 86.

15. Wildavsky, p. 60.

16. Braybrooke and Lindblom, pp. 66–79.

17. Braybrooke and Lindblom, p. 79.

18. Jones, *Clean Air,* and "Speculative Augmentation."

19. Bradley Behrman, "Civil Aeronautics Board," in James Q. Wilson, *The Politics of Regulation* (New York: Basic Books, 1980), pp. 75–120. See Also Martha Derthick and Paul J. Quirk, *The Politics of Deregulation* (Washington, D.C.: Brookings Institution, 1985).

20. David A. Stockman, *The Triumph of Politics* (New York: Avon Books, 1987).

21. Jeffrey H. Birnbaum and Alan S. Murray, *Showdown at Gucci Gulch* (New York: Random House, 1987).

22. For Lindblom's discussion of why policy analysts find incrementalism an attractive strategy, see Braybrooke and Lindblom, pp. 111–143.

23. For a highly readable version of this thesis, see Milton Friedman, *Capitalism and Freedom* (Chicago: University of Chicago Press, 1962). For an excellent treatment of welfare economics, see Stiglitz, pp. 51–97.

24. Lindblom makes this point in all works cited above. See especially Lindblom, *The Intelligence of Democracy.* For a concise statement of the case, see Wildavsky, pp. 165–176.

25. Charles E. Lindblom, *Politics and Markets* (New York: Basic Books, 1977).

26. Stiglitz, pp. 75–95.

27. Daniel Ellsberg, *Papers on the War* (New York: Simon and Schuster, 1972); and Leslie H. Gelb and Richard K. Betts, *The Irony of Vietnam* (Washington, D.C.: Brookings Institution, 1979).

28. Robert Stobaugh and Daniel Yergin (eds.), *Energy Future,* 3d ed. rev. (New York: Random House, Vintage Books, 1983).

29. Stockman, *The Triumph of Politics.*

CHAPTER 3

Multiple Veto Points and the Need for Concurrent Majorities

The American Constitution is rooted in a coherent vision of government that may be termed the classical model, predicated on the need to limit arbitrary power through a complex system of checks and balances.[1] The framers' distrust of popular majorities produced a political system in which significant policy departures are extremely difficult to effect. While nonincremental policy change remains possible under this system, the dominant tendency is to reinforce the tendencies toward inertia and incrementalism present in all systems, as identified in the previous chapter.

This model is meliorative rather than utopian; it makes no claims to generate outcomes in the public interest or to maximize shared societal values. As Charles O. Jones has observed, "The framers were more concerned about preventing tyranny than they were about facilitating policy development."[2] The document was designed primarily to guard against excesses—particularly against the abuse of power by popular majorities. Alexander Hamilton made this orientation explicit in *The Federalist*, No. 73: "The injury which may possibly be done by defeating a few good laws will be amply compensated by the advantage of preventing a number of bad ones."[3]

THE PROBLEM OF FACTIONS

Writing in *The Federalist*, No. 10, Madison saw the formation of interest groups as an inevitable by-product of a free society.[4] Where the incremental model views the struggle among contending interests as potentially yielding the public interest, Madison feared that such a process must inevitably fail to protect the interests of minorities. While operation of the "republican principle" (e.g., majority rule) could be relied upon to check the excesses of minority factions, real danger arises whenever a group or coalition mobilizes a majority, permitting it to pursue its narrow interests at the expense of the common good.[5]

Such majorities can in no way be trusted to exercise self-restraint in deference to the natural rights of minorities: "If the impulse and the opportunity be permitted to coincide, we well know that neither moral nor religious motives can be relied on as an adequate control."[6]

Madison saw only two potential remedies for the mischiefs of faction: to remove their causes or to control their effects. The causes of factions might be removed by imbuing every citizen with the same passions and interests—an impractical ideal at best. Alternatively, factions might be entirely eliminated by limiting the freedom of association under which they thrive, a remedy "worse than the disease."[7]

Plainly, any solution to the problem of factions would have to focus instead on controlling their effects. Popular majorities "must be rendered, by their number and local situation, unable to concert and carry into effect schemes of oppression."[8] This objective was ultimately to be achieved by four means: (1) by creating a new *national* republic, in which majorities would find it difficult to mobilize, (2) by subdividing society into a multiplicity of distinct interests, thus making joint action less likely; (3) by fragmenting power among several independent national institutions; and (4) by further dividing power between the states and the new national government.

A National Polity

One of Madison's keenest insights into the future of the new republic was his recognition that the heterogeneity required for a balanced group struggle is more likely to occur in a large, national system than within any of its component subdivisions.

> The smaller the society, the fewer probably will be the distinct parties and interests composing it; the fewer the distinct parties and interests, the more frequently will a majority be found of the same party and the smaller the number of individuals composing a majority, and the smaller the compass within which they are placed, the more easily will they concert and exercise their plans of oppression. Extend the sphere and you take in a greater variety of parties and interests; you make it less probable that a majority of the whole will have a common motive to invade the rights of other citizens; and if such a common motive exists, it will be more difficult for all who feel it to discover their own strength and to act in unison with each other.[9]

The validity of this proposition is easily verified. For example, while corporations often wield excessive power at the state or local level, where individual businesses provide needed jobs and tax revenues, at the national level such groups must contend with many countervailing interests (see Chapter 5). Of course, as many observers have noted (and Madison himself recognized in advancing the Virginia Plan at the Constitutional Convention), the greater heterogeneity of large politics clearly implies the need to shift as much power as posssible away from the states and to the federal government. The framers were prepared to go only so far in this regard; preservation of a significant role for the states in domestic affairs would provide a further safeguard against tyranny, as will be seen below.

A Multiplicity of Interests

A second device for assuring a heterogeneous polity lay in dividing the new republic into as many distinct interests as possible. While the formation of various economic interests is virtually inevitable in any free society, the new Constitution would go even further to activate a variety of new constituencies:

> The society itself will be broken into so many parts, interests and classes of citizens, that the rights of individuals, or of the minority, will be in little danger from interested combinations of the majority. In a free government the security for civil rights must be the same as that for religious rights. *It consists in the one case in the multiplicity of interests, and in the other in the multiplicity of sects* . . . [Emphasis added].[10]

At the national level, the separation of powers would contribute to the representation of diverse constituencies. The House, the Senate, and the president were not only to be independent institutions; their members would be accountable to entirely different electorates. The House would be responsive to local interests, the Senate to the states (members were originally elected by the state legislatures), and the president to broader national concerns (as filtered through the Electoral College). Thus, in addition to inevitable economic or religious interests, individuals would be further cross-pressured by a new kind of dual citizenship. That distinctive state interests would not wither away under the new republic was further assured by preserving the states as sovereign entities under the new Constitution, with important, albeit ill-defined, responsibilities.

Checks and Balances

At the national level, effective political power would be dispersed among independent branches of government. This would not only help to produce a variety of distinct interests, as discussed above, but would also provide an important check against the accumulation of legislative, executive, and judicial powers in the same hands, which Madison termed ''the very definition of tyranny''[11] In order to guard against a gradual concentration of power in any one branch of government, the new Constitution would create a complex system of checks and balances. In Madison's formulation, ''ambition must be made to counteract ambition. The interests of the man must be connected with the constitutional rights of the place.''[12] The representatives of each branch of government would be given the necessary means to resist encroachments by the other branches.

This would first be accomplished by making the various branches independent of one another. For example, proposals were rejected at the Constitutional Convention that would have made the Senate elected by the House of Representatives. Similarly, the president's tenure in office is not dependent upon the continued confidence of the legislature, as in parliamentary systems. Instead, each branch is elected independently and is accountable to entirely different constituencies.

Equally important, no one branch of government would be able to act alone in the formulation and execution of policy. In this vein, the American system is not so much one of separation of powers as it is a system of separate institutions sharing and contending over important powers.[13] For example, the president is empowered to periodically recommend ''necessary and expedient measures'' to Congress, but majorities of both houses of Congress must give their approval before the president's proposals become law. By the same token, the president has a qualified veto power over acts of Congress, although a two-thirds majority of both houses can override a veto. The Supreme Court has an unqualified veto power in its authority to declare acts of Congress unconstitutional. However, the Court cannot take the initiative on policy issues, being forced to wait for a case to arise between parties with legitimate standing. Moreover, the Court lacks any formal power to compel compliance with its rulings where the other branches of government withhold their full cooperation.

Federalism

A final line of defense against majority tyranny is provided by the institution of federalism. If checks and balances at the national level make for a system of separate institutions sharing powers, the preservation of states as sovereign entities further guarantees that policy-making will typically involve contention between separate levels of government sharing important powers.

The Constitution is deliberately unclear as to the proper division of authority between the states and the federal government. The formal powers of the new national government were limited to those specifically enumerated in Article I, Section 8. A variety of activities were denied to the states (e.g., coining money, entering into foreign alliances, levying export duties without the consent of Congress, etc.) in Article I, Section 10. Beyond these provisions, the Tenth Amendment unequivocally reserved all remaining powers to the states. At the same time, however, Article I, Section 8, paragraph 18 also gave the new national government blanket authority to ''make all laws necessary and proper'' for carrying out its enumerated powers. The inherent ambiguity of this ''elastic clause'' threw open to interpretation just what powers were properly exercised by the federal government and which were to be reserved to the states.

The failure to be specific on this key point was a natural product of practical politics, as persistent disagreements among the framers precluded a clear division of power. At the same time, however, a vague formulation also offered a potential bulwark against tyranny by creating an additional mechanism through which ambition could be made to counteract ambition. As Madison saw it:

> In a single republic, all the power surrendered by the people is submitted to the administration of a single government; and the usurpations are guarded against by a division of the government into distinct and separate departments. In the compound republic of America, the power surrendered by the people is first divided between two distinct governments, and then the portion allotted to each subdivided among distinct and separate departments. Hence a double security arises to the rights of the people.[14]

POLICY-MAKING IN A COMPOUND REPUBLIC

In designing a system to safeguard against the potential excesses of majority factions, the framers sought to fragment political power through a system of checks and balances, both at the national level and across levels of government. In so doing, they virtually guaranteed that a multiplicity of interests would sooner or later come into play for any given issue. As Hamilton described it in *The Federalist*, No. 73, the fundamental objective was to subject all policy initiatives to a protracted process of deliberation involving the widest possible range of interests:

> The oftener a measure is brought under examination, the greater the diversity in the situations of those who are to examine it, the less must be the danger of those errors which flow from want of due deliberation, or of those missteps which proceed from the contagion of some common passion or interest.[15]

One natural result of such a system was a built-in bias against significant policy departures. As will be seen below, nonincremental policy proposals do receive consideration under the American system—much more so than Lindblom suggests—but nonincremental policy *outcomes* are rendered unlikely by the provision of multiple opportunities for minorities to block or erode threatening policies.

Agenda Setting

As predicted by the incremental model, agenda setting does not occur through a process of rational decision making. Priorities are set not through comprehensive analysis of problems but rather through a disjointed process of contention and compromise among multiple contending interests. There is typically disagreement as to what problems should be on the agenda, and there are more problems competing for attention than policy makers can deal with at any one time.

The American system offers various points of access.[16] This permits groups to seek out the most sympathetic arena in which to initiate policy proposals. For example, civil rights groups stymied by a Congress dominated by Southern Democrats in control of key legislative committees in the late 1940s turned their attention instead to the courts, eventually securing the landmark *Brown* decision, which mandated the gradual desegregation of public schools.[17] Similarly, policy innovations often originate at the state level before generating a federal response.

At the same time, however, this multiplicity of access points reflects the fact that to become an effective national policy a proposal must make it onto several institutional agendas. Reformers can begin the process anywhere they want, but they must eventually go through all the decision points. Policy-making in our compound republic is a kind of obstacle course with no clearly marked starting point or finish line.

Thus multiple access points do not necessarily increase the receptivity of the political system to new proposals. Policy makers have only so much time to deal with a wide variety of demands for action, and they are not likely to allocate precious time to proposals that stand little chance of successfully reaching a variety of institutional agendas. While they may introduce a bill or schedule hearings in order to keep a favored idea alive, they will not push hard for an issue unless it stands some reasonable chance of making it all the way through the obstacle course.[18]

Not surprisingly, research suggests that it is difficult for problems to gain agenda status in the American system. It is not enough for a problem to be arguably serious, as evidenced by various statistical indicators. Ordinarily it takes something more to place an issue on the necessary variety of institutional agendas.[19] For example, a dramatic "focusing event" may draw public attention to a problem. The collapse of a bridge may trigger legislation to spend more money on highway maintenance. An assassination attempt will typically lead to a spate of gun control bills. The London smog disaster in 1962 focused public attention on air pollution.

An aroused public opinion can catapult an issue onto a variety of institutional agendas. While this often results from a triggering or focusing event, as discussed above, it can also occur spontaneously. For example, growing public awareness of the seriousness of air pollution led to a sharp increase in support for federal action between 1967 and 1970. This growing public concern helped spawn the environmental movement, as the number of environmental groups active in Washington more than doubled over this period. Similarly, sharp increases in public concern over nuclear war and the arms race in the early 1980s gave rise to the nuclear freeze movement and helped force the arms control issue onto congressional and presidential agendas in 1982 and 1983.

When a problem takes on crisis proportions, it can be action forcing. For example, Social Security reform was forced on the agenda in 1982 by the imminent bankruptcy of the system—a critical problem that would not go away until effective action was taken. Similarly, the energy "crisis" of the 1970s did not develop overnight. A variety of indicators clearly showed that domestic oil discoveries were on the decline even as consumption continued to grow exponentially. The result was a steadily increasing dependence on imported oil, particularly from the politically volatile Middle East. Nevertheless, the issue reached the agenda only with the formation of OPEC (Organization of Petroleum Exporting Countries) and the first oil embargo in 1973, when policy makers could no longer avoid the issue.

There is little support in these examples for the proposition that policy makers will typically confine themselves to proposing relatively small policy departures.[20] To the contrary, relatively small problems (with correspondingly incremental solutions) may not generate the breadth of support necessary to reach a variety of institutional agendas and make it all the way through the process. Instead, problems may be neglected until they become so serious that a crisis is imminent or a dramatic policy failure (e.g., a focusing event) arouses public opinion or forces policy makers to address the issue. To the extent that bold and dramatic action seems necessary to deal with the problem, nonincremental policy initiatives may be particularly attractive, contrary to Lindblom's model.

Empirical research also suggests that a problem has a much better chance of reaching the agenda if a clearly perceived and readily understood solution already exists when events or public concern draw attention to an issue.[21] A problem no one knows how to solve will likely recede from the agenda without securing a governmental response. By contrast, where a ready-made solution does exist, action is much more likely. Here again, nonincremental solutions may be seized upon as readily as marginal policy changes if they seem likely to solve the problem and can be easily explained to the electorate.[22]

Members of Congress often play an important role in agenda setting by acting as policy entrepreneurs. A legislator strongly committed to a given proposal can try to keep the issue alive over time by periodic congressional hearings, hoping to seize any opportunity to link the proposal to a salient problem currently on the agenda. John Kingdon refers to this phenomenon as one of solutions chasing problems.[23]

Legislators may act as policy entrepreneurs for a variety of different reasons.[24] Often they simply want to make good public policy. Alternatively, they may seek to make a name for themselves, which may pay off in reelection or the pursuit of higher office. However, localism is perhaps the most potent factor in legislative entrepreneurship. It should not be surprising when legislators from Pennsylvania or West Virginia advocate an increased reliance on coal as an alternative to petroleum, or when a congressman from Los Angeles pushes for a federal solution to the smog problem.

Under the American system, the president plays a critical role in setting the agenda. While placing an item on the congressional agenda in no way guarantees eventual passage, and some of the president's initiatives will receive short shrift, determined presidents can almost always succeed in placing their highest priorities on the agenda.[25] In this way, President Reagan had been conspicuously successful in controlling the legislative agenda until the onset of the Iran-Contra scandal. While President Carter was widely regarded as less successful in dealing with Congress, he was nevertheless able to place the bulk of his domestic program—energy legislation, airline deregulation, welfare reform, national health insurance, hospital cost containment—on the agenda of Congress.

This presidential influence over the agenda serves to offset the localism of individual legislators. The president has a national constituency and, moreover, will be held accountable by the electorate for the government's performance, particularly in managing the economy, while individual members of Congress are largely absolved from blame by the voters. Responsible for the entire budget, the president is forced to make trade-offs among competing values and programs. Where legislators can specialize in the programs under the jurisdiction of the committees and subcommittees on which they serve, the president will be blamed for policy failures wherever they occur and must thus keep abreast of more policies than any other actor in the system. While different presidents may have very different political views, any president will necessarily adopt a broad, national perspective on issues that sets him apart from members of Congress, with their localized constituencies, and from bureaucrats, with their narrow programmatic interests.[26]

Policy Adoption

As suggested by the incremental model, policy adoption in the American system is typically a process of contention and compromise among a multiplicity of actors representing different interests. Beyond the inevitable conflicts arising out of the breakdown of comprehensive rationality, identified in the previous chapter, the representation of numerous interests is built into the American Constitution. Provision for a bicameral Congress assured that new policies would require the assent of two independent legislative bodies, whose members would be accountable to entirely different constituencies.[27]

Responsiveness to local interests was thus built into the Constitution by the framers. What the framers could not foresee, however, was the extent to which all legislators would eventually come to cooperate in securing reelection. In order to gain favorable name recognition among their constituents, lawmakers engage in ''credit-claiming'' for benefits going to their districts. To win votes, these benefits must be ''particularized''— that is, they must be local in nature, benefiting individual congressional districts narrowly, and they must be readily identifiable as resulting from the efforts of incumbent members of Congress.[28] The result is pork barrel legislation providing concentrated benefits to a variety of congressional districts: water projects, highway funds, federal education monies, or farm price supports for a coalition of commodity interests.

Given these pressures for localism and the undisciplined nature of American legislative parties (to be discussed below), the president's role is critical in mobilizing majorities in support of broader, national interests. While the president has no monopoly on policy initiatives, it remains much easier to secure major policy change under our system in response to vigorous presidential leadership. In asserting such leadership, however, the president suffers from a number of important disadvantages.[29] Within the executive branch, he cannot rely upon his nominal subordinates to comply automatically with his commands. In dealing with Congress, he has no hierarchical authority whatsoever; legislators are nominated and elected in individual states and congressional districts, independent of the president and the national parties. Moreover, representatives' terms of office are staggered, with the full House and one-third of the Senate up for reelection every two years; this serves to reduce the impact of presidential popularity on local congressional races and makes divided party control of Congress and the presidency an ever-present responsibility.

In this regard, all presidencies are subject to inevitable policy cycles. According to Paul Light, all presidents go through a cycle of increasing effectiveness. There is no adequate preparation for the office; all presidents must learn on the job. Over time, performance in office improves as the president gains a feel for the office and his staff acquires expertise. Unfortunately, as presidential performance improves, the president also goes through an equally unavoidable cycle of decreasing influence. Presidential popularity invariably declines with the making of hard choices. Midterm elections produce a loss of seats in Congress for the president's party. In the fourth year (and sometimes even earlier) attention shifts to the campaign for reelection. Once reelected, the president's influence begins to wane almost immediately, as the two-term limit makes him ineligible to run again. While the first year or so of a second term provides some opportunities for legislative action, midterm elections typically produce new losses for the president's party. The administration becomes increasingly irrelevant to the legislative process during the final two years of any president's term, as attention turns to the long campaign to determine who his successor will be.[30]

Even where the president's party controls both houses of Congress, he cannot depend upon automatic support for his program or to sustain a veto. While the public tends to equate the president's program with his party's program in Congress, making for a degree of joint responsibility for performance, the president's separate constituency and fixed term of office remove an important incentive for party cohesion. In a parliamentary system of government, party members cannot defect in large numbers without forcing a dissolution of the government. The continued tenure of the executive depends upon party cohesion; the desire to remain in power is sufficient to keep members in line. In the American system, by contrast, the continued tenure of the executive is assured by a fixed four-year term. While this renders the president independent of Congress in important respects, it also frees individual legislators to defect from the president's program by breaking the linkage between party cohesion and continued control of the White House.[31]

At the same time, the breakdown of party discipline under a separation-of-powers system may have offsetting advantages. Most presidents win on a large percentage of legislative issues, often by securing support across party lines. In distinct contrast to parliamentary systems, where party votes are the only recurring source of cleavage, presidential majorities come in all shapes and sizes and may be altered as necessary from one issue to the next:

> The fact is that the president can have either kind of majority: strictly party or cross-party. He can have a party majority on certain issues, and a cross-party majority on other issues. Moreover, the cross-party majority need not be the same combination on each occasion. All this is another way of saying that the president, freed from exclusive reliance on a single party, is able to present some policy recommendations with considerable chance of success even though his own party would not always be sufficiently united to enact them into law.[32]

However, the internal rules and procedures of Congress provide additional veto points where minorities may block or amend threatening proposals. Perhaps most important in this regard is the division of Congress into numerous committees and subcommittees specializing in narrow policy areas and retaining a great deal of latitude vis-à-vis the party leaderships within each house. This decentralization of power was made even worse in the mid-1970s by a series of internal House reforms that weakened the standing committee chairs and parceled effective power out to a proliferation of new subcommittees. Promoted in response to an influx of new members impatient with the seniority system and eager to move up the ladder as soon as possible, these reforms multiplied the number of veto points through which legislation must pass.[33] In the 97th Congress, for example, the House divided its labor among twenty-two standing committees with 139 subcommittees. The Senate was similarly organized into sixteen standing committees having 102 subcommittees. Jurisdiction over environmental policies, to name one issue area, was spread over five different standing committees in the Senate and twelve of the twenty-two standing committees in the House.[34] Much the same thing could be said of almost any major domestic policy area.

The filibuster provides a final line of defense to threatened minorities. Because there are no formal limits on debate in the Senate, a minority of members may literally talk a bill to death by blocking attempts to close off debate. Until 1975, two-thirds of those senators present and voting had to concur to invoke cloture; in 1975 the requirement was changed to the somewhat less restrictive three-fifths of the entire membership. Traditionally employed by Southern conservatives to block civil rights legislation, the filibuster has been used by a wide variety of interests in recent years. While a filibuster is precluded in the House by strict limits on debate, the existence of a standing Committee on Rules creates yet another decision point through which all bills must pass—and where they can be effectively undermined or defeated.[35]

Policy Implementation

As in the agenda-setting and policy adoption stages, many actors and institutions are inevitably involved in policy implementation, creating once again a process of "due deliberation" that provides new opportunities to block or amend national policies. If administration is inevitably political, as suggested in Chapter 1, it follows that implementation is too important a task for politicians to leave to administrators. Elected officials will eventually succumb to the temptation to intervene in the implementation process: to make sure their districts are receiving a fair share of federal money, to secure specific benefits for individual constituents (e.g., casework), to gain favorable publicity by uncovering scandals in administration, or (in the case of policy entrepreneurs) to make sure execution is consistent with the original spirit of the law. In this vein, one of the earlier proponents of a clear-cut distinction between politics and administration, Woodrow Wilson, clearly recognized the frequent intrusion of Congress into the "details" of administration and condemned the practice as interfering with professional administration![36]

It must be emphasized that the bureaucracy is *not* an independent branch of government under the Constitution. To the contrary, administrative agencies come into being through legislation, and they remain dependent upon Congress throughout their life spans for revenues and statutory authority. Where agency actions overstep the bounds of political support, Congress does not hesitate to discipline them through funding cuts or abridgment of their powers.[37]

While most executive agencies are nominally under the authority of the president, recent research emphasizes the limited powers of the president to force compliance with his directives. In the case of the nominally "independent" regulatory commissions, like the Federal Communications Commission, the Interstate Commerce Commission, or the Federal Reserve Board, the president's formal powers are even further reduced. Such commissions do not fall under the jurisdiction of a cabinet department, remaining instead arms of Congress in the execution of policy. Commissioners serve for fixed terms and cannot be removed under normal circumstances. The president can fill vacancies only as they arise, and then often only under the additional constraint of maintaining a partisan balance among the commissioners.

The president nevertheless retains some important resources to influence policy implementation.[38] To begin with, the president is a very important actor in the budget process, with his budgetary requests typically serving as the starting point for congressional deliberations. President Reagan successfully cut the budget of the Environmental Protection Agency by more than a third during his first term in office, forcing the agency to conform to his vision of limited government by crippling its capacity to regulate. In this same way, he issued an executive order bringing new business regulations under the purview of the Office of Management and Budget, ostensibly to assess their potential impact on federal outlays.[39] Headed under Reagan by conservatives sharing the president's desire to deregulate the economy, OMB has successfully blocked many new regulations affecting industry.

Presidents may also shape agency behavior through new legislation. President Reagan sought to weaken the Clean Air Act in both 1981 and 1982, albeit rather ineptly. His failure to obtain the revisions he sought forced him into the budgetary strategy discussed above.[40] By contrast, however, President Carter was strikingly successful in pursuing his regulatory goals, securing legislation to deregulate the airlines and substantially loosening the regulation of trucks and railroads.

The airline deregulation example points to an additional presidential resource: the appointment power. President Carter appointed advocates of deregulation to vacancies on the Civil Aeronautics Board at every opportunity. With these new appointments, the commission first moved to deregulate informally through new regulations granting airlines more freedom to raise and lower rates and to enter new routes. As rates fell over many routes, the number of air travelers rose, making for greater industry profits. Thus consumers and at least some airlines provided sufficient support for statutory action to secure the Airline Deregulation Act of 1978.[41]

The president's appointment powers are much broader within the cabinet departments, and President Reagan used these powers to great effect, staffing the executive branch to an unprecedented extent with ideological conservatives sympathetic to his programs. While many critics deplored the decline in professional qualifications of administrators resulting from Reagan's use of the "administrative presidency," supporters countered that he brought the permanent government under effective control in carrying out his electoral mandate—a precondition for the existence of "responsible parties" and majority rule (see Chapter 6).[42]

The courts provide another source of uncertainty in the environment of government agencies. With the expansion of standing to sue in recent years, a wide variety of private interests are now entitled to challenge agency actions in the federal courts. For example, environmental groups may sue to force the agency to take stronger action or even to develop new regulations in accordance with its legislative mandate. In bringing suits relating to "nationally applicable standards" under the Clean Air Act of 1970, such a group may shop around for the federal court most likely to be sympathetic to its case. In *Sierra Club v. Ruckleshaus*, to cite one example, the federal district court for the District of Columbia required the EPA to prevent the significant deterioration of air quality in areas (like Yellowstone Park) already meeting the law's health-based air quality standards. This decision was subsequently upheld by the D.C. circuit court of appeals and the U.S. Supreme Court, forcing the development of a complicated and politically controversial new program that was eventually incorporated into the Clean Air Amendments of 1977. At the same time, however, businesses may seek relief from EPA rulings in the federal district court serving their area, often successfully eroding the impact of rulings favoring environmental interests elsewhere in the federal court system.[43]

Federalism introduces another whole set of actors and political struggles into the implementation process. The vast majority of domestic policies are administered intergovernmentally. Under categorical grant programs, the federal government gives revenues to the states on a matching funds basis, usually under a formula that yields substantial federal revenues in return for state participation. The grants are given for narrowly defined purposes, and federal standards constrain how the money may be spent. Even so, the primary responsibility for on-site administration remains with state (and in some cases local) authorities, typically leaving a good deal of discretion to local implementors.

In recent years, the block grant has emerged as an alternative to the categorical grant. Block grants are given for broader purposes than categoricals, and they permit states and localities much more discretion in fashioning their own approaches to problems. In many cases, block grants have been employed to simplify an increasingly labyrinthine federal grant structure, consolidating a variety of overlapping categorical grants into a single block grant and thus permitting more coherent program management by local officials.[44]

Under the Reagan administration, the use of block grants to replace categorical grant programs was greatly accelerated. At the same time, the total amount of federal assistance going to state and local governments was sharply reduced. While these cuts were dictated in large part by the need to reduce the federal deficit, there was also an ideological component to the cutbacks. President Reagan sought a return to an earlier concept of federalism, in which the states would again operate independently of the federal government in determining their own policy priorities and raising their own revenues to pay for them.[45] Such a shift also favors business interests, as corporations often find themselves in a stronger political position at the state and local level (see Chapter 5).

While block grants deliberately place few restrictions on the freedom of action of state and local administrators, in practice the degree of federal control over ultimate policy outcomes is typically quite limited even in categorical grant programs. In this regard, recent research on policy implementation has consistently emphasized the latitude available to state and local actors.[46] Even where narrowly restrictive, federal grants constitute an effort by the national government to intervene in ongoing state and local political processes. Because the states remain sovereign entities under the Constitution, there can be no pretense of a hierarchical system in which national policy mandates are automatically carried out by the states as subordinate political units. Federal grants may shift the balance of power within these political systems, but they cannot eliminate completely the necessity for bargaining with them.[47]

Thus, passage of a law does not put an end to the political process, but rather sets in motion a whole series of new policy struggles. At the national level, interests defeated in the legislative process will attempt to recoup their losses by influencing the administrative process or by going to court to obtain a favorable interpretation of the statute. In implementing the statute, national administrators will be forced to contend with fifty different state political systems, and often countless local governments as well. State officials remain ultimately accountable to their own constituencies, and federal policies will inevitably reflect the socioeconomic and political environments in which are implemented. Under such circumstances, the erosion of national policy mandates is virtually inevitable and coherent policy delivery would seem almost impossible.

POLICY CHANGE UNDER THE CLASSICAL MODEL

Clearly, the classical model adds much to our understanding of the prevalence of incrementalism in the policy process. We can now see that incrementalism is only partly the result of inherent limits on rational decision making. Contrary to Lindblom's expectations, proposals for major policy change frequently receive consideration from policy makers, and at least some of the time they are enacted into law. More often, however, the need to construct concurrent majorities distributed across a series of veto points makes bargaining and compromise imperative, leading to incremental policy outcomes. Legislation must normally be acceptable to both houses of Congress and the president. Within Congress, proposals must pass through a series of committees, subcommittees, floor votes, and the possibility of a Senate filibuster before becoming law. Policies surviving this legislative obstacle course must go on to face additional hurdles: renewed efforts by defeated interests to influence the administrative process and the necessity in most cases for intergovernmental implementation in a federal system.

Ideally, these multiple veto points serve to force majorities to consider the legitimate concerns of minorities. While a broadly distributed and determined majority can eventually work its will, the need to secure a wide range of political support virtually guarantees that intense minorities will be able to soften the impact of policies emerging from this obstacle course.[48]

If large change is possible under the American system, contrary to the tenets of the incremental model, such major policy departures remain the exception rather than the rule. Nonincremental policy proposals may stand as good a chance of reaching the agenda as do more moderate initiatives, but the need to make concessions in order to build concurrent majorities at different stages ordinarily results in legislative outcomes that are vaguely worded and significantly compromised. For a major policy change to make it all the way through the process, something has to happen—a crisis, an aroused public opinion, strong presidential leadership, or some other variables—to make key decision makers at several different points in the system receptive to large change. (For a full examination of some of the factors giving rise to nonincremental policy outcomes, see Part II.)

But the process does not end with the passage of a law, and large change is extremely difficult to sustain in the American system. Court challenges, resistance to effective implementation at local levels, subsequent legislation amending the original law, or the election of new officeholders with a different idea of good public policy can all retard the full implementation of major policy departures. For example, the Clean Air Act of 1970 now appears to have been much more incremental in its impact than was at first thought.[49] The ten-year project to put a man on the moon, often cited as a classic instance of major policy change, now seems like ancient history to a space agency beset with budgetary restrictions and outside investigations in the wake of the Challenger disaster.[50] The tax reform bill of 1986 is widely expected to be amended in future years as special interests once again begin to lobby for exemptions. Even airline deregulation may prove short lived, as Congress responds to increasing concerns about airline safety and constituency complaints of declining quality of service in many locations.

To conclude, the Constitution is designed to subject all proposed policy changes to a process of protracted deliberation and all too often precludes a timely and coherent response to pressing problems, promoting instead obstructionism, localism, and delay. In saying this, however, we must recognize the framers' concern with preventing majority tyranny, and we must be careful not to indict the Constitution for policy failures where conflicts over values and problem definition or limits on the available knowledge base would preclude rational policy-making under any system of government. Where agreement on objectives is combined with adequate knowledge, there is nothing in the classical model to prevent major policy change. Indeed, where the demand for action is strong enough, as with the air pollution case in 1970, it can produce nonincremental change even where the knowledge base remains incomplete.[51]

What can safely be said is that the classical model makes it virtually impossible for the average citizen to monitor the policy process intelligently and hold any specific groups or institutions accountable for policy outcomes.[52] The American system is extraordinarily complex. There is no fixed starting point for the policy process, as issues can reach the agenda in a wide variety of institutional settings. Equally important, there is no clear and definite resolution of most issues. Rather, the virtual necessity of going through all the veto points sooner or later makes it likely that a wide range of actors, distributed among political institutions and across levels of government, will eventually become involved, making accountability difficult to assign. The seriality of the policy process, identified by Lindblom, reinforces this institutional complexity. Issues tend to emerge over and over again in slightly different form, or at different levels of government, as groups defeated at one stage of the process reopen the struggle somewhere else. The abortion controversy provides an excellent case in point, moving from the courts to Congress and back again over the past fifteen years.

The normal flow of issues through a variety of institutional arenas, over a long period of time and in no particular order, requires a high degree of sophistication and sustained attention beyond the capacity of most voters. This gives organized interests a real advantage over unorganized mass publics and turns our attention to yet another set of factors giving rise to incrementalism in policy-making: variations across groups in political resources and the ability to mobilize for effective influence. These sources of political inequality will be the focus of the next two chapters.

NOTES

1. In laying out the elements of this model, the primary focus here will be on *The Federalist Papers,* Clinton Rossiter, ed. (New York: New American Library, Mentor Books, 1961), especially Nos. 10, 47, 51, and 73. In labeling this the "classical model," I have followed the terminology of Peter Woll in his text *Public Policy* (Washington, D.C.: University Press of America, 1974). Characterizing the model as the "separation of powers" or "checks and balances" model highlights only one aspect of the model. Alternatively, calling it the "Madisonian model," as does Robert Dahl in *A Preface to Democratic Theory* (Chicago: University of Chicago Press, Phoenix Books ed., 1963), gives full credit for the model to James Madison

at the expense of the other two authors of *The Federalist*, Alexander Hamilton and John Jay.

2. Charles O. Jones, *An Introduction to the Study of Public Policy*, 3d ed. (Monterey, Calif.: Brooks/Cole, 1984), p. 6.

3. *The Federalist*, No. 73, p. 443.

4. "Those who hold and those who are without property have ever formed distinct interests in society. Those who are creditors, and those who are debtors, fall under a like discrimination. A landed interest, a manufacturing interest, a mercantile interest, a moneyed interest, with many lesser interests, grow up of necessity in civilized nations, and divide them into different classes, actuated by different sentiments and views." *The Federalist*, No. 10, p. 79.

5. *The Federalist*, No. 10, p. 80.

6. *The Federalist*, No. 10, p. 81. Similarly, Madison writing in *The Federalist*, No. 51: "If men were angels, no government would be necessary. If angels were to govern men, neither external nor internal controls on government would be necessary."

7. *The Federalist*, No. 10, p. 78.

8. *The Federalist*, No. 10, p. 81.

9. *The Federalist*, No. 10, p. 83. On this point, see also Grant McConnell, *Private Power and American Democracy* (New York: Knopf, 1966), pp. 91–118.

10. *The Federalist*, No. 51, p. 324.

11. *The Federalist*, No. 47, p. 301.

12. *The Federalist*, No. 51, p. 322.

13. This insight is drawn from Richard E. Neustadt, *Presidential Power*, rev. ed. (New York: Wiley, 1980), p. 26.

14. *The Federalist*, No. 51, p. 323.

15. *The Federalist*, No. 73, p. 444.

16. David B. Truman, *The Governmental Process* (New York: Knopf, 1951), pp. 507–508.

17. J. W. Peltason, *Fifty-Eight Lonely Men* (Urbana: University of Illinois Press, Illini Books ed., 1971). For a more comprehensive account of the civil rights movement, see Taylor Branch, *Parting the Waters* (New York: Simon and Schuster, 1988).

18. John W. Kingdon, *Agendas, Alternatives, and Public Policies* (Boston: Little, Brown, 1984), pp. 109–110.

19. Kingdon, pp. 95–108.

20. Kingdon, pp. 83–88.

21. Jack L. Walker, "Setting the Agenda in the U.S. Senate: A Theory of Problem Selection," *British Journal of Political Science*, 7 (October 1977), pp. 423–445.

22. The Kemp-Roth bill provides an excellent illustration here. Plainly a nonincremental policy departure, it proposed to cut federal income tax rates by 10 percent per year for three years in order to lower marginal tax rates and improve incentives to work and invest. The proposal became the centerpiece of Ronald Reagan's domestic agenda in the 1980 presidential campaign and was enacted into law in 1981 as its "supply-side" orientation offered a potential solution to the high levels of inflation, unemployment, and interest rates occurring simultaneously, in violation of conventional economic theories.

23. Kingdon, especially pp. 122–151 and 174–204.

24. Kingdon, pp. 129–130.

25. Kingdon, pp. 23–28.

26. This is not to say that the president's position can be properly equated with the public interest. See Alfred de Grazia, "The Myth of the President," in Ronald C. Moe (ed.), *Congress and the President* (Pacific Palisades, Calif.: Goodyear, 1971), pp. 88–108.

27. *The Federalist,* No. 62, pp. 376–382. It should be noted that the direct popular election of United States senators was not instituted until 1913, with the ratification of the Seventeenth Amendment to the Constitution.

28. David R. Mayhew, *Congress: The Electoral Connection* (New Haven, Conn.: Yale University Press, 1974).

29. In Neustadt's oft-cited phrase, the president's powers add up to little more than "the power to persuade." See *Presidential Power,* pp. 26–43.

30. Paul Light, *The President's Agenda* (Baltimore: Johns Hopkins University Press, 1982), pp. 36–40.

31. Leon D. Epstein, *Political Parties in Western Democracies* (New York: Praeger, 1967), pp. 315–350.

32. Epstein, pp. 347–348.

33. For a good account of the reform process, see Norman J. Ornstein, "The Democrats Reform Power in the House of Representatives, 1969–75," in Allan P. Sindler (ed.), *America in the Seventies* (Boston: Little, Brown, 1977), pp. 2–48.

34. Henry C. Kenski and Margaret Corgan Kenski, "Congress Against the President: The Struggle Over the Environment," in Norman J. Vig and Michael E. Kraft (eds.), *Environmental Policy in the 1980s* (Washington, D.C.: Congressional Quarterly Press), 1984), pp. 97–120.

35. Jones, *An Introduction to the Study of Public Policy,* p. 119. For a comprehensive and insightful, albeit somewhat dated, discussion of congressional procedures, see Lewis A. Froman, Jr., *The Congressional Process* (Boston: Little, Brown, 1967).

36. Woodrow Wilson, "The Study of Administration," *Political Science Quarterly,* 2 (1877), pp. 197–222.

37. For an argument that all delegations of legislative authority are inherently tentative, see Paul H. Appleby, *Policy and Administration* (University: University of Alabama Press, 1949), pp. 26–65. For some excellent case studies illustrating this point, see Erwin G. Krasnow, Lawrence D. Longley, and Herbert A. Terry, *The Politics of Broadcast Regulation,* 3d ed. (New York: St. Martin's, 1982).

38. Krasnow, Longley, and Terry, pp. 66–75.

39. George C. Eads and Michael Fix, *Relief or Reform?* (Washington, D.C.: Urban Institute, 1984).

40. Richard J. Tobin, "Revising the Clean Air Act: Legislative Failure and Administrative Success," in Vig and Kraft, pp. 227–249.

41. Bradley and Behrman, "Civil Aeronautics Board," in James Q. Wilson (ed.), *The Politics of Regulation* (New York: Basic Books, 1980), pp. 75–120.

42. J. Clarence Davies, "Environmental Institutions and the Reagan Administration," in Vig and Kraft, pp. 143–160.

43. On the structure of the federal courts and its impact on policy-making, see especially Jack W. Peltason, *Federal Courts in the Political Process* (New York: Random House, 1954); Richard J. Richardson and Kenneth N. Vines, *The Politics of Federal Courts* (Boston: Little, Brown, 1970); Robert A. Carp and C. K. Rowland, *Policymaking and Politics in the Federal District Courts* (Knoxville: University of Tennessee Press, 1983); Lettie M. Wenner, *The Environmental Decade in Court* (Bloomington: Indiana University Press, 1982); and R. Shep Melnick, *Regulation and the Courts* (Washington, D.C.; Brookings Institution, 1983). For a critique of judicial activism, see David L. Horowitz, *The Courts and Social Policy* (Washington, D.C.: Brookings Institution, 1977). On the expansion of standing to sue in recent years, see Karen Orren, "Standing to Sue: Interest Group Conflict in the Federal Courts," *American Political Science Review,* 70 (September 1976), pp. 723–741.

44. On the evolution of the grants system, see Michael D. Reagan and John G. Sanzone, *The New Federalism,* 2d ed. rev. (New York: Oxford University Press, 1981).

45. Early in his first term, President Reagan proposed a "New Federalism," in which various programs now operated jointly by the states and the federal government would be taken over by one level of government or the other. Under the Reagan plan, for example, the states would assume complete responsibility for the Aid to Families with Dependent Children program, while the federal government would assume sole funding and administration of the Medicaid program. Resistance from governors and mayors stalled this initiative, which has since been dropped.

46. For a good review of this literature, see Robert T. Nakamura and Frank Smallwood, *The Politics of Policy Implementation* (New York: St. Martin's, 1980), pp. 7–28. For a clear model of this process, see Carl E. Van Horn, *Policy Implementation in a Federal System* (Lexington, Mass.: Lexington Books, 1979).

47. Martha Derthick, *The Influence of Federal Grants* (Cambridge, Mass.: Harvard University Press, 1970), pp. 193–215.

48. For the classic statement that the classical model provides protection to intense minorities, see Willmoore Kendall and George W. Carey, "The 'Intensity' Problem and Democratic Theory," *American Political Science Review,* 62 (March 1968), pp. 5–24. For a very different assessment, see Dahl, *A Preface to Democratic Theory.*

49. Contrast Charles O. Jones, *Clean Air* (Pittsburgh: University of Pittsburgh Press, 1975) with Walter A. Rosenbaum, *Environmental Politics and Policy* (Washington, D.C.: Congressional Quarterly Press, 1985), or Melnick, *Regulation and the Courts.*

50. Paul R. Schulman, "Nonincremental Policy-Making: Notes Toward an Alternative Paradigm," *American Political Science Review,* 69 (December 1975), pp. 1354–1370.

51. See Jones, *Clean Air.*

52. On this point, see Stephen Kemp Bailey, *Congress Makes a Law* (New York: Random House, Vintage Books, 1964), pp. 235–240.

CHAPTER 4

The Unequal Group Struggle

In Chapter 2 we saw that policy-making is typically a process of mutual adjustment among a multiplicity of groups active on an issue rather than the product of a process of rational choice or decision. According to Charles Lindblom, this process of "disjointed incrementalism" will yield good public policies, better in any event than would be produced by a misguided attempt at rational decision making. However, the normative case for Lindblom's model rested upon two unrealistic assumptions: that almost every social interest would have its watchdog, and that competition among social interests would be "atomistic": that is, no single actor or coalition would possess political market power.

In reality, neither of these optimistic assumptions about group activity is warranted. We therefore turn our attention in this chapter to a model that addresses directly these important sources of political inequality. In contrast to the incremental model, group theory treats the array of active interests and the distribution of political resources as the fundamental variables that combine to determine the group equilibrium. The task of the political scientist is to identify the relevant groups and specify their relative strength. As Arthur Bentley observed:

> It is only as we isolate these group activities, determine their relative values, and get the whole process stated in terms of them, that we approach to a satisfactory knowledge of government.[1]

Group theory (or the group struggle model, as it is identified by some proponents)[2] shares with incrementalism the fundamental insight that public policy is less the result of rational, conscious choice than the political resultant of the interplay of numerous contending groups. However, the group theorists emphasize, much more than Lindblom, that this process of mutual adjustment is at the same time a struggle for advantage:

> What may be called public policy is actually the equilibrium reached in the group struggle at any given moment, and it represents a balance which the contending factions are constantly striving to weight in their favor.[3]

Where Lindblom treats the interplay of groups as essentially an adaptive or coordinative mechanism for arriving at collective decisions under difficult conditions, the group theorists see politics as combat among contending groups determined to prevail. If the multiplicity of contending interests typically forces individual groups to accept less than total victory in this struggle, any model that treats mutual accommodation as an end in itself will fail to do justice to the intensity of the group conflict. To Lindblom, the proper subject matter of public policy analysis is the quest for rational policy under severe constraints. To the group theorist, it is *power*—the need to acquire power in order to prevail over other actors, and the importance of variations in resources across groups.[4]

THE GROUP BASIS OF POLITICS

The central premise of group theory is that public policy results from a struggle among contending interests. According to the group theorists, most human activity takes place through groups of one kind or another—schools, churches, business firms, labor unions, voluntary associations, and so on—and effective political action by isolated individuals is so rare as to be discounted. At the same time, groups are formed to advance the collective interests or shared preferences of individuals. Where they fail in these aims, they will lose members, shrinking in size and influence or even failing to survive. To the group theorists, individuals remain "the bedrock materials from which groups are organized."[5]

The primary actors in this struggle are organized interest groups mobilized to represent an almost bewildering array of economic interests, demographic groups, and ideological viewpoints. For example, at the national level a variety of organizations lobby on behalf of farmers, businesses, and organized labor. In recent years, a wide variety of groups have mobilized to represent previously unorganized interests: consumers, environmentalists, women, and the aged, among others. The legalization of political action committees in the post-Watergate reform period has not only enhanced the role of corporations and labor unions in electoral politics but also given rise to a large number of ideological groups, drawing large numbers of previously unaffiliated individuals into the group universe.

While group theory has been criticized for treating policy makers as little more than passive referees of the group struggle,[6] in reality this model treats various governmental actors as active participants in the process, with their own group interests and resources. As Earl Latham observed, the government official "does not play the part of inert cash register, ringing up the additions and withdrawals of strength."[7] Rather, executive agencies have institutional interests to protect. At a minimum, they will seek to defend, and if

possible expand, their budgetary base. Beyond this, bureaucratic agencies will seek to enhance their autonomy in administering programs under their control, and they will guard
against encroachments by other departments on their organizational turf. Different agencies will not only have different institutional interests but will also tend to see different
facets of the same issue—for example, they will tend to define the public interest differently. In general, executive agencies will strive to expand their influence with other
policy makers in order to better advance their organizational interests, and they will typically see the expansion of their influence as being in the larger public interest.[8]

According to Latham, such public groups differ from their private counterparts primarily through their possession of an important kind of status he termed "officiality."
Whereas government possesses a monopoly on the legitimate use of coercion, and government alone has the power to authoritatively allocate values for society, governmental actors are granted formal powers unavailable to other actors. However, officiality is not to
be equated with power. The statutory authority of most executive agencies to compel behavior is quite limited. Given an incomplete arsenal of powers, governmental actors must
struggle to shape policy, along with private interest groups.[9]

Clearly, a wide range of groups must be considered as potentially relevant in a group
analysis of the policy process on a given issue: traditional pressure groups, political action
committees, bureaucrats, party leaders, informal groups within Congress, and so on.
Analysis cannot be confined to private interests, but must be expanded to include a variety
of actors possessing official status as well:

> The group struggle, therefore, is apparent in the universe of unofficial groups and it is
> apparent in the universe of official groups. But these are not separate universes. They are
> one. . . .[10]

THE SYSTEMATIC BIAS TO THE GROUP UNIVERSE

Group theory has frequently been criticized for equating the group equilibrium with the
public interest.[11] The assumption that all affected interests would sooner or later be represented in the group struggle, thus yielding an outcome in the public interest, has been
most prominently (and somewhat unfairly) associated with the work of David Truman. In
The Governmental Process, Truman suggested that policy makers would be forced to consider the interests of unorganized, "potential groups," inasmuch as these groups might
mobilize at any point to influence policy.[12] Because Truman's book is widely recognized
as the single most important and influential work on the role of interest groups in the policy process, it is often treated as the definitive statement of the theory.

Truman was almost alone among group theorists in taking such an optimistic view of
the group struggle, however.[13] Bentley, Latham, and Gross saw the model as offering a
particularly realistic and unsentimental description of how the policy process actually
worked. Politics was characterized as a struggle to determine who gets what. In this struggle, organized groups are "structures of power" designed to "concentrate human wit, energy, and muscle for the achievement of received purposes."[14] Far from arguing that the

group struggle would automatically produce outcomes in the public interest, group theorists saw the public interest as an amorphous concept at best, virtually impossible to define in the abstract and seldom, if ever, clearly identified for a specific issue.[15]

Because the group struggle model makes no assumption that all groups with a stake in a given issue will succeed in mobilizing, most group theorists have viewed formal organization as an advantage in dealing with unorganized interests. While "potential groups" may receive some consideration from policy makers, there is much more incentive to respond to the pressures of the effectively mobilized. According to Truman, formal organization is evidence that a group has attained a threshold level of cohesion and shared values. It also provides for a division of labor that makes possible effective action. Finally, it suggests a degree of permanence, implying that the group is an important element in the environment whose wishes will have to receive at least some consideration.[16] Where unorganized mass publics are vulnerable to a short attention span, organized groups will have longer memories and a greater degree of expertise. To summarize:

> In this group struggle, there is an observable balance of influence in favor of organized groups in their dealings with the unorganized, and in favor of the best and most efficiently organized in their dealings with the less efficiently organized. . . . Or, to put it another way, organization represents concentrated power, and concentrated power can exercise a dominating influence when it encounters power which is diffuse and not concentrated, and therefore weaker.[17]

The Free Rider Problem

In a seminal contribution to group theory, political economist Mancur Olson observed that all potential groups must first overcome a "free rider" problem if they are to organize at all.[18] Because the benefits of interest group activity are typically available to potential members whether they actually join the group or not, self-interested individuals will find it rational not to contribute, hoping instead to benefit from the efforts of others. This free rider problem is particularly severe for large, diffuse interests—consumers, taxpayers, or environmentalists, for example—as the larger the size of the group, the less likely it is that any one individual's contribution will make a difference to the group's success. By contrast, in very small groups, like the three major domestic automobile manufacturers, the importance of each member's contribution to the group's success is so apparent—and the individual's personal stake in the outcome so much larger—that collective action is much more likely.

Moreover, as Robert Salisbury has shown, it is most difficult to form interest groups when they are most needed—for example, when their members face hard economic times. Group membership is an economic transaction; entrepreneurs (like Ralph Nader) offer potential members a mix of tangible and intangible benefits in exchange for dues. To survive in the long run, the group must (eventually, at least) take in more in dues than the costs of servicing the membership. Because group membership is something of a luxury for many individuals, membership dues will be one of the first expenses sacrificed in hard times. Thus, Salisbury found, interest groups are most likely to form in prosperous times and most likely to fail (or at least lose members) in times of group hardship, when they might make a greater difference in members' lives.[19]

A Class Bias to Participation

The obstacles facing large, diffuse groups are reinforced by a socioeconomic bias to all forms of political participation, including interest group membership. Entrepreneurs seeking to mobilize the poor face particularly serious difficulties inasmuch as potential members have little income and leisure time to spend on group memberships that will typically yield benefits, if at all, only in the distant future. Not surprisingly, as E. E. Schattschneider observed, in the interest group struggle "the heavenly chorus sings with a strong upper-class accent."[20]

The Permanence of Institutions

A final bias to the group universe favors institutions of all kinds over membership groups. Corporations provide perhaps the best example here. Lobbying as individual organizations, they do not face a free rider problem in getting off the ground. Where membership groups are vulnerable to economic cycles, with membership rolls rising in good times and falling in hard times, institutions are much more likely to have the surplus profits to devote to lobbying regardless of the economic circumstances.

Institutions thus tend to be much more permanent than membership groups.[21] The free rider problem never goes away for membership groups; once a group has gotten off the ground, it still must motivate members to remain in the group over the long haul. A comparative study of the group universe in 1960 and 1981 found the vast majority of corporations active in the earlier period still on the scene later. By contrast, most of the citizens' groups in the 1960 sample were no longer to be found, and most of the citizens' groups in the 1981 sample were born over the past ten to fifteen years, suggesting that the recent explosion of new citizens' groups may have accomplished little more than to replace a whole generation of earlier groups that failed to survive, with the net effect that the group universe was not significantly more balanced in 1981 than it was two decades earlier.[22]

THE BALANCE OF FORCES

According to this model, policy—which is to say, the final equilibrium of the contending groups—will be a function of the balance of forces active on the issue. Specifically, the group equilibrium will depend on the resources available to the various participants and the extent to which each is able to translate these resources into effective influence.[23]

Money is not the only resource available to interest groups in this regard. For example, organized labor is able to partially offset the growing monetary advantage of business by contributing manpower to the campaigns of Democratic candidates. Nuclear freeze groups, operating on a shoestring budget, successfully forced the arms control issue onto the agenda in 1981 through grass roots mobilization of public opinion. In 1970, environmental groups were similarly able to arouse public opinion to push Congress into passage of a much stronger Clean Air Act than originally anticipated.

Intangible Resources

The pollution and nuclear freeze cases just cited suggest that often various intangible resources can be at least as important to a group's success as money and manpower. For example, a group's influence will depend in part on its reputation as a reliable source of information or *expertise*. Interest groups often act as ''service bureaus'' for legislators already sympathetic to their cause, providing information on alternative policies and, in turn, educating their members on the need to accept the compromises emerging from the bargaining process. A reputation for honesty and accuracy is essential, lest groups forfeit access to policy makers.[24]

Another intangible resource is the group's prestige or *legitimacy*. Senior citizens' groups possess extraordinary legitimacy, for example, partly because the serious problems they face (large medical bills in their retirement years) are widely regarded as not of their own making, and partly because eventually all of us must confront problems associated with aging. If effect, Medicare and Social Security have come to be perceived not as largess for a segment of the population, but rather as universal entitlements sooner or later available to all. By contrast, welfare recipients are readily characterized (rightly or wrongly) as failures living off the toil of others: men too unskilled or irresponsible to hold a steady job, women abandoned by their husbands or having children out of wedlock, welfare queens taking advantage of the system by collecting multiple benefits. The contrast is striking, and it helps to explain why the aged were relatively insulated from major program cuts during President Reagan's term in office, while AFDC and Food Stamps were cut repeatedly.[25]

Finally, a group's *strategic position* in society can be a critically important resource. A group has leverage to the extent that society depends upon goods or services it routinely provides. For example, Charles Lindblom has recently argued that corporations occupy a ''privileged position'' in capitalistic societies (see Chapter 5).[26] Because government officials need prosperity to remain in office, they are naturally solicitous of the needs of business. Business leaders are accorded automatic access while other groups must compete to make their views heard. Even where business groups are inactive on an issue, they may exercise indirect influence as policy makers take into account the effects of proposed policies on economic growth, plant location, or incentives to invest.

Such resources, however impressive, constitute only the potential for influence. They are worth nothing until they are translated into effective influence. In this regard, *internal cohesion* is a critically important variable. Internal divisions reduce a group's credibility in claiming to speak for its constituency and may prevent the group from taking any position at all. For example, peak associations organized to represent the shared class interests of American business (e.g., the Chamber of Commerce or the National Association of Manufacturers) find it difficult to act on many economic issues because such issues tend to divide the business community. Because these groups typically require near unanimity among their members before taking a stand, they are much more likely to lobby on issues that only peripherally affect business, like farm price supports or welfare reform.[27]

In this same vein, the *political skill of the group's leadership* is also a variable, and thus not to be taken for granted. In the case study of tariff lobbying in the 1950s, cited above, many business lobbyists were found to be timid and poorly informed. Afraid that efforts to persuade unsympathetic legislators would be perceived as unreasonable "pressure," they focused most of their attention on members of Congress already sympathetic to their cause. These same lobbyists were found to lack even the most rudimentary data as to which legislators remained undecided, and thus potentially persuadable, on the issue.[28] While such timidity is no longer the norm for business lobbyists in this era of expanded corporate involvement in politics, it nevertheless serves as a reminder that seemingly overwhelming resource advantages do not translate automatically into effective power.

THE GROUP STRUGGLE AND THE EVOLUTION OF POLICY

The group struggle model differs from incrementalism on a number of critical points. At a fundamental level, the model treats the interplay among groups as a struggle for power rather than a cooperative attempt to make the best possible collective decisions. This emphasis on social combat rather than mutual adjustment inevitably shifts attention to important issues of political equality largely ignored by Lindblom: in particular, the question of what groups succeed in mobilizing and the critical importance of variations in resources from one group to another. Not surprisingly, the group struggle model provides a very different description of each of the stages of the policy process.

Agenda Setting

In contrast to incrementalism, group theory does not assume that all (or even most) important issues will reach the agenda. To the contrary, there will typically be a struggle over the agenda, which will take place on at least two levels: an initial struggle over the scope of conflict—over whether the issue is properly public or private and over where in government the issue should be taken up—and a second struggle over how the issue should be defined.

The question of whether a given problem is properly public can never be neutral, for at bottom it is a question of who is going to participate in the group struggle. If policy represents an equilibrium of contending groups, it follows that the ultimate outcome will be a function of what interests are included in the balance. According to Schattschneider, all political conflicts feature not only the immediately contending interests, but also an "audience" with the potential to intervene, tipping the balance one way or the other. Thus it is the losers in private conflicts that have an incentive to approach government, broadening the scope of conflict to include new participants. Schattschneider termed this phenomenon the "socialization of conflict." By contrast, the winners in the private struggle have every incentive to "privatize" conflict, arguing that the issue is not properly a public problem for government to resolve.[29]

The same thing can be said for the question of where in government a public problem should be placed. Blacks in the South in the early 1960s had every incentive to draw the federal government into the civil rights struggle. By contrast, Southern whites, who dominated local political systems by disenfranchising black voters, argued that civil rights questions were properly dealt with at the state level. Similarly, business interests typically favor pollution controls at the state and local level, where they possess tremendous leverage by virtue of their capacity to affect local employment and tax base. By contrast, environmental groups prefer action at the federal level, where business influence is less pronounced. In addition, they prefer not to spread scarce resources thinly over fifty state political systems.

In short, the placement of an issue can never be neutral, for it critically affects who will participate in the group struggle. Arguments about whether an issue is properly public may be couched in analytic terms, and appeals to the Constitution or other powerful symbols may be made to influence the placement of an issue at one level of government rather than another, but all such arguments are ultimately a smoke screen for efforts to secure tactical advantage.

Finally, there will be a struggle over precisely how the issue is to be defined. Most issues can be defined in more than one way, if for no other reason than that public problems typically involve trade-offs among important values. Which value will be paramount is of critical importance in influencing the final outcome. As Schattschneider observed, the definition of alternatives is the supreme instrument of power.[30]

Two examples from Chapter 2 again provide excellent illustrations. An economist would define air pollution as an externality, emphasizing the need to make polluters (and their customers) pay for the adverse effects on third parties. However, this is by no means the only way the problem can be defined. Electric utilities and their customers will minimize the damage to third parties and point to lack of clear-cut evidence that they are in fact responsible for the problem. At the same time, they will point to very real impacts on utility rates resulting from the requirement of expensive emissions control devices, with adverse effects to local consumers and possible ripple effects on overall employment levels in the area. These arguments will have added force under our system of government (see Chapter 3) because these local interests will be vigilantly represented in Washington by a representative and two senators concerned with securing their reelection.

Much the same thing could be said of the abortion controversy. It is obviously of critical importance whether this issue is defined as one of fetal right to life or freedom of choice for pregnant women. Indeed, the struggle over policy is focused almost entirely around how the issue should be defined. For example, arguments that the abortion decision is an inherently "private" one, to be made by a woman in consultation with her physician and her spouse, are really attempts by pro-choice forces to define the issue in favorable terms by characterizing it as an inappropriate subject for regulation.

Policy Adoption

The central premise of this model is that policy represents an equilibrium of contending groups. The precise balance will be a function of what groups participate in the struggle on a given issue, what resources they bring to bear, and how effectively they translate these resources into effective influence.

Where incrementalism assumes that all (or at least most) affected interests will be represented in the group struggle, group theory recognizes that some groups (particularly institutions, relatively small groups, and the affluent) will be much more likely than others to mobilize. There is thus no guarantee that the group equilibrium will be properly balanced, or even that groups will be active on both sides of the issue.

It follows that the configuration of active groups is a critically important variable in determining the final legislative outcome. Broadly speaking, two distinct patterns of demand may be identified.[31] Where many groups are active on all sides of the issue (as with the tariff issue in the 1950s), the demand pattern may be termed *conflictual*. This is the ideal state of affairs according to both incrementalism and group theory: a pattern of atomistic competition in which no individual group can independently influence the outcome. (This is analogous to the inability of individual firms to affect prices in a perfectly competitive market.)

Ironically, where no groups possess market power, the contribution of any one group to the final outcome will be limited, and the impact of lobbying activities can appear quite marginal. In this vein, during the decade of the 1960s, group theory fell into disrepute in the wake of Bauer, Pool, and Dexter's major case study of business lobbying on the tariff issue of that period, which seemed to suggest that pressure groups were overrated as political actors.[32] The authors found a multiplicity of groups active on all sides of the tariff issue, cancelling out each other's influence and leaving legislators seemingly free to make roll call voting decisions.

However, an inability to impute observable influence to any individual group or coalition on the tariff issue is precisely what should have been expected under the circumstances. When the political marketplace is operating ideally (as it seems to have been in the tariff case), policy will represent an equilibrium of many groups, with no individual interest exerting disproportionate influence. To infer from this that interest groups are unimportant is analogous to studying a perfectly competitive market, finding that no firms wield market power, and concluding that the laws of supply and demand are fundamentally flawed.

Under such circumstances, the legislative outcome typically takes the form of a statute delegating broad discretion to the bureaucracy. Faced with powerful groups active on both sides of the issue, legislators try to avoid electoral repercussions by passing controversial issues along to the administrative process, in which some or all of the expected groups can be expected to participate. Thus the legislative mandate will tend to be highly ambiguous, important but contentious terms will remain undefined, and groups active on all sides of the issue can usually find at least some support for their position.[33] Theodore J. Lowi has pejoratively termed this phenomenon "interest group liberalism."[34] According to Lowi, while the primary motives for interest group liberalism are electoral, such actions are all too conveniently rationalized by appealing to the myth that the interplay of contending groups will automatically yield a rough approximation of the public interest.

By contrast, where all the active groups are mobilized on one side of the issue, the demand pattern may be said to be *consensual*. Under such circumstances, group pressures are one-sided and overwhelming. The active groups gain their objectives with no real need to compromise, and the influence of organized interests is easily recognized. A good example here is the Sugar Act, which governed sugar production and pricing in this country for more than two decades after World War II. The act limited sugar production in an attempt to prop up domestic prices. Total production was then divided into domestic and foreign shares, with specific production quotas (i.e., licenses to produce given amounts of sugar) granted to individual producers and to various foreign countries. The periodic extensions of the Sugar Act were notorious for being among the most heavily lobbied bills in Congress, yet none of the active groups ever lobbied against the bills. Rather, they all sought a piece of the action in the form of a license to produce sugar for sale in the United States.[35]

Where the demand pattern is consensual, as in the Sugar Act case, policy-making may be characterized as "distributive" in nature. That is, benefits are distributed to all comers; none of the active participants needs to lose. Sometimes this is because there is a surplus to distribute, as when strong economic growth generates higher than expected income tax revenues. More often, it is because those who must bear the costs of these policies are not active participants in the group struggle due to the free rider problem or a lack of information. Distributive policies typically concentrate benefits on organized interest while spreading the costs—so thinly as to go almost unnoticed—over taxpayers or consumers. Such was the case with the Sugar Act, which benefited domestic producers by propping up the price of sugar and carefully restricting foreign competition—all at the expense of American consumers.

It might also be noted that within the realm of distributive politics, a pathological form of rational decision making is made possible by the failure of potential opposition to mobilize. The major domestic sugar producers and refiners all shared a desire to escape the rigors of the competitive market. They sought to stabilize the price of sugar at a high level. Given this objective—which was clear, specific, and agreed upon by all involved—the obvious solution was a mix of import quotas, domestic production quotas, and price supports. From the perspective of society as a whole, such a policy cannot be characterized as rational; certainly taxpayers and consumers would not have agreed to the stabilization of sugar prices above market levels as a desirable social objective. But consumers and taxpayers were not mobilized, at least until 1974, when the Sugar Act was finally defeated. For more than twenty years, value-maximizing decisions in pursuit of sugar industry goals were made possible by the consensual configuration of demand on the issue.

The Sugar Act is not an isolated case. To the contrary, a study of congressional roll call voting found groups active on both sides of the issue in only 12 percent of the cases. Similarly, a study of congressional hearings over a sixteen-year period found groups testifying on only on side of the issue fully 55 percent of the time.[36]

Policy Implementation

As in the policy adoption stage, the group equilibrium will be a function of what groups participate in the administrative process, what resources they possess, and how effectively they employ them. In general, the number of active participants will be smaller in the administrative process than in the struggle in Congress over passage of a law. Implementation is an ongoing, day-to-day process, and thus costly to monitor. It is much easier for most groups to mobilize resources for an effort, however protracted, to pass a law. To then monitor the bureaucracy, all day every day, to protect against adverse interpretations of the statute, is beyond the resources of most groups. Moreover, unorganized mass publics may be aroused in the short term by scandals or grass roots lobbying efforts; in the long term, however, they will be subject to an "issue attention cycle," as their interest wanes or moves on to other matters.[37] Over time, the agency must come to terms with the relatively small circle of organized groups with a stake in their day-to-day operation.

Thus, as Lowi argued, proponents of interest group liberalism are naive in assuming the interplay of contending groups can serve as a substitute for concrete policy decisions. There is no reason to believe all affected interests will be represented in the legislative process, and there is even less reason to believe all the active groups will go on to participate in the administrative process. To the contrary, the costs of participation increase at each stage: it is easier to force an issue on the agenda than it is to pass a law (witness the efforts of the nuclear freeze movement in this regard), and it is easier to secure passage of a statute than it is to monitor its enforcement.[38]

The regulation of business by independent commissions provides a good illustration here. Many regulatory agencies go through a life cycle, culminating with capture by their ostensible clientele.[39] During the gestation phase, demands for regulation are brought to government by victimized groups (for example, shippers overcharged by railroads on monopolistic routes). Eventually an agency is created to correct the abuses, over the opposition of the industry in question. The youth phase of the agency provides an opportunity for effective regulation. The agency is brand new and staffed with highly committed individuals. Moreover, popular indignation remains high, permitting the agency to return to Congress in subsequent years for additional money or expanded powers. Vigorous regulation in the consumer interest will occur at this stage, if at all.

With the passage of time, the agency enters the maturity phase of its life cycle. With the inevitable waning of mass public arousal, the agency is soon left with a narrowly restricted clientele: the industry it is supposed to regulate. As in the formulation stage, the configuration of demand is a critical variable in determining the group equilibrium. Faced with a single constituency, as in the example above, the agency has little choice but to accommodate itself to its clientele. Dependent on industry support to maintain its budgetary base, the agency is soon co-opted. "Capture" takes place, and the agency becomes an advocate of the industry rather than its regulator.

Under such circumstances, policy subsystems, or "iron triangles," tend to develop, in which administrative agencies, congressional committees, and organized clientele groups dominate policy formulation.[40] Relationships are symbiotic within these policy subsystems, as the major participants all share a common interest in program expansion.

Interest groups gain tangible benefits from agency programs, and legislators cultivate the support of these organized interests in their continuing quest to secure reelection. Administrative agencies gain a supportive clientele in their efforts to expand their budgets and protect their statutory authority. This phenomenon is most marked for distributive issues, in which the statute is written to benefit a consensual configuration of active groups, thus removing the necessity to go through a life cycle before agency "capture" occurs.[41]

By contrast, where the agency is faced with multiple constituencies, capture is much less likely. The agency can play one group off another or form short-term coalitions to attain policy objectives. This does not mean that the agency will necessarily dominate policy-making under these circumstances. Here it is worth reiterating that the arsenal of powers available to most agencies is incomplete, suggesting that "officiality," albeit an important resource, is not to be equated with power. While it is tempting to visualize policy implementation as an equilibrium process with the agency at the center, responding to a variety of vector forces representing various group pressures, such a view attributes too much control to the agency. Ordinarily, agencies cannot accomplish their policy objectives without the political support of at least some of the groups in their environment, which includes not only private interest groups but also relevant congressional committees, other executive agencies affected by the agency's actions, and, at times, the president.[42] Thus it is probably more accurate to visualize implementation as an equilibrium process with *policy* at the center, and to treat administrative agencies as just one of the groups contending in an effort to influence the outcome.

POLICY CHANGE AND THE GROUP STRUGGLE MODEL

In contrast with the incremental model, the group struggle model makes no explicit assumptions about the dimensions of policy change. The model does not assume that policy makers will necessarily restrict their attention to alternatives differing only marginally from previous policies. Nor does it assume that contending interests will necessarily seek some kind of accommodation in the broader public interest. Rather, the model assumes only that policy represents the equilibrium of contending groups, with the precise outcome a function of the relative strengths of contending actors.

Even so, certain elements of this model reinforce Lindblom's contention that policy change will typically be gradual at best. Mancur Olson has recently argued in this regard that the proliferation of special interest groups over time can make advanced industrial societies subject to what he terms "institutional sclerosis." More specifically, where a society's organized groups represent relatively narrow interests, the public interest becomes a collective good subject to the free rider problem; while all groups might benefit from policies in the broader national interest (in particular, policies encouraging competition and greater economic growth), each individual group finds it rational to pursue policies advancing its narrow economic interests. The end result is economic inefficiency, as the group struggle gives rise to protectionist policies favoring established interests (small groups, institutions, etc.) over broad, diffuse interests. Often, public policies fostering free markets would promote greater competition and correspondingly higher rates of economic growth, but such policies must inevitably threaten these established interests. Moreover, decision making via interest group interaction will be time consuming, further retarding the system's ability to respond to changing economic circumstances.[43]

Insofar as special interest groups tend to proliferate over time, this pattern of institutional sclerosis can help explain why economic growth rates are slower for nations (like the United States and Great Britain) with a long history of economic and social stability. By contrast, new nations and nations whose social institutions have been destroyed by wars (like Japan and Germany) will be at an earlier stage of interest group development and thus free of institutional constraints on economic growth.

Nations characterized by a high level of interest group mobilization may still achieve economic efficiency where organized interests represent very large (or what Olson terms "encompassing") interests. Sweden would be a good example here, as the government formulates public policies in consultation with large organizations monopolizing the representation of various economic interests. In contrast with the United States, where a multiplicity of groups frequently compete to speak for business interests, in Sweden business is represented by a single organization; the same is true for labor, agriculture, education, and the other major social interests.[44] Under such circumstances, a group's interests are of necessity broadened; its actions will now have a significant effect on the national interest, thus reducing the effects of the free rider problem. In short, where the state interacts with a small number of very large groups, the free rider problem plaguing the pursuit of the public interest is minimized. By contrast, where the state interacts with many narrow interests, the free rider problem plaguing the pursuit of common interests is maximized, and policy change will be correspondingly retarded.[45]

While Olson's theory provides an intuitively appealing explanation for economic stagnation in some advanced industrial societies, the empirical evidence in support of his thesis is mixed. Central to his argument is the proposition that groups will tend to proliferate over time, barring wars or other shocks to the system, and that this proliferation will be associated with a reduction in economic efficiency. At no time, however, does Olson present data to show that interest groups do in fact proliferate over time for any societies. Nor does he show that countries exhibiting different levels of economic growth are actually characterized by different levels of interest group development. In this regard, Robert Salisbury has suggested that interest groups are highly vulnerable to economic fluctuations and that many fail to survive; this proposition is borne out by recent empirical surveys of the universe of national groups, which identify a high mortality rate for membership groups of all sorts.[46]

Moreover, Olson's thesis presumes an ability to define and agree upon the public interest; in his view, policies promoting higher rates of economic growth are plainly in the public interest, albeit not in the narrow interest of particular groups. However, as we saw earlier in this chapter and in Chapter 2, the public interest is an amorphous concept at best. Disagreements over values and limitations on available knowledge preclude rational decision making for most policies, giving rise instead to a clash of interests. Economic growth is an important value, but it is only one value among many; not all groups in society benefit from economic growth, and the protection of the environment, a more equitable distribution of income, or a desire for security against the impersonal and highly dynamic vicissitudes of the market might all be reasonably considered more important by some interests. Nor is there agreement on what policies would best promote economic growth even if that criterion were to be accepted as the benchmark guiding policy choices.[47]

If the relationship between interest group mobilization and incrementalism remains unclear in the aggregate, we can speak with more confidence of the relationship between policy outcomes and the configuration of organized interests on individual issues. Where the demand pattern is conflictual and atomistic, policy-making will conform to the broad patterns Lindblom identified, although the participants will tend to be less cooperative and more combative than he would suggest. As noted earlier, the typical outcome here will be interest group liberalism, as described by Lowi. However, where the configuration of group demand is conflictual, the balance of forces will inevitably come into play, making the final group equilibrium a function of what groups participate, what resources they bring to bear, and how effectively they translate these resources into influence. While the dominant tendency here is clearly toward legislative delegation, the precise form of that delegation will reflect the relative power of the various participants. Under the right circumstances, such a configuration of demand can even give rise to nonincremental policy changes, as will be discussed later in this section.

Where the configuration of groups is consensual, by contrast, program expansion and budgetary growth can be rapid, but the fundamental purposes and directions of policies will be resistant to change. Distributive policy subsystems are characterized by extraordinary stability as legislators, bureaucrats, and clientele groups share common interests in the maintenance of programs and the privatization of conflict. At a minimum, new participants mean dividing the available pie into more slices. At worst, they threaten the symbiotic nature of the policy subsystem by forcing at least a degree of responsiveness to interests that would otherwise have passively borne program costs.

However, the configuration of demand is never fixed, and groups outside the policy subsystem benefit from the socialization of conflict. In spite of all the obstacles to mobilization identified by the group theorists, the composition of the group universe is not static. As David Truman observed, at any given time the group universe is in a kind of tenuous equilibrium. A disturbance to that equilibrium can set in motion a flurry of group formation as new groups form in response to the disturbance, generating countermobilization by interests threatened by the new group forms, and so on. A major change in the group universe cannot help but affect the prospects for policy change.[48]

Recent surveys of groups active at the national level strongly suggest that the interest group universe has become much more balanced in recent years, with the formation of a variety of new groups representing consumers, environmentalists, women, senior citizens, and others. A variety of disturbances, mostly associated with advanced industrialization, have contributed to this phenomenon: the increasing number of women entering the work force, the growing threat of air and water pollution, the steady increase in life expectancy due to medical advances, and so forth.[49] In large part, these new groups have been able to circumvent the free rider problem by securing sources of funding outside their memberships: seed money from large foundations, gifts from wealthy philanthropists, grants from government agencies seeking to mobilize a supportive clientele, or support from previously organized interests sympathetic to their causes. The rise of these outside funding sources, which really became widely available only in the 1960s, may constitute the most important disturbance of all in the long run. The vast majority of the new groups forming in recent years needed such outside money to get off the ground, and many remain heavily dependent on such sources for their continued survival.[50]

The mobilization of these new groups has profoundly affected the policy process in recent years. On issue after issue, previously autonomous policy subsystems have been penetrated by new interests, giving rise to more complex "issue networks" in which a multiplicity of actors contend over policy.[51] Similarly, regulatory agencies are now much more likely to operate in a highly pluralistic environment. Agencies once co-opted by their industrial clientele now find themselves confronted with lobbying and litigation by a variety of public interest groups.

Where a policy subsystem is penetrated by previously unmobilized interests, the result is not nonincremental policy change, at least in the sense that Lindblom would use the term. Rather, a lopsided pattern of demand favoring established interests is replaced with a more balanced and atomistic configuration in which no single group or coalition wields excessive power. Put another way, the penetration of policy subsystems will inevitably transform what was a distributive policy process into a classically incremental one. The importance of such a development should not be underestimated, however. Whatever its faults, incremental policy-making (where a wide range of interests are in fact mobilized) is vastly preferable to the ostensibly rational but highly unrepresentative distributive arena.[52]

Nonincremental policy changes will tend to occur instead where the demand pattern is already conflictual and a fundamental change occurs in the group equilibrium that tips the balance toward the proponents of policy change—for instance, new groups mobilize on the side of change, or there is a significant shift in the balance of resources among existing groups. These factors can occur together, as in the late 1960s and the early 1970s, when new groups mobilized to represent consumer and environmental interests at the same time the legitimacy of corporate interests was eroded by campaign finance scandals.

All this suggests that perhaps the most important sources of incrementalism—at least according to this model—are inevitable obstacles to mobilization and inequalities in political resources across groups. Were all groups politically active, and were political resources distributed more evenly across groups, the mix of policy outcomes across a wide range of issues would look very, very different than it does now. If the group universe is more balanced now than at any time in the past, it nevertheless remains true that many potential groups remain unorganized. The veritable explosion of new groups over the past twenty-five years is almost exclusively a middle-class phenomenon that has done little to remedy the systemic bias against economically disadvantaged interests.[53] And at least one study has found the composition of the group universe more biased toward corporate interests now than it was in 1960, when Schattschneider first pointed to the scope and bias of the pressure system.[54]

This is because the free rider problem never goes away for large, diffuse groups; not surprisingly, the mortality rate for such groups is much greater than that for corporations and other institutions. At best, these interests tend to be represented by staff organizations with no real rank-and-file memberships, or by checkbook organizations (like political action committees, PACs) that have a nominal membership but provide few, if any, opportunities for members to interact with one another or to hold group leaders accountable for group performance.[55]

Moreover, important differences in political resources remain across groups, making for an unbalanced group struggle. Perhaps most significant in this regard are persistent gaps on the various intangible dimensions; strategic position, expertise, and legitimacy. When a dearth of valued resources is combined with a failure to mobilize—as with AIDS victims or welfare recipients, for example—pressures for major policy change will be virtually nonexistent. Where an interest opposed to fundamental change possesses a wide range of tangible and intangible resources, as is often the case with business groups in the United States, the obstacles to real reform can be almost insurmountable.

NOTES

1. Arthur F. Bentley, *The Process of Government* (Chicago: University of Chicago Press, 1908), p. 300.
2. This term was first applied by Bertram Gross in *The Legislative Struggle* (New York: McGraw-Hill, 1953), and by Norman Wengert in *Natural Resources and the Political Struggle* (Garden City, N.Y.: Doubleday, 1955). Both these authors attempted to build on the pioneering work of Arthur F. Bentley, *The Process of Government,* cited in note 1.
3. Earl Latham, "The Group Basis of Politics: Notes for a Theory," *American Political Science Review,* 46 (June 1952), p. 390. See also Earl Latham, *The Group Basis of Politics: A Study of Basing-Point Legislation* (Ithaca, N.Y.: Cornell University Press, 1952). The model developed in this chapter draws extensively on Latham's formulation, which is in many ways the clearest and most insightful statement of the model.
4. See Gross, *Legislative Struggle,* pp. 4–5:

   > It would be possible to describe this process with more euphemistic words, such as "adjustment" or "bargaining." Both could probably be interpreted in a manner that would give the full flavor of the group conflict. Yet "adjustment" overemphasizes the end result of given conflicts and does too little justice to the motives and methods of the actors in the drama. "Bargaining," while better oriented toward the activities of the participants, is too narrow a concept. Just as "competition" has long since proved itself as one of the most expressive terms in economics, "struggle" is the most useful term with which to describe the process of government.

5. See David Truman, *The Governmental Process* (New York: Knopf, 1951), p. 48; Gross, p. 5.
6. Raymond A. Bauer, Ithiel de Sola Pool, and Lewis Anthony Dexter, *American Business and Public Policy,* 2d ed. (Chicago: Aldine-Alterton, 1972).
7. Latham, "Group Basis," p. 391.
8. See Graham T. Allison, *Essence of Decision* (Boston: Little, Brown, 1971); Morton H. Halperin, *Bureaucratic Politics and Foreign Policy* (Washington, D.C.: Brookings Institution, 1974); Aaron Wildavsky, *The Politics of the Budgetary Process,* 4th ed. (Boston: Little, Brown, 1984); and Matthew Holden, Jr., " 'Imperialism' in Bureaucracy," *American Political Science Review,* 60 (December 1966), pp. 943–951.
9. Latham, "Group Basis," pp. 389–396.

10. Latham, *Group Basis of Politics,* p. 49.
11. See E. E. Schattschneider, *The Semi-Sovereign People* (New York: Holt, Rinehart, and Winston, 1960); Theodore J. Lowi, *The End of Liberalism* (New York: Norton, 1969); and Mancur Olson, Jr., *The Logic of Collective Action* (New York: Schocken Books, 1970).
12. Truman, *The Governmental Process,* p. 114. On a visit to Rutgers University some years ago, Professor Truman made clear to me in private conversation his feeling that his critics—myself included—have taken his argument too far on this point. In advancing the concept of "potential groups," he did not believe that all social interests would mobilize automatically when threatened or that the group universe would necessarily be balanced or representative of all interests. Rather, he sought to counter then contemporary criticisms of the "pressure system" as necessarily favoring special interests over the average citizen. His point (and it is an important one) was rather that interest groups afford a vehicle through which the average citizen may seek to influence policy-making—a vehicle, it might be added, every bit as legitimate as the political party. See *The Governmental Process,* Chapter 16, "Group Politics and Representative Democracy," pp. 501–535.
13. A similarly optimistic view of the process is taken by Norman Wengert in *Natural Resources and the Political Struggle* (Garden City, N.Y.: Doubleday, 1955). On pp. 67–68, for example, Wengert defends the group struggle in language strikingly similar to Lindblom's defense of incrementalism:

> The concepts of the governmental process which underlie this study of natural resources and the political struggle accept group conflict and strife as inevitable—even necessary and desirable. Through continuing struggle among a multiplicity of groups a working definition of the public interest may be achieved. Like the idea of competition in economics, group struggle is the means by which alternative politics and programs are brought to public attention and submitted to the searching analysis and criticisms of those who oppose them. But more than that, the necessity of gaining effective support for particular proposals subjects them to scrutiny, review, and most importantly to modification so that as the process operates the proposals that can muster support are those which move from the narrow particularist interest in the direction of the larger, common interest. This is, in a sense, "the free trade in ideas" which Justice Holmes regarded so highly, for implicit in his view was the belief that through many "sellers" of ideas would the integrity of "consumer" choice be maintained. It is, also, the essential characteristic of the political process in America.

However, like Truman, Wengert goes on to say (p. 68) that the process often works imperfectly, with no one to represent the unorganized and inarticulate, and with propaganda and manipulation often more in evidence than efforts at education or appeals to reason.
14. Latham, "Group Basis," p. 382.
15. To Wengert, for example, it is not necessary to define and agree upon the public interest; rather, what serves to temper the group struggle is the need for all groups to justify their demands in terms of some broader conception of the public interest (*Natural Resources and the Political Struggle,* p. 66). Here too, he echoes Truman. Of the orginal group theorists, Truman and Wengert come the closest to equating the group equilibrium with the public interest. Over the past two decades or more, the thrust of interest group theory and empirical research has been to emphasize obstacles to group mobilization and inequalities in resources across groups.
16. Truman, pp. 112–115.
17. Latham, "Group Basis," p. 387.
18. Mancur Olson, Jr., *The Logic of Collective Action* (New York: Schocken Books, 1970), pp. 1–

52. See also James Q. Wilson, *Political Organizations* (New York: Basic Books, 1973); and Terry M. Moe, *The Organization of Interests* (Chicago: University of Chicago Press, 1980).

19. Robert H. Salisbury, "An Exchange Theory of Interest Groups," *Midwest Journal of Political Science,* 8 (February 1969), pp. 1–32.

20. Schattschneider, *Semi-Sovereign People,* p. 35. See also Wilson, *Political Organizations;* and Salisbury, "An Exchange Theory of Interest Groups."

21. Robert H. Salisbury, "Interest Representative and the Dominance of Institutions," *American Political Science Review,* 78 (March 1984), pp. 64–77.

22. Kay Lehman Schlozman and John T. Tierney, *Organized Interests and American Democracy* (New York: Harper and Row, 1986), pp. 58–87.

23. This list of group resources is drawn from David Truman's insightful discussion in *The Governmental Process,* pp. 506–507.

24. Bauer, Pool, and Dexter, pp. 350–357.

25. Theodore R. Marmor, *The Politics of Medicare* (Chicago: Aldine, 1973).

26. Charles E. Lindblom, *Politics and Markets* (New York: Basic Books, 1977).

27. Bauer, Pool, and Dexter, pp. 332–340.

28. Bauer, Pool, and Dexter, pp. 341–357.

29. Schattschneider, *Semi-Sovereign People,* pp. 1–19.

30. Schattschneider, *Semi-Sovereign People,* pp. 62–77.

31. The following paragraphs draw heavily from Michael T. Hayes, *Lobbyists and Legislators* (New Brunswick, N.J.: Rutgers University Press, 1981). For the seminal typology of policies, upon which my own work is based, see Theodore J. Lowi, "American Business, Public Policy, Case Studies, and Political Theory," *World Politics,* 16 (July 1964), pp. 677–715.

32. Raymond A. Bauer, Ithiel de Sola Pool, and Lewis Anthony Dexter, *American Business and Public Policy,* 2d ed. (Chicago: Aldine-Atherton, 1972).

33. Hayes, *Lobbyists and Legislators,* pp. 93–127.

34. Lowi, *The End of Liberalism,* pp. 55–97.

35. On the Sugar Act, see Hayes, pp. 12–14, and the sources cited therein.

36. John W. Kingdon, *Congressmen's Voting Decisions* (New York: Harper and Row, 1973), and Robert L. Ross, "Relations among National Interest Groups," *Journal of Politics,* 32 (February 1970), pp. 96–114. For a more detailed analysis, see Robert L. Ross, "Dimensions and Patterns of Relations among Interest Groups at the Congressional Level of Government," Ph.D. dissertation, Michigan State University, 1962.

37. Anthony Downs, "Up and Down with Ecology—The Issue Attention Cycle," *The Public Interest,* 28 (Summer 1972), pp. 38–50; see also Murray Edelman, *The Symbolic Uses of Politics* (Urbana: University of Illinois Press, 1964).

38. John E. Chubb, *Interest Groups and the Bureaucracy* (Stanford, Calif.: Stanford University Press, 1983).

39. Marver P. Bernstein, *Regulating Business by Independent Commission* (Princeton, N.J.: Princeton University Press, 1955).

40. Douglas Cater, *Power in Washington* (New York: Random House, 1964); J. Leiper Freeman, *The Political Process,* 2d ed. (New York: Random House, 1965); and Randall B. Ripley and Grace A. Franklin, *Congress, the Bureaucracy, and Public Policy,* 2d ed. rev. (Homewood, Ill.: Dorsey, 1976).

41. Not all cases of business regulation conform to the capture theory. However, a similar pattern of industry domination occurs where the industry actively seeks regulation in order to restrict entry into a market and to shore up an otherwise unstable cartel. Where the capture scenario presumes that regulation imposes concentrated costs and broadly distributed benefits, the cartel (or "economic") theory of regulation sees regulation as offering concentrated benefits to an in-

dustry at the expense of consumers. See George J. Stigler, "The Theory of Economic Regulation," *Bell Journal of Economics and Management Science,* 2 (1971), pp. 359–365; and James Q. Wilson, "The Politics of Regulation," in James Q. Wilson (ed.), *The Politics of Regulation* (New York: Basic Books, 1980), pp. 357–394.

42. For an excellent case study of the administrator's dependence on the configuration of groups in the agency's environment, which makes clear the divergence between power and "officiality," see Earl Latham, *The Politics of Railroad Coordination, 1933–1936* (Cambridge, Mass.: Harvard University Press, 1959). See also Krasnow, Longley, and Terry for some recent case studies illustrating this phenomenon.

43. See Mancur Olson, *The Rise and Decline of Nations* (New Haven, Conn.: Yale University Press, 1982), especially pp. 1–74.

44. Graham K. Wilson, *Business and Politics* (Chatham, N.J.: Chatham House, 1985), pp. 103–113.

45. Olson, *Rise and Decline,* pp. 47–53.

46. See Salisbury, "An Exchange Theory of Interest Groups." See also Schlozman and Tierney, *Organized Interests and American Democracy,* pp. 78–82.

47. See Robert H. Salisbury, "Are Interest Groups Morbific Forces?" *Political Science Paper No. 56,* Washington University in St. Louis, July 1980. Prepared for presentation to the Conference Group on the Political Economy of Advanced Industrial Societies, held in conjunction with the annual meeting of the American Political Science Association, Washington, D.C., August 1980.

48. Truman, pp. 26–33.

49. See Henry J. Pratt, *The Gray Lobby* (Chicago: University of Chicago Press, 1976); Joyce Gelb and Marian Lief Palley, *Women and Public Policies* (Princeton, N.J.: Princeton University Press, 1982); and Jeffrey M. Berry, *Lobbying for the People* (Princeton, NJ: Princeton University Press, 1977). See also Schlozman and Tierney.

50. Jack L. Walker, "The Origins and Maintenance of Interest Groups in America," *American Political Science Review,* 77 (June 1983), pp. 390–406.

51. Hugh Heclo, "Issue Networks and the Executive Establishment," in Anthony King (ed.), *The New American Political System* (Washington, D.C.: American Enterprise Institute, 1978), pp. 87–124.

52. Another disturbance, of indefinite duration, is the enormous federal deficit generated by the Reagan administration's 1981 tax cuts. The unprecedented magnitude of these deficits, in combination with their persistence, forces policy makers of all stripes to look for ways to reduce spending. Even liberals interested in expanding the welfare state must look for compensating spending cuts someplace else. This reinforces the rise of issue networks, as discussed above. Previously autonomous policy subsystems will be under continuous scrutiny, even where newly formed citizens' groups do not penetrate their defenses, as successive presidents look for wasteful or inefficient programs to cut (or even eliminate) in the search for savings.

53. Andrew S. McFarland, "Recent Social Movements and Theories of Power in America." Paper delivered at the 1979 annual meeting of the American Political Science Association, Washington, D.C., August 31, 1979.

54. Schlozman and Tierney, *Organized Interests and American Democracy.*

55. See Michael T. Hayes, "The New Group Universe," in Allan J. Cigler and Burdett A. Loomis, *Interest Group Politics,* 2d ed. (Washington, D.C.: Congressional Quarterly Press, 1986), pp. 133–145; and Hayes, "Interest Groups: Pluralism or Mass Society?" in Cigler and Loomis, *Interest Group Politics,* 1st ed. (Washington, D.C.: Congressional Quarterly Press, 1983), pp. 110–125.

CHAPTER 5

The Privileged Position of Business

In this chapter, we will examine another source of political inequality that reinforces the tendencies toward incrementalism identified in the preceding chapters. The proposition to be examined here is that business as a class exercises disproportionate power within capitalistic societies, approaching ruling elite status. In particular, business acquires a kind of veto power over proposals threatening to capitalist interests to the extent that all actors in the system need prosperity, which only business can provide and which it can also withhold.

THE MARKET AS PRISON

The most influential theorist in this regard is Charles Lindblom,[1] introduced in Chapter 2 as the author of the theory of disjointed incrementalism. Because Lindblom's earlier model was so optimistic regarding the potential for attaining the public interest through the interplay of contending groups, his conversion to the ranks of elite theorists had a magnified impact within the discipline.

According to Lindblom, the free market constrains policy makers to reject out of hand virtually all policy changes detrimental to business. Within capitalistic economies, any attempt to alter fundamental institutions automatically triggers punishment in the form of unemployment or a sluggish economy:

> Do we want business to carry a larger share of the nation's tax burden? We must fear that such a reform will discourage business investment and curtail employment. Do we want business enterprises to reduce industrial pollution of air and water? Again we must bear the consequences of the costs to them of their doing so and the resultant declines in investment and employment.[2]

63

More fundamental reforms, such as worker participation in management or public in-volvement in corporate decision making, cannot be raised at all, according to Lindblom, lest they undermine business confidence.

A variation on this theme is advanced by Ralph Miliband.[3] Where Lindblom charac-terizes the market as a kind of prison, which operates to preclude any reforms threatening to business interests, Miliband sees the problem as one of "imperfect competition" among social interests.[4] He explicitly acknowledges that business groups do not always dominate policy-making:

> Had business predominance been absolute, it would be absurd to speak of competition at all. There *is* competition, and defeats for powerful capitalist interests as well as vic-tories. . . .[5]

According to Miliband, the advantage to business in this competition among interests is rooted in the extraordinary degree of commitment to capitalism within the advanced in-dustrial democracies. Disagreements among the viable contenders for elective office are typically confined to secondary issues, leaving the fundamental question of the form of economic organization unaddressed. Debate is thus confined to the proper degree of state intervention in an economy that all agree will remain capitalistic.[6]

THE SOURCES OF BUSINESS POWER

Within Lindblom's formulation, there would seem little point in assessing the relative ad-vantages of different actors in the group struggle. In his view, business is a qualitatively different kind of actor occupying a special place within capitalist systems: on economic is-sues, policy-making is imprisoned by the need to induce business performance. At best, policy may be accurately conceived as an equilibrium of a multiplicity of contending groups only for a highly restricted, unimprisoned zone of policy-making.[7]

If the policy process is instead characterized, following Miliband, as an imperfect competition among social interests, then business can be treated as only one of many ac-tors in the system, albeit an arguably advantaged one. Viewed in this light, what is strik-ing about the arguments of both Lindblom and Miliband is how well they fit into the framework of the group struggle model advanced in Chapter 4. While the group theorists recognized the importance of tangible resources (like money), they placed a greater em-phasis on a variety of intangible factors, particularly strategic position, legitimacy, and expertise.[8]

Intangible Resources

Both Lindblom and Miliband play down the substantial business advantage in financial resources over the other actors in the system, emphasizing instead these same intangible factors. In short, their argument is that business possesses extraordinary legitimacy, expertise, and strategic position within a capitalistic society, giving it an almost insurmountable advantage over any other actor in the system. Whether business in merely the strongest actor in an ongoing group struggle (a Goliath among Davids in Miliband's formulation),[9] or a qualitatively different kind of actor rendering the whole concept of a group struggle meaningless for most issues, is simply a matter of how far one wants to push the argument. The sources of business power are essentially the same for both authors.

Foremost among these is what the group theorists termed strategic position. It will be recalled from Chapter 4 that a group has leverage to the extent that society depends upon goods or services it routinely provides. In this vein, according to Lindblom, business managers serve in effect as a second set of public officials in capitalist economies insofar as a wide range of activities affecting the entire public are delegated into their hands: decisions regarding what is to be produced, how labor and other factors of production will be allocated to different lines of production, what technologies will be employed, where plants will be located, and so on. While all these activities are defined as private by the market (and by most economists), they have momentous consequences for the average citizen, affecting the overall level of economic growth and the prospects for employment in different locations and lines of work.[10]

In this regard, some scholars have emphasized the power this gives to a relatively small number of giant corporations to affect the performance of the economy. Viewed from this perspective, the real problem is the "corporate revolution" in American capitalism in the twentieth century that gave rise to an economy dominated by giant (and generally uncompetitive) firms.[11] The end result is not so much a single power elite as a system of multiple elites in which the leading corporations wield excessive power.[12]

This is not Lindblom's argument, however. To Lindblom, the central problem is the delegation of properly public functions into private hands, and with it the forfeiture of command as a means of control. This makes the performance of the economy dependent upon the response of business managers to changes in the business climate, regardless of whether the economy is dominated by a few large firms or atomistically competitive. Relations between the state and business managers are not hierarchical; corporations must be induced to perform the functions upon which society depends. This is where the "market as prison" analogy comes into play: in making public policies, government officials must always take into account the effects of their proposals on the incentives facing business managers.

This dependence of the state on business for the maintenance of prosperity gives rise to a second significant advantage. Government officials need reliable information when formulating public policies. This is all the more true when the subject matter is highly technical, as is typically the case with business regulation. Business managers typically possess a near monopoly on expertise relating to production processes; for example, until the late 1970s the United States government was dependent upon the petroleum industry for estimates of available oil and gas reserves.[13] Possession of such information guarantees business executives automatic access to policy makers while other groups in society must compete to make their voices heard.

The critical importance of expertise was verified by a recent study of interest group involvement in energy policy-making. Under the Ford administration industry groups (nuclear, oil and gas, etc.) had virtually monopolized access to the energy bureaucracy. President Carter sought to reverse this pattern and made clear his commitment to environmental protection, even appointing environmental activists to many positions. Despite this major change in personnel and top-level attitudes, the vast majority of contacts between bureaucrats and clientele groups still involved industry representatives, and most of these contacts were initiated by the agencies themselves. The need for technical information— and for a sense of how proposed regulations would affect business performance—overrode the administration's very real commitment to move policy in a new direction.[14]

A final advantage to business stems from the extraordinary legitimacy granted to business managers in a capitalist society. Part of this follows from the delegation of public functions into private hands, discussed earlier. To the extent that business executives serve as a second set of public officials in such societies, they are responsible for decisions of great consequence to all citizens and thus are naturally accorded high status. Another important aspect of legitimacy, however, is the degree to which a group's demands are compatible with the values held by policy makers and the larger society. In this regard, business possesses an enormous advantage. Because capitalism is so entrenched within Western democracies, the narrow class interests of business come to be equated with the broader national interest. By comparison, all other groups, particularly organized labor, are perceived as narrow sectoral interests:

> If the national interest is in fact inextricably bound up with the fortunes of capitalist enterprise, apparent partiality towards it is not really partiality at all. On the contrary, in serving the interests of business and in helping capitalist enterprise to thrive, governments are really fulfilling their exalted roles as guardians of the good of all.[15]

Tangible Resources

While both Lindblom and Miliband minimize the importance of tangible resources as a source of business power, the financial advantage of business over other actors is very large and growing steadily larger. With the legalization of political action committees in the mid-1970s, the total amount of business contributions to candidates has grown dramatically, much faster than that of any other group. By the early 1980s, corporate and trade association PACs had amassed a better than two-to-one dollar advantage over organized labor, business's closest competitor on this dimension. Even more impressive, this total for all business groups exceeded the combined resources of all the other groups in the system, including labor.[16]

This remarkable monetary advantage to business interests enables corporations and trade associations to gain access to a broader range of legislators than almost any other group. Although most PAC contributions do not make a significant difference in determining the outcome of a given race, single issue groups typically focus on close races where they can at least claim to have affected the election. Organized labor limits its contributions to Democratic candidates, who tend to be more receptive to labor issues. By contrast, business can afford both to reward its friends and to neutralize its potential opponents. Business PACs tend to favor incumbents over challengers, with only a slight bias toward Republican candidates. The net result is that the average Republican candidate receives a relatively homogeneous pot of contributions from business groups and sympathetic conservative and New Right groups. By contrast, the contributions going to Democrats show a rough balance between liberal groups (including organized labor) and business PACs.[17]

Effective Influence

It will be recalled from Chapter 4 that such resource advantages, however impressive in the abstract, cannot be equated with influence. Whether such resources are translated into effective influence will ultimately depend upon at least two additional variables: the political skill of the group's leadership and its internal cohesion.

Lindblom and Miliband both take corporate political skill for granted. Research suggests that this is a potentially serious mistake. While contemporary business lobbyists are among the best organized and most successful actors on the Washington scene, a major study of business groups in the 1950s and 1960s found business representatives to be ill-informed, timid, and generally inept, to the point of calling into question the group struggle model then serving as the prevailing paradigm within the discipline.[18] Skilled leadership must be understood as a variable rather than a constant, differing across groups and over time.

Similarly, Lindblom fails to see internal cohesion as a significant problem for business groups. To the contrary, he sees business as possessing an advantage through prior organization. In distinct contrast to groups relying on a mass membership base, corporations do not face a free rider problem. They are already organized for the purpose of producing and marketing economic goods. [19]

By contrast, Miliband concedes the existence of internal divisions within the business community but points to what he sees as greater divisions plaguing organized labor. But his main line of defense is to distinguish between the grand issues affecting business as a class and secondary issues affecting individual industries.[20] As we shall see in the following sections, this distinction between grand and secondary issues plays a major role in the theory of corporate power. It not only responds to objections stemming from the persistence of internal divisions within the business community on a broad range of issues, but also provides a way to reconcile a theory of corporate predominance with the substantial evidence of business defeats on individual issues. In short, business defeats on secondary issues, however numerous, need not refute the theory, for business can be seen to control the agenda through the suppression of any significant assault on the more important issues of capitalism, private property, and corporate autonomy in making production and investment decisions.

THE IMPORTANCE OF THE AGENDA

In placing primary emphasis on the control of the agenda, corporate power theorists may be classified as *neo-elite theorists*. The controversy over whether a power elite dominates policy-making has a long history, with most of the early studies focusing on decision making within various local communities. The controversy between the power elite theorists and their intellectual antagonists, commonly referred to as pluralists, passed through at least three stages: an early phase more or less dominated by the elite theorists, a second period in which the pluralist critique of the elite theorists' methodology carried the day (at least within political science), and a final stage in which a new generation of elite theorists (the "neo-elitists") attempted to reinvigorate elite theory by shifting the focus of attention to the political agenda. While the corporate power controversy has not followed this same pattern precisely, an understanding of these arguments helps to place the arguments of Lindblom and Miliband in proper perspective.

Early elite theorists sought to uncover the existence of ruling elites within particular communities by asking local residents (or a subset of socioeconomic "notables") "who really runs this town?" Pluralist critics, most notably Robert Dahl, objected that phrasing the inquiry in such terms made it likely that some elite would be identified, whether its members actually ran things or not. Such an approach erred in equating power with reputation for influence.[21]

A more reliable approach, according to Dahl, would focus on actual instances of decision making. Dahl suggested a rigorous test of the ruling elite hypothesis. First, for the theory to be testable, some identifiable elite (e.g., business, the "military-industrial complex," or some other minority of the population) must be specified at the outset. Next, a broadly representative sample of issues must be examined, to guard against the temptation to impute elite dominance from atypical issues likely to be restricted to a small circle of decision makers (such as the decision to drop the atomic bomb on Japan in 1945). Finally, a study of actual decision making on these issues must be conducted to determine whether the hypothesized elite does in fact prevail with any degree of regularity.

Within political science, the Dahl test was widely accepted as providing a more reliable methodology for the identification of potential ruling elites. Not surprisingly, apparent power elites were harder to find when Dahl's more rigorous standards of analysis were employed. The power elite theorists waned in influence, and the pluralists (and their cousins, the group theorists) came to dominate the discipline by the early 1960s.

Some years later, Peter Bachrach and Morton S. Baratz challenged the pluralist model by shifting the focus of attention to the agenda-setting stage. According to this critique, the pluralists had erred by confining their attention to who wins and loses in cases of observed decision making. They suggested that elites in fact control access to the agenda, suppressing issues they find particularly threatening (e.g., "grand issues") and permitting only those issues to arise that are relatively harmless to elite interests. Thus observed defeats for elites at the formulation stage do not constitute evidence of a pluralistic polity, for these defeats by definition occur on secondary issues of low importance to the power elite.[22]

Bachrach and Baratz termed this process of controlling the agenda "nondecision-making." Nondecision-making typically takes on one of two forms, which Bachrach and Baratz term Barrier I and Barrier II.[23] Nondecisions are observable (Barrier II) where a challenge to the established order is made manifest, an overt struggle occurs, and elites successfully suppress the issue by manipulating existing institutions or rules of the game. A good example here is the oil depletion allowance, a tax break favoring large oil companies for many years. In the 1940s and 1950s, when the speaker of the House and the Senate majority leader were both from Texas, appointments of new members to the key tax committees (Ways and Means in the House and Finance in the Senate) were made conditional upon pledged support for the continuation of the depletion allowance. Not surprisingly, efforts by liberals in Congress to repeal the provision were easily killed in committee during this period.[24]

Nondecision-making is more subtle where no overt struggle occurs. Rather, potential challenges to the existing order remain latent because proponents either feel that there is no hope of winning or that their demands are illegitimate. In the latter case, childhood political socialization is seen as playing a major role in indoctrinating citizens to support the existing political and economic order and to accept the prevailing distribution of income as reflecting a rough correlation between work or achievement and eventual reward.[25] While these Barrier I nondecisions are no less real than the overt struggles characterizing Barrier II, they are by definition impossible to observe and thus to verify:

> Suppose the observer can uncover no grievances, no actual or potential demands for change. Suppose, in other words, there appears to be universal acquiescence in the status quo. Is it possible, in such circumstances, to determine empirically whether the consensus is genuine or instead has been enforced through nondecision-making? The answer must be negative. Analysis of this problem is beyond the reach of a political analyst. . . .[26]

CORPORATE POWER AND THE AGENDA

The impossibility of empirically verifying Barrier I nondecisions makes it difficult to prove or disprove a significant portion of the neo-elitist argument. While the overt suppression of manifest challenges can be identified, some of the most interesting and significant examples of nondecision-making would seem to take place in Barrier I. Not surprisingly, this has led to problems for neo-elite theorists, as pluralist critics charge them with focusing on ''nonevents'' or seeking to avoid the responsibility of supporting their theory with hard empirical evidence. The neo-elitist response to these charges is essentially that confining one's attention to observable decisions is akin to looking for lost coins under a street lamp because the light is better there.[27] Being fundamentally unresolvable, the dispute between the pluralists and the neo-elitists drags on with no end in sight.

This same problem plagues Lindblom and Miliband. Their argument that the needs of a market economy serve to constrain policy makers is ultimately a Barrier I hypothesis: certain kinds of challenges to the prevailing (e.g., capitalist) order do not arise because they are understood to be incompatible with the maintenance of that order. Citizens depend upon the proper functioning of the economy for their livelihood and have been socialized to support the capitalist system through their schools and churches, through corporate advertising, and ultimately through a basic need to conform to conventional values in the hope of ''getting ahead.'' Thus fundamental challenges to the capitalist order simply do not arise; conflict is limited to secondary issues of how and when to intervene in an economy that all agree will remain at bottom capitalistic. As Lindblom succinctly puts it:

> Our thought is imprisoned. We cannot venture intellectually—a few exceptions aside— beyond what seems normal and natural. We uncritically accept what the market provides.[28]

Although Barrier I decisions are inherently unobservable, Lindblom nevertheless attempts to infer their occurrence from a systematic survey of the world's political and economic systems. He begins by differentiating capitalist or market-oriented economies from systems characterized by central economic planning. He then goes on to distinguish authoritarian and democratic political systems. (Here he adopts Dahl's terminology, labeling the more or less democratic systems as "polyarchies.") Interestingly, examples of both kinds of economies can be found within the ranks of authoritarian political systems. Communist states (except for Yugoslavia) provide the most obvious examples of authoritarian regimes with central planning systems. A surprising number of systems combine authoritarian politics with capitalistic economies, however; the application of Chicago school free market theories to Chile under the Pinochet regime provides a particularly striking example here.[29]

By contrast, the pattern for democratic systems is altogether one-sided. At least according to Lindblom's classification, which will be questioned below, there are no cases of democratic polities with centrally directed economies. This remarkable finding cries out for an explanation in his view:

> Can we explain the refusal of polyarchies to experiment with central planning of production on the assumption that polyarchal citizens and their leaders simply know, for all the superficial appeal of central planning, that it is not in fact a better solution to their problems than the market system? They could not possibly know that to be true. No one knows it to be true—or false. It is a matter of dispute. *One would think that at least one polyarchy would experiment, even if for the worst of reasons.* But they do not dispute, let alone experiment. It is a deeply puzzling phenomenon. [Emphasis added][30]

The historical correlation between democracy and capitalism may be attributable to the fundamental respect for individual rights and civil liberties underlying both systems. A political system emphasizing individual liberty will tend to nourish an economic system permitting individuals to acquire property, engage in productive activity, and trade with their counterparts in other lines of commerce. At least one theorist has argued that this relationship must hold in reverse as well: a system of central planning of economic activity must ultimately be coercive in ways that are incompatible with a free society.[31]

Lindblom acknowledges this historical connection between economic and political liberties but does not find it a sufficient explanation for such a strong linkage between democracy and capitalism. He finds his own explanation for this phenomenon in the privileged position of business within capitalist economies:

> If all past and existing polyarchies are dominated by business and property, it is to the dominating minority that we may owe its ties to the market system. That is to say, it is

possible that genuine democracy would not be dependent on the market system. Only existing polyarchies are, and that only because, although they are libertarian, they are controlled undemocratically by business and property.[32]

BUSINESS INFLUENCE ON OBSERVED DECISIONS

For the neo-elitists, a focus on the agenda-setting process was necessitated by the failure of previous elite theorists to find convincing evidence of the existence of a power elite through the examination of representative instances of policy-making. In the same way, an emphasis on Barrier I nondecisions permits corporate power theorists to minimize the failure of business to dominate policy-making on observable issues. This is not to say that business is a weak actor on the national scene. All students of government-business relations would concede that business groups possess important resources and that they win their share of victories in the policy process.[33] However, a cursory examination of regulatory policies enacted in recent years is sufficient to demonstrate that business fails to qualify as a ruling elite under the Dahl criteria.

In the fifteen-year period between 1964 and 1979, more than sixty new consumer health and safety laws were passed by Congress, a figure more than five times the total for the New Deal period.[34] This wave of social regulation brought the federal government into a wide range of new activities. In the pollution area, for example, the Environmental Protection Agency was created and given the responsibility for controlling air and water pollution and toxic wastes. The Occupational Safety and Health Administration was created to reduce workplace hazards. The automobile industry was forced to comply with tough new emissions standards, steadily increasing fuel economy regulations, and a variety of new safety requirements. Moreover, affirmative action requirements brought the federal government into personnel decisions for many businesses.

Secondary Issues?

Such business defeats are not evidence of business weakness according to the corporate power theorists. To say that business holds a privileged position within capitalist economies is not to say that the state cannot intervene at all in the functioning of a market economy. To the contrary, Miliband saw some infringements on private property as the "ransom" that business must pay to maintain the broader right of private ownership of the means of production.[35] Seen in this light, business defeats on a variety of regulatory fronts over the past two decades may be characterized as losses on secondary issues. If anything, the argument runs, business defeats on these secondary issues serve to consolidate its strength on the grand issue by mitigating the harsher consequences of reliance on impersonal market forces and thus putting a humane face on capitalism.

This argument loses force upon closer examination, however. Business defeats on such secondary issues are typically attributed to internal divisions within the business class. Internal divisions tend to surface where regulation targets individual industries or affects different industries in different ways. By contrast, issues threatening the shared interests of business as a class (for example, the rise of the labor movement early in this century) should lead to business unity and effective mobilization.

From this perspective the new wave of social regulation poses serious problems for the theory, inasmuch as most of these recent laws transcended individual industries to focus on the economy as a whole. Where the Interstate Commerce Commission was created in 1887 to regulate the railroads, and the Civil Aeronautics Board dealt exclusively with the airlines, more recent laws regulating emissions, toxic waste disposal, workplace safety, or affirmative action apply at least potentially to all lines of commerce. These new regulations threatening the shared class interests of all business did stimulate an impressive corporate countermobilization in the later 1970s, as predicted by the theory, culminating in the election of Ronald Reagan in 1980 and a period of emphasis on easing regulatory burdens. However, the business ascendance of the early 1980s failed to completely reverse the regulatory tide of the preceding period. While there is no question that the Reagan administration was more sympathetic to the needs of business than its predecessors, it managed at best to ease the burdens of a regulatory apparatus that remains intact, albeit somewhat scarred by repeated assaults.[36]

To the extent that such laws threatened business class interests, they were not really secondary issues at all. They should not have reached the agenda, and once there they should have produced an immediate (and more effective) business response. Government regulators are now in a position to significantly circumscribe managerial autonomy in a wide variety of areas including the adoption of specific production technologies (e.g., scrubbers for coal-burning utilities), the environment of the workplace (through OSHA), and personnel decisions (via affirmative action). If these matters are to be characterized as secondary issues, then one is forced to question just what qualifies as a grand issue.

Business groups clearly possess a variety of tangible and intangible resources making them highly significant actors in the policy adoption stage, but it must be acknowledged that they lose far too often to be termed a ruling elite under Dahl's rigorous standards. Faced with such a pattern of evidence, Lindblom and Miliband are forced to fall back on the neo-elitist conception of elite control of the agenda. While the need to induce business performance almost certainly constrains the political agenda to some degree within capitalistic societies, it is hard to document the extent of this control since Barrier I nondecisions are by their very nature immune to systematic observation.

Policy Implementation

If business influence is easily overstated in the agenda-setting and policy adoption stages, it would seem to be much greater in the eventual implementation of policies. Policy implementation is a costly and protracted process. Most organized groups will lack the resources and staff to monitor the day-to-day activities of administrative agencies, and mass publics initially aroused by an issue will tend to lose interest with the symbolic passage of a statute ostensibly protecting their interests. By contrast, industries affected by a law will be much more likely to participate in the administrative process. They will typically have a greater stake in the issue inasmuch as most regulatory statutes concentrate the costs of compliance on industry while spreading the benefits over the public as a whole.[37] Moreover, individual corporations, and often trade associations as well, stand already organized and ready for political action. They possess both the money and staff necessary for sustained attention to the process, and their considerable expertise on technical matters of production virtually guarantees them access to administrators.[38]

Moreover, the American Constitution provides additional advantages for business at this stage. Under our federal system of government, most domestic policies are characterized by intergovernmental implementation; federal agencies are forced to negotiate with a multiplicity of state and local agencies to secure reasonable conformity with legislative intent. Here Madison's argument for a national republic is prescient: the smaller the polity, the more vulnerable it is to domination by a single faction. All the factors allegedly operating to give business a privileged position in capitalist societies are much stronger at the state and local levels, where governments are especially vulnerable to the strategic position of business. State and local economies are often heavily dependent upon individual industries for employment opportunities and tax base, and the competition among these units of government to attract new business creates a considerable incentive to lower business taxes and reduce regulatory burdens.[39]

IMPERFECT COMPETITION

Plainly, corporations possess significant advantages in the group struggle, particularly ample financial resources, expertise, a high degree of legitimacy most of the time, and an unparalleled strategic position within society. If these advantages do not quite add up to a ruling elite status for business, they are nevertheless sufficient to guarantee an unbalanced competition among competing social groups. At the same time, it must be acknowledged, corporations have failed to control the institutional agenda, and while business is clearly a very important factor in the policy adoption stage, corporate power remains insufficient to guarantee favorable outcomes in all cases. Contrary to the Barrier I hypothesis advanced by both Lindblom and Miliband, business power would seem greatest not at the agenda-setting stage, but rather in policy implementation.

It is thus necessary to delineate carefully the extent of business power. In this regard, at least three generalizations can be drawn with confidence. First, corporate influence on any given issue will depend upon the configuration of demand, as we saw in Chapter 4. Where business is on the defensive, as is the case much of the time, it cannot necessarily keep threatening issues from arising, but its significant resource advantages may permit it to erode policies in the adoption and implementation stages. Where business groups are on the offensive, by contrast, seeking restrictions on competition, tax breaks, or other advantages, they are (like any other group) most successful in the distributive arena, where potential opponents have failed to mobilize due to the free rider problem or a lack of information.

Second, it is misleading to treat business as a monolithic entity. While business does mobilize as a class on some issues, most policies tend to affect individual industries or to impact on different industries in different ways. In this regard, it is important to recognize that some industries may consistently exercise more power than others. Where the three major domestic automakers have been ineffective in fending off a variety of regulations regarding auto safety, fuel economy, and air pollution in recent years, the major multinational oil companies have long occupied something approaching a "privileged position" within American politics, suppressing threatening issues and obtaining a variety of tax breaks, subsidies, and restrictions on competition.[40]

Finally, business power waxes and wanes over time. Lindblom and Miliband both imply that business's legitimacy and strategic position provide an inherent and timeless advantage over other interests within capitalistic societies. In reality, however, business involvement in politics has typically been a response to specific threats. The rise of labor unions at the turn of the century, followed by the political success of the Progressive movement, stimulated a major business mobilization in the early 1900s. With the election of Warren G. Harding in 1920, business activity declined until the emergence of the New Deal in 1933. The ensuing period of business mobilization lasted roughly until the late 1940s, when passage of the Taft-Hartley Act remedied what business groups saw as the prolabor bias of the Wagner Act and the National Labor Relations Board. The election of Dwight Eisenhower in 1952, with his cabinet of eight millionaires and a plumber, reinforced the temptation for business to lapse once again into political quiescence.[41] This period, it should be noted, provided the background for Bauer, Pool, and Dexter's influential study of trade policy that found business groups ill-informed, timid, and generally inept in approaching policy makers.[42]

Business influence in national politics reached its nadir in the middle 1970s. Disclosures of illegal corporate contributions to the Nixon reelection campaign eroded the legitimacy of big corporations in the eyes of voters and policy makers. Substantial Democratic gains in the 1974 midterm elections, in the wake of the Nixon pardon, gave liberals working control of both houses of Congress. Finally, the explosion of new citizens' groups, discussed in Chapter 4, substantially expanded the interest group universe to the disadvantage of business, mobilizing women, senior citizens, environmentalists, and consumers in large numbers. The tremendous countermobilization of business in the late 1970s and early 1980s must be understood in historical perspective as a response to these threats.[43] The significant business presence in Washington that we take for granted today is a comparatively recent development, and the history of business involvement in national politics gives every reason to believe that business lobbying will continue to wax and wane over the long term.

The almost cyclical nature of business involvement in national politics may be best understood through a categorization of groups developed by sociologist William Gamson.[44] Gamson distinguishes three kinds of groups, which he terms confident, neutral, and alienated. Confident groups believe the political system is predisposed to favor them. As a result, they tend to rely on persuasion (e.g., the provision of information) in dealing with policy makers. By contrast, neutral groups feel the system is unbiased; they find it necessary to approach policy makers with inducements (e.g., campaign contributions or other forms of political support) in order to gain favorable policies. Where confident groups may be seen as occupying a kind of privileged position within the polity, akin to that attributed by Lindblom and Miliband to business, the relationship between neutral groups and policy makers is instead transactional, resting on some kind of quid pro quo. Alienated groups, the final category, feel the system is so biased against their interests that neither persuasion nor inducements will be effective. Such groups are forced to rely instead upon sanctions, particularly demonstrations and social protests, in order to compel policy makers to deal with their demands.[45]

In Gamson's terms, business groups can properly be understood as oscillating between confident and neutral status. In the Eisenhower years, for example, business had every reason to believe the system was biased in its favor, making substantial political mobilization unnecessary. (This may also explain Bauer, Pool, and Dexter's finding that business lobbyists eschewed pressure tactics in the 1950s, choosing instead to act as service bureaus for legislators already sympathetic to their cause.) When faced with a serious political threat, as in the middle 1970s, business became a neutral group. The rise of corporate PACs in the last decade was thus predictable given the tendency for such groups to approach policy makers with inducements, as Gamson suggested.

If business does not constitute a ruling elite in American politics, it is safe to say that it has never constituted a genuinely alienated group. Oscillation between confident and neutral status suggests a number of conclusions regarding the power of business groups. First, business is indeed a very powerful actor within the system, capable at times of attaining a level of influence consistent with a systemic bias. However, this high level of business influence does not come to business automatically, but must rather be nurtured and sustained through a good deal of hard work. Finally, business as a class is no less vulnerable to the free rider problem than any other group, as suggested by its tendency (like many other actors in the system) to revert to political quiescence whenever external threats to its collective interests recede.

CORPORATE POWER AND POLICY CHANGE

According to the corporate power thesis, the privileged position of business in capitalist societies ultimately reinforces those factors already operating within any system to produce incremental policy change. In particular, large changes threatening to business class interests—for example, frontal assaults on capitalism as a form of economic organization—are not merely precluded but rendered inconceivable. Where Lindblom sees our thought as imprisoned, Miliband observes that Western governments are composed of leaders who simply ''cannot see'' capitalism for what it is in his view: ''an inherently coercive form of organization of society that cumulatively constrains men and all their institutions to work the will of the minority who hold and wield economic power.'' Thus the deficiencies of capitalism are perceived not as cause for changing the system itself but rather as ''remediable within its confines—in fact *only* remediable within its confines.''[46]

On this point, Lindblom and Miliband may be criticized for a tendency to characterize all policy change short of the abolition of capitalism as little more than incremental tinkering with a corrupt system. For example, Miliband acknowledges the nationalization of various industries, the imposition of national health insurance, and the creation of a welfare state by the postwar Labour government in Britain, but minimizes these reforms as little more than ''a certain humanization of the *existing* social order.''[47] Because he identifies the fundamental issue as the locus of control over economic power, Miliband sees all policy changes short of systemic transformation as inherently conservative.

Likewise, Lindblom's inability to find any polyarchies engaged in economic planning raises serious questions as to how he defines economic planning. In fact, there is a wide range of variation among the Western democracies in this regard. Their economies may be considered as ranging along a continuum, with the United States at one extreme; all the other Western governments play a greater role in managing their economies than is true here. At the other extreme, the various "neocorporatist" nations (Norway, Sweden, and Austria) make decisions regarding production, investment, and income distribution through consultation between the central government and monolithic organizations representing the major economic sectors. Seen in this light, the United States is distinctive in its lack of any single, unified group with the recognized authority to speak for business in dealing with the state.[48]

Of course, economic planning as practiced by the neocorporatist nations is much less coercive than is the case for authoritarian systems. In the neocorporatist countries, governments are formed through free elections and the major interest groups are free at any time to withdraw from their partnership with the state.[49] When Lindblom asserts that no Western democracies engage in central planning of their economies, one is forced to conclude that he is referring to a kind of authoritarian and coercive planning that is incompatible with democratic values. Put another way, central planning within a democratic society would probably have to look something like the neocorporatist model.

Ultimately, the kind of authoritarian central planning idealized by Lindblom presumes both a knowledge base and a level of consensus on objectives unlikely to be attained with any regularity in most democratic polities. In short, it presumes a capacity for rational decision making; indeed this is the very basis of its appeal. Seen in this light, Lindblom's inquiry, noted earlier in this chapter, as to why no polyarchy had experimented with central planning may be reworded to ask why no polyarchies have experimented with rational economic decision making. The answer to this question need not lie entirely in excessive corporate power, as Lindblom now believes. Rather, much of the explanation lies in the inherent limitations on rationality he identified in his earlier works on disjointed incrementalism. If decision making in a democracy is best understood as a process of bargaining and compromise among contending interests, as Lindblom long asserted, then one would expect central planning to take on a form very much like that observed in the neocorporatist societies. One would also expect, by Lindblom's (earlier) reasoning, to find movement toward such a system occurring gradually at best; here again this is pretty much what we find in these nations. Where Miliband and the recent writings of Lindblom suggest that changes short of systemic transformation are merely incremental, the early writings of Lindblom serve to remind us that incremental changes, accumulated over time, can add up to systemic transformation.

NOTES

1. Charles E. Lindblom, *Politics and Markets* (New York: Basic Books, 1977). See also Lindblom's "The Market as Prison," *Journal of Politics,* 44 (May 1982), pp. 324–336.
2. Lindblom, "Market as Prison," pp. 324–325.

3. Ralph Miliband, *The State in Capitalist Society* (New York: Basic Books/Harper Colophon Books, 1969).
4. Miliband, Chapter 6, "Imperfect Competition," pp. 146–178.
5. Miliband, pp. 164–165.
6. Miliband, pp. 68–69.
7. Lindblom, "Market as Prison," pp. 334–335.
8. David B. Truman, *The Governmental Process* (New York: Knopf, 1951), pp. 506–507. See also S. E. Finer, "The Political Power of Private Capital," Part I, *Sociological Review*, 3 (December 1955), pp. 279–294; and Part II, *Sociological Review*, 4 (July 1956), pp. 5–30. For an excellent review of corporate political resources, see also Edwin M. Epstein, *The Corporation in American Politics* (Englewood Cliffs, N.J.: Prentice-Hall, 1969), pp. 187–242.
9. Miliband, p. 165.
10. Lindblom, *Politics and Markets*, pp. 171–175. See also Charles E. Lindblom, *The Policy-Making Process*, 2d ed. (Englewood Cliffs, N.J.: Prentice-Hall, 1980), pp. 72–73; and Miliband, pp. 147–155. Finer termed this same phenomenon "surrogateship." See Finer, "Political Power of Private Capital," Part I, p. 285.
11. See Gardiner C. Means, *The Corporate Revolution in America* (New York: Collier Books, 1964); Adolph A. Berle, *The 20th Century Capitalist Revolution* (New York: Harcourt, Brace, and World, 1954); Adolph A. Berle, *Power Without Property* (New York: Harcourt, Brace, and World, 1959); Morton S. Baratz, "Corporate Giants and the Power Structure," *Western Political Quarterly*, 9 (June 1956), pp. 406–415; and Peter Bachrach, *The Theory of Democratic Elitism* (Boston: Little, Brown, 1967).
12. Baratz, p. 415.
13. Walter A. Rosenbaum, *Energy, Politics, and Public Policy*, 2d ed. (Washington, D.C.: Congressional Quarterly Press, 1987), pp. 45–48 and 73–75.
14. John E. Chubb, *Interest Groups and the Bureaucracy* (Stanford, Calif.: Stanford University Press, 1983).
15. Miliband, p. 75.
16. Lindblom, *Politics and Markets*, pp. 194–196. See also Kay Lehman Schlozman and John T. Tierney, *Organized Interests and American Democracy* (New York: Harper and Row, 1986), Table 10.5, p. 249.
17. Thomas Byrne Edsall, *The New Politics of Inequality* (New York: Norton, 1984). See also Larry J. Sabato, *PAC Power* (New York; Norton, 1984); and Philip M. Stern, *The Best Congress Money Can Buy* (New York: Pantheon Books, 1988).
18. Raymond A. Bauer, Ithiel de Sola Pool, and Lewis Anthony Dexter, *American Business and Public Policy*, 2d ed. (Chicago: Aldine-Atherton, 1972).
19. Lindblom, *Policy-Making Process*, p. 81; *Politics and Markets*, pp. 196–197.
20. Miliband, p. 157.
21. Robert A. Dahl, "A Critique of the Ruling Elite Model," *American Political Science Review*, 52 (June 1958), pp. 463–469.
22. Peter Bachrach and Morton S. Baratz, *Power and Poverty* (New York: Oxford University Press, 1970).
23. Bachrach and Baratz, pp. 52–60.
24. Bruce I. Oppenheimer, *Oil and the Congressional Process* (Lexington, Mass.: D. C. Heath, Lexington Books, 1974).
25. Miliband, pp. 179–264; Lindblom, *Politics and Markets*, pp. 201–213.
26. Bachrach and Baratz, p. 49.
27. See, for example, Richard M. Merelman, "On the Neo-Elitist Critique of Community Power,"

American Political Science Review, 62 (June 1968), pp. 451–461. For a response by Bachrach and Baratz, and a reply by Merelman, see *American Political Science Review,* 62 (December 1968), pp. 1268–1269.

28. Lindblom, "Market as Prison," p. 334.
29. Lindblom, *Politics and Markets,* pp. 161–169. See also pp. 93–160.
30. Lindblom, *Politics and Markets,* pp. 161–162 and 168.
31. Friedrich A. Hayek, *The Road to Serfdom* (Chicago: University of Chicago Press, 1944).
32. Lindblom, *Politics and Markets,* p. 168.
33. See, for example, Epstein, pp. 230–242; Finer, "Political Power of Private Capital," Part II, p. 25; and David Vogel, "The Power of Business in America: A Reappraisal," *British Journal of Political Science,* 13 (January 1983), pp. 19–43.
34. Michael D. Reagan, *Regulation* (Boston: Little, Brown, 1987), pp. 85–111. See also Vogel, and two works by Murray L. Weidenbaum, *Business, Government, and the Public* (Englewood Cliffs, N.J.: Prentice-Hall, 1977), and *The Future of Business Regulation* (New York: American Management Association, Amacom Books, 1979).
35. Miliband, p. 78.
36. For example, efforts to weaken the Clean Air Act in 1981 and 1982 failed as the administration (and its business allies) ran into opposition from environmentalists determined to strengthen the act and public opinion polls showing sustained support for strong antipollution laws. With legislative revision of the law blocked, the administration mounted a new assault on the agency through the budgetary process, reducing EPA's appropriations and staff by roughly a third during Reagan's first term in office. By 1983, highly publicized scandals involving top-level officials at EPA had forced an end to this strategy as well, resulting in personnel shakeups and a restoration of much of the agency's funding. While the agency was badly damaged by the ordeal, it did survive, and the panoply of environmental laws remains on the books, awaiting more vigorous enforcement under future administrations. See Richard J. Tobin, "Revising the Clean Air Act: Legislative Failure and Administrative Success," in Norman J. Vig and Michael E. Kraft (eds.), *Environmental Policy in the 1980s* (Washington, D.C.: Congressional Quarterly Press, 1984), pp. 227–249. See also Robert V. Bartlett, "The Budgetary Process and Environmental Policy," and J. Clarence Davies, "Environmental Institutions and the Reagan Administration," in the same volume, pp. 121–160.
37. James Q. Wilson, "The Politics of Regulation," in James Q. Wilson (ed.), *The Politics of Regulation* (New York: Basic Books, 1980), pp. 357–394.
38. Chubb, pp. 89–125.
39. C. K. Rowland and Roger Marz, "Gresham's Law: The Regulatory Analogy," *Policy Studies Review,* 1 (February 1982), pp. 572–580.
40. On automobile regulation, see Robert W. Crandall, Howard K. Gruenspecht, Theodore E. Keeler, and Lester B. Lave, *Regulating the Automobile* (Washington, D.C.: Brookings Institution, 1986). On the power of the major multinational oil companies, see Robert Engler, *The Brotherhood of Oil* (New York: Mentor Books, 1977); Anthony Sampson, *The Seven Sisters* (New York: Viking, 1975); and Robert Sherrill, *The Oil Follies of 1970–1980* (Garden City, N.Y.: Doubleday, Anchor Press, 1983).
41. L. Harmon Zeigler and G. Wayne Peak, *Interest Groups and American Society,* 2d ed. (Englewood Cliffs, N.J.: Prentice-Hall, 1972), pp. 215–234.
42. Raymond A. Bauer, Ithiel de Sola Pool, and Lewis Anthony Dexter, *American Business and Public Policy,* 2d ed. (Chicago: Aldine-Atherton, 1972).
43. Thomas Byrne Edsall, *The New Politics of Inequality* (New York: Norton, 1984), pp. 107–140. David Truman, in his "disturbance theory" of group formation, hypothesized that interest

groups will mobilize in response to economic hard times or external threats. While this disturbance theory does not adequately account for the mobilization of most mass membership groups (see Robert H. Salisbury, "An Exchange Theory of Interest Groups," *Midwest Journal of Political Science,* 8 (February 1969), pp. 1–32), it appears to fit the cyclical mobilization of business groups quite closely. See also David Vogel, *Fluctuating Fortunes* (New York: Basic Books, 1989).

44. William A. Gamson, *Power and Discontent* (Homewood, Ill.: Dorsey, 1968). See also Gamson's later book, *The Strategy of Social Protest* (Homewood, Ill.: Dorsey, 1975).

45. In addition to Gamson's work, cited above, see also Michael Lipsky, *Protest in City Politics* (Chicago: Rand McNally, 1970); and Jack L. Walker, "Protest and Negotiation: A Case Study of Negro Leadership in Atlanta, Georgia," *Midwest Journal of Political Science,* 7 (May 1963), pp. 99–124.

46. Miliband, p. 74.

47. Miliband, pp. 109–110.

48. G. Wilson, *Business and Politics,* pp. 103–126 and 130.

49. G. Wilson, *Business and Politics,* p. 104.

CHAPTER 6

Is There an Alternative to Incrementalism?

Taken together, the four models we have covered thus far add a great deal to our understanding of the policy process, and we now have a reasonably coherent picture of the major forces contributing to incremental policy outcomes. All four of these models treat the policy process as a form of group struggle, and all four would predict incremental outcomes from the interplay of contending interests under normal circumstances, albeit for different reasons. There is little question that participants frequently make use of aids to calculation of the sort identified by Lindblom, building on past policies, analyzing ends and means together, converging on solutions through a series of policy cycles, and so on. However, incremental policy outcomes also stem from a variety of factors—in particular, the Constitution, inequality in political resources, and capitalism as a form of economic organization—that are not commonly associated with incrementalism as a deliberate decision strategy.

To the extent that some degree of imperfect competition among social interests is virtually inevitable, incremental outcomes cannot be equated with the public interest. We are compelled to explore whether there is any realistic alternative to policy-making by group struggle. Accordingly, this chapter will focus on the responsible parties model, long advocated by a wide variety of political scientists, which provides what is arguably the most popular and enduring alternative vision of policy-making.

It is also a particularly significant model for our purposes because the case for responsible parties is rooted in a critique of the normative premises underlying the incremental, group struggle, and classical models. In theory, at least, responsible parties would offset the fragmenting and decentralizing tendencies imposed by the Constitution, and by making periodic elections the pivot point in the policy process, would shift decision-making power away from organized interest groups (and corporations) and into the hands of rank-and-file voters, many of whom are now left out of the group struggle. Moreover, a system of programmatic and disciplined political parties would be highly responsive to changes in mass public opinion and correspondingly open to nonincremental changes in policy.

Ultimately, as this chapter will show, the responsible parties model fails to provide a practical alternative to policy-making through group struggle, at least within the American political context. This discovery is not as discouraging as it might at first appear, however. While the group struggle may give rise to an imperfect competition among contending interests, the normative case for the responsible parties model is not without important vulnerabilities of its own, suggesting that a system of organized interest groups may provide a better vehicle for the representation of citizen preferences than a system of competitive political parties. Moreover, a good deal of incrementalism would likely persist even under an ideal system of responsible parties. Accordingly, the chapter will conclude with a hardheaded and unsentimental defense of the American political system as it has been described in Chapters 2 through 5.

RESPONSIBLE PARTIES AND THE EVOLUTION OF POLICY

Calls for strengthening the party system date back at least to the 1940s.[1] The evolution of policy within a system of responsible parties would diverge considerably from the patterns suggested by the four preceding models.

Agenda Setting

Within this model, issues are perceived and defined by political parties during electoral campaigns. The parties take positions on a variety of issues in an attempt to attract voters. In turn, the voters decide between the parties on the basis of issue differences rather than personalities or other considerations. Under such ideal circumstances, the winning party has a clear mandate and the legislative majority necessary to carry it through. Its platform is now the agenda until the next election.

Policy Adoption

In the postelection period, the winning party must be "responsible"—that is, it must live up to the promises it made during the previous election. For this to happen, the political parties must be disciplined: they must possess some means to keep members in line on party votes. Thus in contrast to the classical model reviewed in Chapter 3, party divisions provide the only recurring cleavage in this model. In a true parliamentary system, the failure of the majority party to keep its members together on a critical vote would result in the dissolution of the government. Grafted onto the American constitutional system, responsible parties would at least vote together a good deal more often than they do now.[2]

Policy Implementation

To the extent that important decisions must inevitably be made by bureaucrats, effective majority rule requires that administrators somehow be held accountable to elective politicians. Otherwise, elections lose their meaning, as the bureaucracy becomes a kind of permanent government, insulated from popular control. If the parties are to keep their electoral promises, the bureaucracy must be made responsive to the government in power. This is typically accomplished through party control of patronage, making administrators accountable to elected politicians with the power to hire and fire.

Policy Change

It follows from the foregoing that policies change primarily through elections according to this model. Parties offer clear policy alternatives to voters; party turnover necessarily leads to policy change. While the degree of policy change will depend upon how far apart the two parties are on any given issue, a change in party control signals the substitution of one party's platform for another. Such a system would clearly be more responsive to mass preferences than the classical model, and it would facilitate nonincremental policy change.

MAJORITY RULE AND RESPONSIBLE PARTIES

The responsible parties model retains an enduring appeal, beyond its capacity to produce nonincremental policy change, because it rests on the fundamental principle of majority rule—in distinct contrast to the classical model examined in Chapter 3. Indeed, self-government is ultimately incompatible with any other principle, according to proponents of this model, for a truly democratic polity must always operate in accord with the wishes of a majority of its enfranchised citizens. The preferences of the majority, whatever the merits of its position, are taken as inherently preferable to any alternative system of minority rule.[3]

The test of good policy here is thus procedural and not substantive, resting on two fundamental democratic values: *popular sovereignty*, which holds that all decision-making power must ultimately rest with the people themselves, and *political equality*, which maintains that every adult citizen must have an equal say in all decisions. The latter principle is also referred to as the one-person-one-vote principle: all citizens have a vote, and all votes count the same.[4]

Decision making by majority rule can be criticized for failing to adequately safeguard the interests of minorities, as the one-person-one-vote principle provides no mechanism whatever for taking into account differences in intensity of preference among citizens voting on an issue. Critics charge that such a system allows apathetic majorities to impose their will on intense, and often more directly affected, minorities. In the extreme case, as

Madison argued, undisciplined majorities may even go so far as to deprive minorities of certain natural rights.[5]

Unfortunately, every means of constraining majorities ultimately proves to be incompatible with one or both of the two fundamental democratic values identified above. For example, forbidding certain kinds of actions through a bill of rights circumscribes the freedom of action of majorities and thus violates the principle of popular sovereignty. Similarly, mechanisms for weighting voting according to intensity—severe problems of impracticality aside—violate the principle of political equality. Requiring an extraordinary majority (say, two-thirds) before certain kinds of actions may be undertaken necessarily permits a minority to block action, and thus in a sense to rule. In short, given an absolute commitment to democratic values, majorities must be trusted to exercise self-restraint.[6]

VOTERS, PARTIES, AND ISSUES

The responsible parties model requires political parties that offer the voters clear choices on the issues of the day and voters who choose between the parties solely on the basis of these issue differences. While both the voters and the parties in the United States have frequently been charged with failing to meet these requirements, these criticisms have lost much of their validity in recent years. Recent research suggests that the two parties are becoming increasingly issue oriented and distinct while issue voting now appears to be much more prevalent than previously thought.

Parties and Issues

Various critics of this model have argued that political parties, particularly in the United States, do not function to offer voters clear alternatives on important issues. According to Anthony Downs, for example, in a two-party system, competitive parties will find it rational to move to the electoral center, adopting identical positions on policy issues.[7] What is especially troubling for the responsible party theorist is Downs's contention that parties will fail to offer the voters a clear choice where voters are perfectly informed and decide solely on the basis of the issues.[8]

Meaningful differences between the parties may be further obscured by the persistence of factions within each of the major parties. Southern Democrats have long been much more conservative than their Northern colleagues, frequently defecting to form a "Conservative Coalition" with Republicans in Congress. Urban, Northeastern Republicans similarly ally themselves with liberal Democrats on a number of issues.

Although the Conservative Coalition is still a force to be reckoned with—in 1981, for example, a number of Southern Democrats joined with Republicans to help pass President Reagan's tax cut and budget proposals—the evidence suggests that these internal divisions are becoming much less pronounced. With the rise of real two-party competition in much of the South, and with a sharp decline in the ranks of moderate Republicans in recent years, the two parties are becoming increasingly distinct. Southern Democrats elected to Congress over the past decade often tend to be relatively liberal by a variety of measures, and even the more conservative Southern Democrats now tend to be more liberal than the average Republican.[9]

The critics thus tend to understate the differences between the parties. Republicans and Democrats differ on a wide range of political issues, particularly at the elite level. Surveys of delegates to the national party conventions point to major differences between the parties on such issues as national health insurance, racial integration, arms control, the size of the defense budget, tax cuts, and the importance of a balanced budget relative to domestic needs.[10] This ideological divergence is reflected in the congressional candidates offered by the two parties. Congress would be strikingly more liberal if all the Democratic candidates won their races in any given year, and correspondingly more conservative if all the Republican candidates were elected. Democrats are much more likely than Republicans to support a larger role for the federal government on most issues, particularly the regulation of business, and to support legislation providing welfare benefits or public service employment for the poor. Where Republicans champion supply side fiscal policies, Democrats are much more likely to cling to Keynesian approaches.[11]

These sharp differences between the parties on a variety of issues are often masked by the failure of congressional elections to produce decisive majorities for one side or the other.[12] However, where elections do produce a major change in the ideological composition of Congress—usually in combination with a landslide at the presidential level—a window of opportunity is opened for major policy changes. For example, the 1964 Johnson landslide gave the Democrats a two-thirds majority in both the House and Senate, opening the way for passage of a variety of Great Society programs. Similarly, the election of Ronald Reagan in 1980 brought with it Republican control of the Senate and a working bipartisan majority in the House, making possible sweeping tax cuts and an assault on a wide range of New Deal and Great Society programs. Where such an election produces a long-term realignment of voting loyalties between the parties, as was the case in the 1930s, it can lead to major policy changes that become institutionalized for a generation or more.[13]

Despite this evidence of significant differences between the parties, there is a widespread tendency in recent years to minimize their importance in the policy process. Most textbooks in the field pay scant attention to the parties, except perhaps to comment on their weakness. As we have seen, however, the explanation for this neglect does not lie with the failure of the parties to offer voters a clear choice. While internal divisions continue to plague both parties, these divisions have become much less pronounced in recent years. The parties are in fact very different, and they are becoming more—not less—distinct.

Voters and Issues

A second line of criticism of the model emphasizes the failure of voters to decide elections on the basis of issues. In particular, candidate appeal can overwhelm issues in some elections. Dwight Eisenhower's extraordinary popularity proved too much for the Democrats in both 1952 and 1956, for example. More recently, the 1984 election appears to have been largely a referendum on President Reagans's leadership, with public opinion polls consistently showing the president to be much more popular than his policies.[14]

While the importance of issues relative to other factors varies from election to election, the baseline level of issue voting would appear to have been underestimated by early researchers. The classic voting studies focused on the Eisenhower years, a period noted for its lack of ideological politics. Issue voting appears to have increased steadily since that time, however. With the two parties becoming increasingly distinct, as we have just seen, the voters' perceptions have followed accordingly. Beginning with the 1964 election, the voters have come to see the two parties as taking very different positions on a whole range of issues. By various statistical measures, voters (like the parties) have become more ideological and issue oriented over the past two decades.[15]

THE DECLINE OF PARTY IDENTIFICATION

Although issue-oriented voters and parties are a prerequisite for popular control of public policy, these recent developments do not necessarily bode well for the responsible parties model. The parties seem to be less and less a factor in voters' decisions at the same time they are becoming more distinct ideologically. In recent years, the proportion of the electorate identifying with one of the major parties has declined steadily, with a particularly sharp drop among strong party identifiers. Moreover, while early voting studies found independent voters to be poorly informed and apathetic, the new independents prove to be as well informed on candidates and issues as those voters identifying with one of the parties. Increasingly, candidates have been forced to tailor their appeals to this important group of voters.[16]

In addition, the power of party identification to influence the voting decision seems to be declining. For example, fewer than half of those identifying with one of the parties report having consistently voted for the presidential candidate of their party over several elections, in distinct contrast with the pattern for the New Deal years.[17] Likewise, split-ticket voting has increased steadily in recent decades, giving rise to very different voting patterns at the presidential and congressional levels.[18] Republicans have won four of the past five presidential elections (three of these by landslide margins), while the Democrats have retained control of the House of Representatives throughout the period and the Senate for fourteen out of twenty years.

This decline in the power of party identification would not necessarily be incompatible with a system of responsible parties if the rise of a large bloc of highly informed, issue-oriented independent voters merely signaled that the parties must increasingly compete for votes, as required by the model. However, surveys of the electorate suggest that the two parties have increasingly come to appear irrelevant to most voters.[19] This cannot be explained by a failure of the two parties to offer distinct approaches to contemporary public problems, as we have just seen. Nor does movement away from the electoral center by both parties appear to make them unattractive alternatives for most voters, as one might expect; to the contrary, the evidence suggests that voters are not actively disillusioned with the parties. Rather, as the parties have become less important both as electoral and policy-making institutions over the past twenty years, the voters have simply begun to look elsewhere for levers to control policy outcomes.[20]

THE DECLINE OF THE PARTIES AS ELECTORAL INSTITUTIONS

As we saw in Chapter 3, barriers to majority rule built into the Constitution have weakened the national parties from the beginning of the republic. Federalism decapitates the parties as electoral institutions; members of the House and Senate are nominated and elected locally, with little or no effective interference from the national parties. Name recognition and local issues are typically more important in these races than national party platforms. Each race is independent and idiosyncratic, making it virtually impossible to impute any clear mandate to the aggregate results of congressional elections. Even where a particular election becomes something of a referendum on the president's program, which is by no means the normal case, individual members of the president's party may still avoid close identification with it.[21]

If the institutional weaknesses of the American parties were largely built into the Constitution by the framers, in recent years the parties have acted as their own worst enemies. Never strong, centralized hierarchies, the parties have become even weaker over the past two decades, both as electoral and policy-making institutions.[22] At the national level, reforms resulting in a proliferation of presidential primaries have taken the parties' most important nominations out of the hands of party professionals and given power instead to rank-and-file voters, in some states failing even to restrict participation to self-identified party adherents.[23] In the same way, direct primaries for a variety of lesser offices weaken the power of the party organizations.

With the decline in party organizations, there has been a corresponding increase in candidate-centered campaigns. Party support is less and less important when candidates can approach the voters directly through the media. In turn, the resulting increase in the costs of campaigning for office creates a fertile field for organized interest groups. Interest group involvement in congressional elections has grown dramatically over the past fifteen years with the passage of campaign finance reforms facilitating the development of political action committees (see Chapter 3). While both parties have strengthened their national committees and congressional campaign organizations in recent years, substantially increasing their financial contributions to congressional candidates, they have failed to keep pace with the dramatic growth of PAC contributions. House candidates in recent elections received approximately 40 percent of their funds from political action committees, with most of the remainder coming from individual contributors.[24]

With the rise in candidate-centered campaigns, voters have paid correspondingly less attention to the parties, as Martin Wattenberg has observed:

> As party leaders have come to act more and more on their own initiative and to communicate with voters directly through the media, the public has increasingly come to see the

crucial short-term domestic and foreign issues only in terms of the candidates. It is candidates rather than parties that are now viewed as being responsible for solving, or failing to solve, our current political problems. Therefore, the parties are receiving much less credit or blame for political outcomes than they did several decades ago.[25]

THE DECLINE OF THE PARTIES
AS GOVERNING INSTITUTIONS

The responsible parties model requires that parties be more than just issue oriented; they must also be disciplined if they are to keep their promises once elected. This in turn requires that party leaders have a mix of rewards and punishments sufficient to keep members of their parties in line on key votes.

In the American system, however, legislators are relatively free to ignore party pressures when faced with counterpressures from constituents or organized interests. The demands of party must always compete with constituency pressures, and party loyalty collapses entirely on many issues. By comparison with parliamentary systems, American parties have never been particularly cohesive. By a strict measure of party voting, in which at least 90 percent of the voting membership of one party is aligned against the same percentage of the opposition—less than one-fifth of all House roll call votes would qualify as party line votes in a good year. Even with a more relaxed standard, requiring only that a majority of the two parties vote in opposition to one another, only about 40 percent of all House roll calls would constitute party votes in an average year.[26]

A bicameral Congress further guarantees that House and Senate members of the same party will be subject to very different local pressures and institutional perspectives, thus impeding the development of a coherent party program. Moreover, this reinforces the ever-present possibility of divided government, which has occurred with increasing frequency in recent years as the decline in party identification has led to a rise in ticket splitting. While divided government occurred only 14 percent of the time from 1897 to 1954, it has occurred two-thirds of the time since 1954.[27] President Eisenhower faced a hostile Congress from 1954 onward. Presidents Nixon and Ford faced Congresses controlled by the opposition throughout their terms. By contrast, President Reagan enjoyed a Republican Senate through his first six years in office, but his party never controlled the House, and midterm losses in 1986 gave control of the Senate back to the Democrats as well. Only under presidents Kennedy, Johnson, and Carter (a total of twelve years) has one party controlled the presidency and both houses of Congress.

American political parties clearly fail to fulfill the conditions of the responsible parties model, and there is little reason to believe that they will reform themselves along these lines in the foreseeable future. While the two parties are issue oriented and distinctive enough to provide voters with a clear choice on most issues, the American Constitution in combination with recent party reforms makes responsible party government virtually impossible. Significant movement toward a more responsible party system would require amending the Constitution—at a minimum, to require voting for the president, vice president, and members of Congress as members of teams—but congressional incumbents of both parties, increasingly insulated from the exogenous effects of presidential races on their own campaigns for reelection, would be unlikely to support such reforms.[28] And it is hard to imagine even the most far-reaching constitutional reformer proposing an end to the institution of federalism, which does so much to subject national policies to local pressures in the implementation process.[29]

THE PARTIES AS "POTENTIAL GROUPS"

Where elections fail to set the policy agenda, the parties are forced to compete with a variety of other groups in a struggle over policy. Perhaps the best way to conceptualize the role of the congressional parties under such circumstances is to think of them as "potential groups," in David Truman's terms.[30] Parties are collections of like-minded individuals; Democrats and Republicans do tend to adopt distinctively different outlooks on a wide range of issues. Party affiliation is not an idle choice for most legislators; it is a reflection of their worldview, inclining them to vote with their party in the absence of counterpressures. Within Congress, party affiliation shapes not only general policy orientations, but also a legislator's choice of friends, sources of cues on issues outside his or her expertise, memberships in informal groups, relationships with the respective party leaderships, and even receptivity to different kinds of lobbyists.[31]

At the same time, however, the parties (like interest groups) face a severe problem in mobilizing for collective action. Most legislators would like to see their party triumph on a wide range of issues, but find it rational to defect in response to constituency or interest group pressures. In dealing with this free rider problem, the coercive powers of the party leadership are negligible, and the selective incentives available as inducements are limited at best.[32] Moreover, because the need to secure reelection is common to all members, the leadership takes an understanding view of periodic defections from party positions.

At the same time, the parties are not without important resources in the struggle over policy. While they cannot compete with political action committees as sources of campaign funding, they do secure a significant degree of allegiance from their members in the absence of coercion; legislators are drawn to a party for the philosophy it offers, and they see the demands of their party as entirely legitimate, if not always compelling. Beyond this, the parties occupy an enviable strategic position as gatekeepers for the elective institutions of our government. At the national level, elected officeholders—that is to say, those granted the formal authority to draft legislation, appropriate revenues, and levy taxes under our system of government—must first secure the formal nomination of one of the two major parties.

Unfortunately, as we saw in Chapter 4, political resources represent at best only the potential for power; they are worthless if they cannot be translated into effective influence. The crippling disadvantage of the parties is their inability to maintain cohesion. If major shifts in the party composition of Congress provide unique opportunities for nonincremental policy departures that can alter the political landscape for a generation, more often the parties disintegrate, playing at best a peripheral role in the process. Under such circumstances, even the most adroit leadership can normally do little more than make the most of a weak hand.

PARTIES AND THE RESPONSIBILITY
FOR PERFORMANCE IN OFFICE

If American political parties cannot function as responsible parties, they might nevertheless provide voters with the opportunity to exert meaningful control over policy outcomes through elections. Competitive political parties perform an invaluable function within any representative government by facilitating the assignment of responsibility for past policies. Where voters can hold an identifiable team of incumbents accountable for performance in office, they can register their approval or disapproval at the polls. Officeholders must consider the potential effects of every action on their perceived performance as a team, since the party out of power will have every incentive to comb its record for issues that may rally discontented voters.

No other institution can take the place of the parties in this regard. In one-party systems, like those characterizing the American South throughout much of this century, the functions normally performed by competitive parties are left to the whim of a single party. While stable, bipolar factions within the dominant party may approximate the performance of competitive parties on occasion, more often there are no permanent groupings that can be identified by voters.[33] Under such circumstances, voters are unable to assign any responsibility for performance in office. By the same token, there is no institutionalized opposition with incentive to criticize the performance of the current administration. Rather, elections center around personalities instead of issues, and electoral coalitions are short-term marriages of convenience, constructed through the manipulation of patronage, government contracts, or other private favors.[34]

To perform this critically important function, the parties need not be programmatic. Nor is it necessary for voters to control policy in advance, as in the responsible parties model, by sending an unambiguous mandate that binds the winning party in the postelection period. Rather, the most important characteristic of competitive parties in this regard is simply their permanence. As the late V. O. Key observed:

> The great virtue of the two-party system is, not that there are two groups with conflicting policy tendencies from which voters can choose, but that there are two groups of politicians.[35]

The remarkable longevity of the two American parties would seem to assure that voters will always be able to replace incumbent officeholders where necessary with some alternative team of politicians. In this vein, the 1980 election appears to have been a referendum on the Democratic party's stewardship over the preceding four years. Faced with an apparent decline in American power to shape international events and a failing economy characterized by high inflation, unemployment, and interest rates, voters sought to punish the party in power. While candidate Reagan offered unusually concrete remedies in the form of a massive defense buildup and a series of income tax cuts designed to stimulate the economy, it is not clear that his election constituted a mandate for these specific policies. However, many voters acted decisively to replace the current administration with a distinctively different group of politicians.[36]

What makes the decline of the American parties particularly alarming is that the same factors operating to preclude a responsible parties system also operate to impede (if not quite preclude) the effective assignment of responsibility for policy outcomes. The combined effects of federalism and the separation of powers render a collective judgment of the parties, such as occurred in 1980, the exception rather than the rule. In the absence of disciplined and truly national parties, voters tend to absolve individual members of Congress from responsibility for the effects of current policies. For congressional elections to take on clear meaning, as they seem to have done in 1980, large numbers of voters throughout the United States must put aside local issues and personalities and think in terms of national party differences.

Similarly, while the stability of the two-party system at the national level guarantees the existence of an opposition with at least some incentive to criticize incumbents, the fragmentation inherent in the American system makes the task of the party out of power extremely difficult. In the wake of a defeat at the presidential level, there is typically no single figure in a position to speak with authority for the party. Where potential rivals for the next presidential nomination advocate distinctively different policy directions, it can be almost impossible to unite behind a coherent party program.

Under normal circumstances, then, the American voter finds it extremely difficult to hold anyone accountable for policy outcomes. As the only elected official in our system with a national constituency, the president provides voters with their only real opportunity to signal policy preferences through elections. But the president cannot offset the weakness of the parties in providing voters with a mechanism for majority rule, except in those rare instances (as was the case with President Reagan) where the president's legislative objectives are unusually clear, consistent, and effectively communicated to the public. Under such circumstances, the president's program becomes the party's program in the eyes of the public.

Even then, it must be added, divided party control of Congress and the White House—which has occurred for sixteen of the last twenty years—can create a situation in which stalemate over major issues is almost inevitable and responsibility for resulting policy failures is impossible to assign. As James L. Sundquist recently observed, the United States has entered into a new era of ''coalition government'' in recent years, in which the White House and Congress are controlled by different parties most of the time. Under such circumstances, it becomes almost impossible to produce coherent and effective responses to the policy problems of the day:

> In the American form of coalition government, if the president sends a proposal to Capitol Hill or takes a foreign policy stand, the opposition-controlled House or houses of Congress—unless they are overwhelmed by the president's popularity and standing in the country—simply *must* reject it. Otherwise they are saying the president is a wise and prudent leader. That would only strengthen him and his party for the next election, and how can the men and women of the congressional majority do that, when their whole object is to defeat him when that time arrives? By the same token, if the opposition party in control of Congress initiates a measure, the president has to veto it—or he is saying of his opponents that they are sound and statesmanlike, and so is building them up for the next election.
>
> So when President Reagan sent his budgets to the Congress, the Democrats who con-

trolled both houses had to pronounce them "dead on arrival," as they did. And when they came up with their alternatives, the President had to condemn them and hurl them back. Eventually, when the stream of recrimination and vetoes ran dry each year, some kind of budget was necessarily adopted; but it did not reflect the views of either party, and in terms of the consensus objective of deficit reduction it was a pale and ineffective compromise. Neither party would take responsibility, neither could be held accountable, each could point the finger at the other when things went wrong.[37]

AN UNSENTIMENTAL DEFENSE
OF THE AMERICAN POLITICAL SYSTEM

To conclude, a system of responsible parties is rendered almost inconceivable under the American system, and the same factors preventing the development of disciplined and cohesive parties also operate to impede popular control over policy through retrospective voting. The end result is an extraordinarily complex system involving a multiplicity of actors spread over distinct levels of government that can make it almost impossible for the average voter to understand the process or hold anyone effectively accountable for policy outcomes. Under such circumstances, public policy tends to be determined less by the outcome of periodic elections than by the interplay of organized interests—a group struggle in which many citizens are unrepresented and corporate interests often wield disproportionate power.

However, if majority rule—and a heightened capacity for nonincremental change—is precluded under our system by checks and balances built into our Constitution, it must nevertheless be remembered that the American system is antimajoritarian by design. While the normative case for a more majoritarian politics has an undeniable appeal, particularly to many political scientists, no system rooted in the principles of one-person-one-vote and political equality can effectively deal with the problem of differences in intensity across voters. As noted earlier in this chapter, all attempts to reflect differences in intensity under such a system must violate one or both of these two principles. As Madison clearly understood, any system of majority rule must ultimately rest upon a trust in the majority to exercise self-restraint.

Moreover, in evaluating our current system of imperfect competition among social interests against the lofty standard of majority rule, we now know two things that we did not know at the outset: first, no matter how we reform the system, a good deal of incrementalism will occur anyway due to inevitable inequalities in political mobilization and inherent limitations on rational decision making; and second, the sources of incrementalism we can do something about—the Constitution and our capitalistic economic system—are themselves rooted in important values. In short, we must give something up to gain more policy responsiveness, and if we choose to make this trade-off, the ultimate gains will necessarily be limited.

When the American political system is judged fairly—that is, when it is compared with realistic alternatives and not with a utopian ideal—a number of points may be raised in its favor. First, it can be argued that participation in the group struggle offers interested citizens more control over public policy outcomes than a system of majority rule. A "one-vote-many-policies'' problem would preclude a clear and directive mandate from the voters to the winning party under even a perfectly functioning system of responsible parties.[38] Each voter has but one vote to express a wide variety of issue preferences; unless their positions correspond to the platform of one of the two parties across the board, they will be cross-pressured and forced to settle for whichever party pleases them more on balance. This preference may stem from that party's positions on a majority of the issues, or it may only reflect the party's stand on one or two issues of critical importance to the individual voter. While the winning party is preferred, for one reason or another, by a majority of voters, it is misleading to infer a majority preference for any given plank in the winning party's platform. If responsible parties are in fact a necessary condition for the attainment of majority rule, it would seem that they are insufficient to guarantee it.

By contrast, where policy is the outcome of a group struggle, the average citizen can signal a variety of preferences with great precision by joining several interest groups. A two-party system is often applauded for framing the choices available to the electorate and producing automatic majorities in favor of one party or the other. The other side of this coin, however, is that the parties do this by limiting the alternatives available to the electorate. Competitive parties confront the citizen with a duopoly (or in multiparty systems, an oligopoly) in the supply of public policies. Seen in this light, the responsible parties model offers a narrowly circumscribed vision of popular control over public policy—one in which citizens are able to influence policy only through elections, and in which they are precluded from expressing their views with any real precision.

Second, while many people fail to join organized interest groups, and thus fail to get into the game at all, a system that requires some time and effort on the part of those seeking to influence policy provides at least a crude vehicle for measuring differences in intensity of preference among citizens. While recognizing that citizens may fail to participate for a variety of reasons having nothing to do with intensity—the free rider problem and a lack of money, among others—it is still arguable that a system making some provision (however crude) for differences in intensity is superior to one (like the responsible parties model) that cannot deal with the problem at all.

Third, the system is highly responsive to groups that succeed in mobilizing. The failure of the group equilibrium to fully reflect the interests of any one group should not be taken as evidence of the irrelevance of groups as political actors or of a lack of responsiveness to mobilized interests. To the contrary, the Constitution itself erects no obstacles to participation apart from provision for a national republic, which might be construed as making for broader, national interests more susceptible to a free rider problem. In every other respect, the classical model operates to encourage a responsiveness to local constituencies even where they fail to mobilize as organized interest groups.

Fourth, the proliferation of citizens' groups in recent years has served to make the group universe more balanced and representative than ever before. If this growth has been largely confined to the middle class, and if power remains unevenly distributed across groups, it is nevertheless true that we are probably closer now to a system of ''workable competition'' at the national level than at any time in the past.[39] On a variety of issues, previously insulated policy subsystems have been penetrated by new interests, giving rise to more pluralistic and conflictual issue networks. For example, nuclear power policy was dominated for a quarter century by an iron triangle consisting of the Atomic Energy Commission, the Joint Committee on Atomic Energy, and the nuclear industry. With the rise of the environmental and antinuclear movements of the 1970s, this policy subsystem was opened up in a way unlikely ever to be reversed. Much the same thing could be said of air pollution policy. The aroused mass public opinion that gave rise to technology-forcing legislation in 1970 went through a predictable issue attention cycle. Broad support remains for strong environmental laws, but the issue is no longer salient for most voters.[40] At the same time, however, the institutionalization of the environmental movement has permanently altered the nature of pollution politics, assuring that corporate interests will be counterbalanced in the legislative, administrative, and judicial arenas.

Finally, without equating business interests with the broader public interest, it is fair to say that business groups are an essential component—albeit only one element—of the policy equilibrium, at least on economic issues. Within a capitalistic economy, the vast majority of citizens earn their living within the private sector; under such circumstances, a healthy responsiveness to ordinary citizens in their occupational roles can easily be mistaken for an excessive deference to the sectoral interests of business as a class. A significant role for business in policy-making, and even a degree of imperfect competition among social interests, would seem to be the price we pay for a high standard of living and a good deal of personal freedom. However limited the appeal of these two values to some intellectuals, it is unlikely that most voters would willingly give them up.

NOTES

1. See E. E. Schattschneider, *Party Government* (New York: Rinehart, 1942); and the report of the Committee on Political Parties of the American Political Science Association, *Toward a More Responsible Party System* (New York: Holt, Rinehart, and Winston, 1950). For a review of the arguments of even earlier scholars, see Austin Ranney, *The Doctrine of Responsible Party Government* (Urbana: University of Illinois Press, 1954).
2. Grafted onto the American system, the model would presumably also produce competition between two parties, as it does now. Responsible parties theorists in this country, on the whole, would like to see the two American parties become more programmatic and disciplined. At the same time, they see considerable merit in a two-party system that produces an automatic majority for one party or the other, in contrast to the pattern of coalition government so common to many parliamentary systems. In any case, the development of a multiparty system in this country would necessitate some form of proportional representation—and thus elimination of the single-member district, first-past-the-post system we have now. See E. E. Schattschneider, *Party Government* (New York: Rinehart, 1942).
3. Austin Ranney and Willmoore Kendall, *Democracy and the American Party System* (New York: Harcourt, Brace, 1956), p. 29. The case for majority rule does not presume a correlation between the number of people supporting a position and its essential wisdom or "rightness." The majoritarian theorist recognizes that majorities can (and often do) err, but argues nevertheless that any system in which the few are in a position to impose their will on the many is fundamentally undemocratic.
4. Ranney and Kendall, pp. 22–39. See also Robert A. Dahl, *A Preface to Democratic Theory* (Chicago: University of Chicago Press, 1956), pp. 36–38.

5. Ranney and Kendall, pp. 32–37; Dahl, *Preface*, pp. 48–50 and 90–123.
6. Ranney and Kendall, p. 37.
7. Anthony Downs, *An Economic Theory of Democracy* (New York: Harper and Row, 1957), especially pp. 114–141. According to Downs, rational voters choose the party nearest to them on an ideological continuum. However, voting entails costs, leading some voters to abstain if neither party takes a position close enough to theirs. As a party moves in one direction in quest of additional votes, it necessarily risks the loss of voters in the area just vacated. Because there are normally many more voters in the middle of the distribution than in the extremes, the parties are compelled to converge to the center of the spectrum; a party staking out a clear ideological position on the left or right wins relatively few converts while potentially forfeiting large numbers in the center to the opposition. Paradoxically, in a perfectly rational world, both parties would move all the way to the center of the distribution, adopting identical positions on the issues.
8. An economist, Downs assumes that individuals are rational and self-interested. Parties are united only by their desire to capture and retain control of formal governmental offices. They are pure vote-maximizers and, being expedient, will campaign on issues only if that is what the voters seem to want. In so doing, they tailor their platforms to maximize voting support. They do not run for office to accomplish shared policy objectives; rather, they manipulate policy positions in order to attract votes: Winning is the overriding objective.
9. William J. Keefe, *Parties, Politics, and Public Policy in America*, 4th ed. (New York: Holt, Rinehart, and Winston, 1984), pp. 48–50. See also A. James Reichley, "The Rise of National Parties," in John E. Chubb and Paul E. Peterson (eds.), *The New Direction in National Politics* (Washington, D.C.: Brookings Institution, 1985), p. 196. On the virtual disappearance of moderate and liberal Republicans, see Nicol C. Rae, *The Decline and Fall of the Liberal Republicans* (New York: Oxford University Press, 1989).
10. For data on 1976 delegates to the Republican and Democratic national conventions, see "Leadership Survey," a special publication by *The Washington Post*, July 20, 1979.
11. See Keefe, pp. 50 and 140–146. See also Aage R. Clausen, *How Congressmen Decide* (New York: St. Martin's, 1973); and Aage R. Clausen and Carl E. Van Horn, "The Congressional Response to a Decade of Change," *Journal of Politics*, 39 (August 1977), pp. 624–666.
12. See John L. Sullivan and Robert E. O'Connor, "Electoral Choice and Popular Control of Public Policy: The Case of the 1966 House Elections," *American Political Science Review*, 66 (December 1972), pp. 1256–1268; Jeff Fishel, *Party and Opposition* (New York: McKay, 1973); and William R. Shaffer, *Party and Ideology in the United States Congress* (Lanham, Md.: University Press of America, 1980). On the frequent failure of congressional elections to generate clear-cut majorities, see Randall B. Ripley, *Majority Party Leadership in Congress* (Boston: Little, Brown, 1969), pp. 11–14.
13. On the importance of so-called critical elections to nonincremental (and enduring) policy changes, see Benjamin Ginsberg, "Elections and Public Policy," *American Political Science Review*, 70 (March 1976), pp. 41–49; Barbara Deckard Sinclair, "Party Realignment and the Transformation of the Political Agenda: The House of Representatives, 1925–1938, "*American Political Science Review*, 71 (September 1977), pp. 940–953; and David W. Brady, *Critical Elections and Congressional Policy Making* (Stanford, Calif.: Stanford University Press, 1988).
14. Even where the voters find neither candidate appealing, this variable can be critically important to the extent that one of the nominees evokes a highly negative response. In 1964, for example, many voters in both parties questioned Barry Goldwater's competence to be president; George McGovern evoked many of the same doubts in 1972. In 1980, a widespread antipathy toward

President Carter's leadership opened the way for Ronald Reagan's election. On the importance of candidate appeal as a factor in electoral outcomes, see Donald E. Stokes, "Some Dynamic Elements of Contests for the Presidency," *American Political Science Review*, 60 (March 1966), pp. 19–28.

15. Gerald M. Pomper, *Voter's Choice* (New York: Dodd, Mead, 1975), pp. 166–185. See also Gerald M. Pomper, "From Confusion to Clarity: Issues and American Voters, 1956–1968," *American Political Science Review*, 66 (June 1972), pp. 415–428; and David E. RePass, "Issue Salience and Party Choice," *American Political Science Review*, 65 (1971), pp. 389–400.

16. Pomper, *Voter's Choice*, pp. 31–35.

17. Pomper, *Voter's Choice*, pp. 36–38.

18. See data in Keefe, Table 25, p. 169.

19. On this point, see especially Martin P. Wattenberg, *The Decline of American Political Parties, 1952–1980* (Cambridge, Mass.: Harvard University Press, 1984).

20. Wattenberg, p. 125.

21. In 1986, for example, President Reagan's farm policies were extremely unpopular in several Midwestern states, turning local races into potential referenda on administration support for the farmer. Nevertheless, some Republican incumbents actually enhanced their popularity by distancing themselves from the president on the issue.

22. William Crotty points to across-the-board decline in the parties: in the electorate, in campaigns, and within Congress. See William Crotty, *American Parties in Decline*, 2d ed. (Boston: Little, Brown, 1984).

23. Austin Ranney, *Curing the Mischiefs of Faction* (Berkeley: University of California Press, 1975).

24. Keefe, p. 19. For a comprehensive examination of PACs, see Larry J. Sabato, *PAC Power* (New York: W. W. Norton, 1984). According to Sabato, the relationship between PACs and the parties is, at least in part, symbiotic; see *PAC Power*, pp. 141–159. On the advent of stronger national parties, particularly on the Republican side, see Reichley, "The Rise of National Parties."

25. Wattenberg, pp. 125–126.

26. For data on the extent of party voting according to the strict definition of a party vote, see Julius Turner and Edward V. Schneier, Jr., *Party and Constituency* (Baltimore: Johns Hopkins University Press, 1970). The more relaxed standard of party voting was developed by *Congressional Quarterly*, which publishes annual figures on the extent of party voting in both the House and Senate. Party voting was up sharply in 1985, to 50 percent of all Senate votes and 61 percent of all House votes. See "Partisanship in Congress Up Sharply in 1985," *Congressional Quarterly Weekly Report*, January 11, 1986, pp. 86–88.

27. James L. Sundquist, "Needed: A Political Theory for the New Era of Coalition Government in the United States," *Political Science Quarterly*, 103 (Winter 1988–89), pp. 613–614.

28. Sundquist, pp. 631–632.

29. As noted earlier, an effective system of responsible parties also requires party control over patronage. At the national level, the decline of the "spoils" system dates back to the 1880s, with the creation of the civil service system. Since that time, the merit system has been gradually extended throughout the federal bureaucracy, leaving only a small number of positions within each department for political appointments. The autonomy of bureaucratic careerists has been further enhanced in recent years with the rise of public employee unions and, more importantly, the increasing professionalism of administrators. See Frederick C. Mosher, *Democracy and the Public Service* (New York: Oxford University Press, 1968). See also Theodore J. Lowi, "Machine Politics—Old and New," *The Public Interest*, 9 (Fall 1967), pp. 83–92.

The Civil Service Reform Act of 1978 increased somewhat the number of political appointments available to the president. On President Reagan's use of the appointment power to render the bureaucracy accountable to his leadership, see Bert A. Rockman, "The Style and Organization of the Reagan Presidency," and Peter M. Benda and Charles H. Levine, "Reagan and the Bureaucracy: The Bequest, the Promise, and the Legacy," both in Charles O. Jones (ed.), *The Reagan Legacy* (Chatham, N.J.: Chatham House, 1988), pp. 3–29 and 102–142. See also Richard P. Nathan, *The Administrative Presidency* (New York: Wiley, 1983).

At the state and local level, however, one of the major effects of federal categorical grant programs has often been the replacement of patronage systems with civil service systems and the requirement of advanced degrees for many positions. See Martha Derthick, *The Influence of Federal Grants* (Cambridge, Mass.: Harvard University Press, 1970).

30. David Truman, *The Governmental Process* (New York: Knopf, 1951), p. 114.

31. Keefe, p. 140.

32. Mancur Olson, Jr., *The Logic of Collective Action* (New York: Schocken Books, 1970). According to Olson, there are only two ways for most groups pursuing collective goods to overcome the free rider problem: coercion or the provision of selective benefits. Selective benefits are tangible or intangible rewards that are available to group members only if they formally join the group. A good example would be group insurance policies for members. Another would be participation in local chapter activities. See also Lewis A. Froman and Randall B. Ripley, "Conditions for Party Leadership: The Case of the House Democrats," *American Political Science Review*, 59 (1965), pp. 52–63.

33. V. O. Key, Jr., *Southern Politics* (New York: Vintage Books, 1949), Chapter 14, "Nature and Consequences of One-Party Factionalism," pp. 298–311.

34. Key, pp. 304–310.

35. Key, pp. 309–310.

36. In this regard, President Carter's poor showing was reinforced by the loss of several Democratic Senate seats, giving control of the body to the Republicans for the first time in more than three decades. Paul R. Abramson, John H. Aldrich, and David W. Rohde, *Change and Continuity in the 1980 Elections*, rev. ed. (Washington, D.C.: Congressional Quarterly Press, 1983).

37. Sundquist, pp. 629–630.

38. Charles E. Lindblom, *The Policy-Making Process*, 2d ed. (Englewood Cliffs, N.J.: Prentice-Hall, 1980), pp. 105–113. For an excellent illustration of this problem, see Leon D. Epstein, "Electoral Decision and Policy Mandate: An Empirical Example," *Public Opinion Quarterly*, 28 (Winter 1964), pp. 564–572.

39. Recognizing that perfect competition is almost never found in the real world, economists have coined the term *workable competition* to describe industries featuring enough competitors to preclude collusion or other forms of oligopolistic behavior. See H. Craig Peterson, *Business and Government*, 2d ed. (New York: Harper and Row, 1985), pp. 12–27.

40. See Robert Cameron Mitchell, "Public Opinion and Environmental Politics in the 1970s and 1980s," in Norman J. Vig and Michael E. Kraft (eds.), *Environmental Policy in the 1980s* (Washington, D.C.: Congressional Quarterly Press, 1984), pp. 51–74.

CHAPTER 7

Federalism, Corporate Power, and Surface Mining Regulation

The Surface Mining Control and Reclamation Act of 1977, which gave the federal government a major role in the regulation of the strip mining of coal, provides an excellent case study of many of the factors leading to incrementalism under normal circumstances. While a number of compromises were necessary to pass any bill at all, making for an incremental legislative outcome, officials within the new Office of Surface Mining strengthened the law significantly through the process of writing regulations. The new regulations encountered stiff resistance at the state and local level, however, where the strategic position of the surface mining industry was maximized. With the election of Ronald Reagan in 1980, the agency was reorganized and reduced in size, and effective authority was shifted to the states.

This chapter will review the adoption and implementation of the surface mining legislation. Chapter 8 will draw on the models reviewed in the preceding chapters to derive a number of generalizations that will be applied to the agenda-setting, policy adoption, and policy implemention stages in the surface mining case.

TRADE-OFFS AMONG CONFLICTING OBJECTIVES

Rational decision making on the surface mining issue was precluded by a conflict over problem definition and objectives, which made it inevitable that policy-making would take the form of a struggle among contending interests. The issue was particularly difficult to resolve (and remains so) inasmuch as both sides active on the issue represented values important to the society as a whole.[1]

Coal will almost surely play a steadily increasing role in meeting our nation's energy needs over the coming decades. Coal provides a significant percentage of our current energy supply, and it is the single most important source of fuel for the generation of electricity.[2] The invasion of Kuwait by Iraq in the summer of 1990 serves as a powerful reminder of the dangers of relying excessively on oil that is imported from politically unstable regions of the world.[3] While there are significant safety and environmental problems associated with coal (acid rain, global warming, and so on), coal offers one major advantage as a potential alternative to foreign oil: the United States possesses almost 25 percent of the world's known coal deposits.[4] This fact alone almost guarantees a major role for coal over the next twenty-five years.

In extracting coal, strip mining is vastly more efficient than the more traditional deep mining techniques. The capital costs are much lower for strip mining, and the average strip miner can produce about three times as much coal in one day as the traditional coal miner. Moreover, deep mining techniques can recover only about 60 percent of the coal within a given seam, while strip mining can extract almost 90 percent.[5] In short, the surface mining of coal, where possible, vastly increases the productivity of coal producers.[6] Not surprisingly, strip mined coal constitutes a steadily increasing percentage of all coal mined in the United States; in 1980, strip mining accounted for 59 percent of this total.[7]

The real question is not whether coal will be a major energy source, but rather how effectively its environmental effects will be controlled. Reliance on coal brings with it a number of undesirable externalities (see Chapter 2 for a definition of this term). Burning coal to generate heat or electricity contributes to acid rain and global warming.[8] Traditional deep mining methods pose the risk of black lung disease as well as the ever-present danger of explosions or cave-ins. While strip mining avoids these problems, it can produce serious damage to both the land and surrounding water supplies.

There are two primary methods of strip mining, each of which causes significant damage to the surrounding environment.[9] The first, employed primarily in relatively flat terrain, is known as area mining. The earth overlaying the coal seam (the overburden) is scooped away by gigantic earth-moving machines and deposited off to one side. As successive trenches are dug, and the coal extracted, the overburden is deposited in the preceding trenches. This technique permits restoration of the land to a state more or less approximating its original condition *if* the topsoil is carefully segregated from the subsoil and if care is thus taken in replacing these deposits into trenches. All too often this is not done, with the end result that the soil becomes irretrievably damaged for the sustenance of normal vegetation, often yielding an appearance not unlike a moonscape.

By contrast, contour mining techniques are employed where coal is situated in mountainous terrain, as in Appalachia. Under this technique, bulldozers make large cuts in the side of the mountain (hence the term *strip mining*) to remove as much of the overburden as possible. Explosives are then planted in the resulting cliff above the cut and detonated to remove additional overburden. This blasted overburden tumbles down the hill, filling in valleys and polluting streams. As successive cuts are made in the mountainside, sediment continues to accumulate in the valleys below until once-spectacular scenic vistas are transformed into gently rolling areas of scarred hillsides and rubble-filled valleys, suitable (perhaps) for commercial development but not for reforestation.

In addition, auger mining (boring horizontally into exposed coal seams) is often employed to extract as much coal as possible from the seam after contour mining techniques cease to be efficient. Auger mining inevitably generates an acid water discharge that also runs down the mountainside, resulting in highly toxic pools and/or the pollution of nearby streams. Additional water pollution results from the dumping of sediment into streams and the oxidation that results from exposure of sulfur-bearing rock to water and sunlight. The resulting sulfates and sulfides increase the acidity of streams, with devastating consequences for both plants and fish.[10]

In extreme cases, where conventional surface and deep mining techniques are insufficient to extract an adequate percentage of the coal contained within a seam, the mountain may be gradually blasted away, from the top down, through a process known as "mountaintop removal." Harry M. Caudill has summarized the end result of this devastating process:

> The rubble that gathers on the valley floor creeps upward as the mountain is sliced away, until the entire range is obliterated. In its place is a wasteland of displaced soil, slabs of rock and slate, and shattered residues of coal and sulfur. All that is left of what was once a tree-covered, living ridge is a vast mesa where nothing moves except the clouds of dust on dry, windy days, or the sluicing autumn rains that carve new creekbeds across its dead surface. It has become an Appalachian Carthage, the beginning of a New World Sahara.[11]

THE SURFACE MINING ISSUE REACHES THE FEDERAL AGENDA

Prior to 1977, regulation of surface mining took place (where it occurred at all) at the state level. In general, legislation to limit surface mining was most likely to be enacted in states (like Ohio and Pennsylvania) where coal interests were counterbalanced by other economic groups. In states lacking a diversified economy (like Kentucky), the resulting dependence on coal tended to preclude effective regulation.[12]

Between 1940 and 1970, a number of proposals to regulate (or at least investigate) the conduct of surface mining were introduced in Congress. Everett Dirksen introduced the first bill to regulate surface mining in 1940. Proposals to survey the damages from surface mining were introduced by an Arkansas representative in 1949 and 1951, and by the Pennsylvania delegation between 1959 and 1965. In the late 1960s, bills initiating federal regulation were introduced by Sen. Gaylord Nelson (D-Wisconsin) and by Sen. Henry Jackson (D-Washington). The surface mining issue lacked salience during this period, however, and none of these bills was reported out of committee.

The Coal Coalition

The strip mining issue activated a coalition of several major economic sectors that have become increasingly intertwined. Some of the more direct economic connections are entirely predictable. For example, mining equipment manufacturers have an obvious common interest with the coal industry. Similarly, railroads are the primary transporters of coal, and some railroads own and mine their own coal. Primary metals producers (e.g., iron and steel) employ vast amounts of coal in their production process and often own their own "captive" coal mines. Electric utilities rely heavily on coal to generate power.

At the same time, however, some major corporate interests have developed an indirect stake in the fortunes of the coal industry in recent years. Oil companies confronted with the looming exhaustion of domestic supplies have begun to invest in coal; by 1976, almost sixty such companies had acquired some coal reserves, and nineteen of the major vertically integrated oil companies had done so. Even more subtly, a number of major banks either own stock, hold trust accounts, or serve on the board of directors of coal corporations. For example, in 1972 Morgan Guaranty Trust had representatives on the board of directors of ten coal corporations and owned stock in six of them. The Chase Manhattan Bank was a member of both the American Mining Congress and the National Coal Association. At the regional level, banking and coal interests combined to dominate the politics of major cities.[13]

This "coal coalition" was represented at the national level by two interindustry groups, the National Coal Policy Conference and the American Mining Congress, and by national-level trade associations, of which four were particularly prominent: the National Coal Association, the Edison Electric Institute, the American Petroleum Institute, and the American Iron and Steel Institute. Additional support was provided by business peak associations, including both the National Association of Manufacturers (NAM) and the U.S. Chamber of Commerce. In combination, these various industry groups possessed a formidable array of tangible and intangible lobbying resources: money, expertise, extraordinary legitimacy, and strategic position.

The Failure of Nondecision-making

In Chapter 5, I argued that business power is typically insufficient to prevent threatening issues from reaching the agenda and that corporate influence is ordinarily greatest at the implementation stage. The strip mining issue is consistent with both these propositions, as this chapter will show.

For all its apparent lobbying resources, the coal coalition was unable to prevent the strip mining issue from reaching the congressional agenda. In congressional hearings on surface mining held in 1968, the American Mining Congress opposed any federal regulation of the industry. Conceding that some environmental damage had occurred, industry representatives portrayed the problem as the result of a few irresponsible operators and argued that the states were already doing an effective job of regulation. The states were in fact going through a period of regulatory reform, with thirty-eight states either enacting or amending their strip mining laws between 1965 and 1977.[14]

By 1971, when Congress again took up the issue of surface mining, regulation at the state level had been effectively discredited. From 1971 to 1973, twenty bills were introduced to regulate strip mining. Where many officials from coal states had joined with the coal industry in opposing federal intervention in the 1968 hearings, in the 92nd and 93rd Congresses state representatives acknowledge the limitations of state autonomy.[15] Citizens' groups from states with reasonably strong laws advocated some form of federal regulation to prevent local operators from citing competitive pressures from adjacent states with weaker statutes to obtain regulatory relief.[16] For example, in testimony before the

Subcommittee on Minerals, Materials, and Fuels of the Senate Committee on Interior and Insular Affairs, the former deputy director of West Virginia's Department of Natural Resources conceded that

> the surface mining industry in Appalachia is not amenable to social control. . . . In a word, State regulation is no match for the surface mine industry, at least in West Virginia.[17]

Proponents of federal regulation advocated a number of very different approaches to regulation, ranging from outright abolition to prohibition only where adequate reclamation was impossible, as with contour mining in mountainous regions. Confronted with growing support for at least partial abolition of strip mining, the coal coalition modified its original opposition to any form of federal involvement. Much as Schattschneider would have predicted, the industry still sought to place effective responsibility at the state level, where its power was greatest. However, it paid lip service to the need for federal involvement by calling for minimum federal guidelines. The states would still set the actual standards (and enforce them) subject to these national guidelines, and the federal government would intervene only where a state failed to develop an acceptable regulatory program.

While the coal coalition was unable to keep the strip mining issue off the congressional agenda, they did succeed in blocking attempts to abolish strip mining entirely. Legislation outlawing strip mining was sponsored by Rep. Kenneth Hechler (D-West Virginia). While this bill attracted eighty-eight cosponsors in the House, and had the support of a number of environmental and religious groups (especially those from Appalachia), it never had any realistic chance of passage. Most environmental groups recognized that outright abolition was impossible and that the real struggle would center around the form federal regulation would take.

THE STRUGGLE FOR A STRIP MINING LAW, 1971–1977

A major turning point in the battle for federal regulation occurred with the mobilization of the environmental movement in the late 1960s. The survival and institutionalization of the environmental movement in the decade of the 1970s virtually assured that strip mining legislation would remain on the legislative agenda during this period.

The most significant proponents of strip mining regulation at the federal level were thus national environmental and conservationist groups, including the Sierra Club, the Audubon Society, the National Wildlife Federation, the Izaak Walton League, and the Friends of the Earth. A number of the more active of these groups pooled their resources to form an umbrella organization in 1972, the Coalition Against Strip Mining (or CASM). These groups were joined by the American Forestry Association and a variety of sportsmen's associations, religious groups, and Appalachian community development groups.[18] What these groups lacked in money, expertise, and strategic position, they tended to make up for in sheer legitimacy. Participants in the coalition were overwhelmingly middle class and were drawn from all walks of life. The mobilization of various religious groups on the side of federal regulation from 1973 onward added further legitimacy to the movement.[19]

However, from 1969 to 1977 the nation was going through a period of divided government, with Democratic Congresses confronted by successive Republican presidents (Nixon and Ford). Moreover, the 1973 oil embargo marked the beginning of the "energy crisis" and strengthened coal's political position considerably. Nevertheless, support for federal regulation grew stronger in Congress, where Democrats controlled both houses and where Western legislators increasingly feared that their states would become another Appalachia. Westerners dominated the two relevant legislative committees; in 1972, 77 percent of the House Interior Committee members and all of the corresponding Senate committee members were from Western states.[20] Strip mining bills were enacted in both 1974 and 1975 only to be vetoed by President Ford, who looked to coal to reduce America's dependency on foreign oil.

Proponents of federal involvement in the regulation of surface mining would occupy strategic positions within the legislative process in 1977, however. The election of Jimmy Carter to the presidency in 1976 not only promised an end to divided government; it also marked the transfer of power to a new president on record as being committed to the broad goals of the environmental movement. Prospects for passage would also be enhanced by the ascension of a strong environmentalist, Morris Udall (D-Arizona), to the chair of the House Interior Committee.

Moreover, the cohesiveness of the coal coalition had begun to break down as early as 1973. While the demand for coal increased significantly in the wake of the 1973 oil embargo, the 1970 Clean Air Act's ambient air quality standards led many utilities to choose low-sulfur Western coal over Midwestern and Eastern coal that had a higher sulfur content. The high-sulfur coal producers sought to protect their interests through the Seiberling amendment, sponsored by Rep. John Seiberling (D-Ohio), which would have levied a $2.50 tax on every ton of coal mined within the United States. While the revenues from the tax were to go to a fund for the reclamation of abandoned strip mines, the real purpose of the amendment was to "enable the deep coal mining industry to compete effectively with the surface coal mining industry."

> Since the tonnage-per-acre productivity of western (thick seam) strip mining was so high, this provision would produce a huge tax burden on such operations, as their reclamation costs per acre/ton were quite low. But eastern coal operators, both deep and strip, would be able to credit nearly all the tax against the costs of health and safety regulations or reclamation. . . . As might be expected, the NCA-AMC-petroleum-gas-utility coalition adamantly opposed this idea, and even its proponents, like Morris Udall, thought it a bit unjust, since western energy would have to pay the reclamation bill for the East.[21]

Compromises on Key Issues

The requirements for rational policy-making were not satisfied for the surface mining issue during this period. The conflict between environmentalists and coal interests over trade-offs among conflicting objectives was intense, as noted earlier, and the knowledge base was inadequate on several important points. Difficulties in estimating the costs of reclamation led to a conflict over basic facts. Where the Office of Surface Mining placed the costs of reclamation in Appalachia at approximately \$2.54 per ton, the National Coal Association asserted that these governmental estimates understated the true costs by anywhere from \$7 to \$20 per ton. It is similarly difficult to measure the value of externalities to various parties stemming from surface mining.[22] A final dispute centered around the percentage of proven coal reserves that could be profitably extracted through traditional deep mining techniques as opposed to surface mining. In this case, environmental groups won a rare victory over the coal industry on a technical issue, convincing many legislators that the fraction of all coal for which strip mining would be essential is actually quite small. Serious errors in their analysis were discovered only after the law was passed.[23] Given the limitations on rational decision making plaguing this issue, it is hardly surprising that the final legislative product represented at best an incremental outcome in Lindblom's terms.

The Surface Mining Control and Reclamation Act of 1977 brought surface mining under federal regulation for the first time and established a fund for the reclamation of areas damaged by previous surface mining. The regulatory responsibilities were assigned to the Office of Surface Mining (OSM), created by the statute, to be located within the Department of the Interior. OSM was required to develop and enforce interim standards for surface mining while the states developed their own programs.

The states were required to submit programs in conformity with the standards specified in the act by early February of 1979; OSM was required to review these plans and approve or disapprove them by early August of 1979. In cases of rejection, states would have sixty days to submit a new plan. Once a given state's regulatory program had been approved by OSM, the state would be given "primacy": for example, primary responsibility for enforcement would shift to the state, subject to monitoring and oversight by OSM. Whenever a state's program was found to be out of compliance with the terms of the act, OSM would step in and enforce the statute directly until the state program was modified to meet federal requirements.[24]

Reclamation of mines predating the law would be financed through an Abandoned Mine Land Fund, financed by a formula taking into account the amount of coal mined, the type of coal mined, and the mining techniques employed. (This formula was a much amended version of the Seiberling amendment.) States receiving primacy would receive money from this fund to reclaim old mines. In addition, reclamation of new surface mines would be financed by a combination of performance bonds posted by operators as a condition of receiving a permit and fines imposed on violators of the statute's various regulations. The Abandoned Mine Land Fund was placed within the Treasury Department; responsibility for assessing and collecting performance bonds, as well as the finding of violators, rested with OSM.[25]

The formidable power of the coal coalition, combined with the need to build concurrent majorities, forced a number of compromises during the long struggle to enact a law. Both the placement of the new agency within the Interior Department and the provision for eventual state regulatory "primacy" represented important victories for the coal coalition. An ideal bill from the environmentalist's point of view would have given the Environmental Protection Agency the authority to promulgate and enforce strict uniform national standards for surface mining. Environmentalists sought to place the responsibility for standard setting and enforcement at the federal level for obvious reasons: corporate power is maximized at the state level while environmental groups are strongest at the national level. Designating EPA as the primary enforcement agency would give effective power to an agency with a clear environmental mission whose primary organized support came from environmental groups. Accordingly, most environmental groups had given strong support to a bill introduced by Senators Kennedy (D-Massachusetts), McGovern (D-South Dakota), and Nelson (D-Wisconsin), which met these requirements.[26]

By contrast, coal interests preferred legislation that would place the primary standard-setting and enforcement responsibility at the state level, with state standards to be set subject to federal guidelines and subject to approval and review by the Department of the Interior. Where the EPA has a clear environmental mission, the Interior Department has a mandate to manage federal lands for "multiple uses," balancing environmental with commercial and recreational interests. While environmental groups take an ongoing interest in policy-making within the Interior Department, the Bureau of Mines has often been characterized as captured by the various mining industries it ostensibly regulates, including coal. Legislation embodying this approach was supported by the ranking members of the House and Senate Interior Committees and the Nixon and Ford administrations.

These issues had all been resolved to the detriment of environmental interests even before President Carter took office in 1977. Outright abolition was out of the question, as was federal preemption of standard setting and enforcement. Placement of the new agency within the Interior Department rather than EPA was a predictable outcome in view of the fact that the two Interior committees (which had jurisdiction over all surface mining legislation) had long been partners with that department in a stable policy subsystem governing public lands.

The act went on to impose 114 detailed performance standards for mining and reclamation and established a mandatory system of inspection and enforcement, including the levying of civil penalties against violators.[27] However, many of these regulatory standards were significantly weakened in response to coal industry lobbying. Coal interests were particularly successful in shaping the content of legislation reported from the two Interior committees to the House and Senate floor. At the markup stage (which takes place in closed session), their technical expertise gave them a significant advantage over environmental lobbyists.[28] In particular, proposals to designate a variety of areas unsuitable for strip mining were significantly compromised. Strip mining would be permitted in national forests and alluvial valleys.[29] It would also be allowed on steep slopes (as found in Appalachia); producers would not be required to restore the land to the original contour where "sound engineering technology" indicated that such an action was too difficult. Even mountaintop removal would remain legal.[30]

IMPLEMENTATION OF THE ACT UNDER PRESIDENT CARTER

We saw in Chapter 3 that most domestic policies are implemented intergovernmentally. The federal agency with primary responsibility for implementation is forced to interact with at least fifty state agencies (and sometimes local agencies or even private actors as well) that retain a good deal of discretion at the field level. Compliance with federal directives is inherently problematic, as much depends upon the political environment at the state level: the state's economic climate and budgetary resources, political support for the statute's objectives within the state legislature or the governor's mansion, attitudes of local interest groups (and mass public opinion), and the willingness of state-level bureaucrats to comply with federal requirements.

The degree to which federal implementors try to influence the behavior of state agencies will be a function of the attitudes prevailing within the federal enforcement agency and the degree to which federal actors monitor the behavior of state actors and communicate federal displeasure. Prevailing attitudes within the federal agency will be shaped, in turn, by various factors in the national policy environment: the economic climate, budgetary resources, the degree of sustained political support for the statute elsewhere within the political system, and so on.[31]

There is no guarantee that federal bureaucrats will act as "strict constructionists" in enforcing the statute. For example, Title I of the Elementary and Secondary Education Act provided categorical grants to local school districts for programs designed to aid disadvantaged students. Administrators within the Office of Education had long preferred federal grants with virtually no strings attached, however, and had played no real role in developing the "disadvantaged student" rationale for Title I. Predictably, disadvantaged students lacked an organized lobby. As a result, the disadvantaged student provisions were largely ignored for the first decade of the act's history; for all practical purposes, ESEA was a block grant.[32]

Erosion of federal mandates can occur in the opposite direction as well. The Comprehensive Employment and Training Act (CETA) and the Community Development Block Grants (CDBG) were two of the first block grant programs passed by Congress in the early 1970s. Under presidents Nixon and Ford, two Republicans with a strong commitment to federalism, few strings were placed on these grants. This pattern changed when President Carter took office, however. Experiences as governor of Georgia had convinced him that block grants tended to redistribute federal aid away from the poor and toward politically active, middle-class groups. Accordingly, he took steps to place new federal strings on these programs in an effort to target aid to the poor. In effect, Carter turned these programs back into categorical grants.[33]

In the case of the Surface Mining Control and Reclamation Act, the relationship between OSM and the states would be crucial:

> By including procedures for variances from the act's requirements, Congress left to the OSM the task of resolving issues related to the breadth and application of the performance standards. More importantly, the relationship between the new agency and the state regulatory authorities was left ambiguous. The OSM's task is to ensure that the states develop adequate regulatory programs, but responsibility for long-range development and implementation was left to the states. Thus the act contains the seeds for serious tension and conflict.[34]

In this vein, research on federal policy implementation has identified two very different approaches to economic regulation. The "enforced compliance" strategy takes a legalistic and adversarial approach, writing highly detailed rules that are rigidly enforced. Within this strategy, federal directives are viewed as commands to be obeyed, and rules are interpreted literally. By contrast, the ''negotiated compliance'' strategy seeks compliance with the spirit of the law through bargaining with the regulated industry. Rules are interpreted flexibly as allowance is made for situational factors; the industry itself is seen as possessing significant expertise and experience that may override the letter of the law in specific instances.[35]

Research on organizational behavior suggests that securing obedience to formal commands is problematic under the best of circumstances; within most organizations, subordinates must somehow be induced to behave in desired ways.[36] In any case, as we saw in Chapter 3, the federal government is in no position to issue formal commands to state and local governments under normal circumstances. On most issues, federal bureaucrats have little choice but to adopt a negotiated compliance approach in dealing with state agencies.

The danger of the negotiated compliance approach, however, is its vulnerability to regulatory ''capture.'' As we saw in Chapter 4, regulatory agencies are frequently co-opted by the industries they nominally regulate; this phenomenon is often foreordained by the configuration of organized interests within the agency's environment. All agencies need sustained political support in Congress to protect their budgetary resources and statutory mandate. For many regulatory agencies, the regulated industry is the only organized group taking a sustained interest in its policies. Under such circumstances, a negotiated compliance strategy may facilitate capture, while the enforced compliance strategy at least recognizes the need to maintain some distance between the regulators and the regulated.

Writing the Federal Regulations

Interior Secretary Cecil Andrus set up an interagency task force to prepare for implementation of the statute in 1977, even before the final legislation had passed Congress; the task force thus played a role in working out technical details in the final stages of congressional consideration. The surface mining task force was drawn from approximately twenty executive agencies. This large group was further subdivided into ''task groups'' with responsibility for the development of particular programs.[37]

Conditions in the national political environment favored a vigorous approach to regulation. President Carter strongly supported the program, as did Morris Udall, chair of the House Interior Committee. Economic conditions were favorable as well; the national economy was performing strongly during this period, and the coal industry was doing extremely well in the wake of the energy crisis.[38] There was thus little reason to be concerned with the effects of regulation on the health of the industry. Finally, as is often the case for brand new agencies, many members of the task force were strongly committed to the agency's environmental mission.[39]

The coal industry clearly lacked legitimacy in the eyes of the task force. While the task force actively solicited the views of environmental interests, representatives of the coal industry were given a formal and polite reception at best. As one industry representative put it:

> You have to believe that there was an intent not to have contact. I don't know how you could believe anything else. . . . I could generally get through to them, yeah. I'd be de-

layed a lot of times, but we had contact with them. But it was always initiated from our side. . . . We go down and we talk with them, and we see our answer in the Federal Register.[40]

The task force members similarly tended to distrust the state regulatory agencies in light of the prior history of surface mining regulation. State opposition to the new program was anticipated and thus discounted by OSM officials.[41]

There was a ninety-day deadline for the development of interim regulations; permanent program regulations had to be in place within one year. Moreover, conflict in Congress over the B-1 bomber issue held up appropriations for the agency for seven months, delaying the hiring of new personnel. In the meantime, the task force acted as an unofficial agency. Ironically, these constraints operated to give the group an unusual degree of latitude, as the need to accomplish a great deal in a short period of time forced potential opponents into acquiescence on many issues.[42]

The task force adopted an enforced compliance approach to dealing with the states and the coal industry. Wherever possible, the task force chose to impose design standards rather than more flexible performance standards in writing regulations. Where design standards require that firms adopt specific technologies (e.g., sedimentation ponds meeting certain specifications) in meeting statutory requirements, performance standards permit firms to satisfy the requirements in whatever manner they find cost-effective. The task force clearly believed that allowing such flexibility would give operators leeway to escape full compliance with the act.

In response to mounting complaints from the coal industry and various states, OSM eventually agreed to include a new provision within the regulations creating what was termed the "state window." Under this provision, states submitting regulations to OSM for approval could provide for alternative means to meet various statutory requirements if they clearly specified the alternative means and presented data to justify the departure from mandated design standards. Environmental groups were vehemently opposed to the state window provision, and OSM made significant changes in the wording of the provision in the wake of meetings with various environmental lobbies. While federal regulators continued to point to the state window provision as evidence of their willingness to be flexible, state and coal industry representatives felt the provision was now so narrowly worded as to be meaningless.[43]

By March of 1979, OSM had published both the interim and permanent program regulations. (The agency failed to meet the statutory deadline for producing these regulations due to the funding delays noted earlier, which forced the task force to act in an unofficial capacity for almost seven months.) The end result was a considerable strengthening of many of the provisions of the statute.[44] Environmental interests regained in the process of writing regulations much of what they had lost in the committee markup stage of the legislative process. An incremental legislative outcome had been transformed into something considerably stronger by the Surface Mining task force.

This would mark the point of greatest leverage for environmental interests, however. Environmental groups lacked the resources to monitor enforcement at the state level; by contrast, coal interests would be most effective there. The industry's technical expertise would be much in demand, and their strategic position would be maximized at the state level. Finally, as we have seen, an enforced compliance strategy is ill-suited to a statute requiring intergovernmental implementation. The states would eventually rebel against federal efforts to dictate their behavior in minute detail given what they saw as unique situational factors that necessitated a high degree of flexibility in enforcement and their own storehouse of experience in surface mining regulation.

Implementing the Regulations

In keeping with its enforced compliance strategy, OSM adopted a rigid and legalistic approach to enforcement:

> As members of the task group saw it, changing the behavior of mine operators was no different from influencing the behavior of ordinary criminal offenders. Principles of deterrence applied to both. They knew of the industry's history of lawlessness, which they largely attributed to the states' failure to establish *credible* regulatory programs. [Emphasis in original.][45]

Thus, the act mandated that OSM biannually conduct unannounced inspections at every legal surface mining operation in the country during the interim period preceding state primacy. In addition, private citizens could trigger an inspection by OSM if they had good reason to suspect a mining operation was out of compliance with the regulations. All observed violations were to receive formal notices of violation, and where violations were not remedied within the specified time limit, the mines were to be closed by formal cessation orders.[46]

While it proved to be impossible for OSM to inspect every mine in the United States, given limitations on money and staff, the number of inspections and citations jumped significantly in the early Carter years as compared with the previous experience under state regulation. During its first six months of operations, OSM inspected only 10 percent of all mines. This record improved to 25 percent during the next six-month period, and peaked at 50 percent between June of 1979 and March of 1980. Coal industry objections were offset by environmental group complaints that the agency was not meeting its statutory requirements to inspect all surface mines twice a year.[47]

Enforcement was not uniform across the nation, however. In particular, a sharp difference in enforcement patterns emerged between Western and Eastern mines. Appalachian surface mining was dominated by small operators who resented federal intrusion and often put up a good deal of resistance to federal mine inspectors, in some cases even engaging in physical violence against them. By contrast, Western operators tended to be large corporations who accepted the basic legitimacy of at least some federal regulation (or feared the adverse consequences of bad publicity) and could afford to retain highly trained technical experts who specialized in meeting the reclamation requirements of the statute. To some degree, cooperation on the part of the industry bred a conciliatory strategy by the agency; in addition, federal inspectors in the West were acutely aware that corporate reclamation officials often possessed as much technical expertise as they did or more. Where OSM often felt compelled to make an example of particularly belligerent small operators in the Eastern region, federal inspectors often had much in common with the corporate technical experts they dealt with in the West. Accordingly, regulation took the form of negotiated compliance within the Western region, in distinct contrast to the rest of the country.[48]

Growing Industry Resistance

Coal industry representatives felt, with some justification, that they had been denied equal access during the process of writing interim and permanent regulations. Accumulated resentments over a string of defeats at this stage, combined with dismay over the steadily rising volume of mine inspections and citations for violations (including at least some cessation orders), led the industry to mount a counterattack against OSM. This counterattack took several forms, including an advertising campaign in major newspapers (particularly the *New York Times* and the *Wall Street Journal*), congressional testimony, attempts to draw other executive agencies into the conflict, and litigation.

Congressional oversight hearings were conducted by the Senate Committee on Energy and Natural Resources in both 1979 and 1981, and by the Subcommittee on Energy and Environment of the House Committee on Interior and Insular Affairs in 1979, 1981, and 1982. Industry witnesses emphasized the nation's need for coal in the wake of the energy crisis and claimed that the regulations were excessively detailed and burdensome, thus significantly increasing the costs of coal and retarding its extraction. Small operators charged that the act made it impossible to operate at all, forcing them out of business. As evidence of OSM's rigidity, industry representatives noted that the states were not granted extensions to statutory deadlines for compliance even though OSM had missed its own statutory deadlines for producing interim and permanent regulations by several months. Industry representatives were united in calling for an extension to the deadlines for industry compliance and for passage of a bill that would have overturned many of the regulations written by OSM. (This legislation, the so-called Rockefeller amendment, will be discussed in more detail below.)[49]

In pursuing this counterattack against OSM, the industry also sought to socialize the conflict to include potentially sympathetic agencies within the executive branch. During the long process of writing the permanent regulations, industry representatives approached the Department of Energy, seeking an ally in their effort to have some of the proposed regulations nullified. The DOE in turn approached the Council of Economic Advisers (a staff agency charged with advising the president on macroeconomic policy). CEA officials were able to force a meeting with OSM, at which they urged relaxation of some rules that might have an inflationary impact on the economy. OSM was able to resist these pressures only because significant errors were discovered in the CEA's quantitative analysis of regulatory impacts; however, this controversy delayed the publication of the permanent regulations by six months.[50]

The industry brought a number of lawsuits against OSM between 1978 and 1980, raising a number of substantive points and arguing that the secretary of the interior had failed to consider adequately the effects of the act on the economy, inflation, and the nation's coal supply. These various court challenges had mixed results for the industry. The statute was consistently upheld as constitutional by the courts, and most of the substantive motions were denied. The industry did win on some specific regulations where OSM was seen as going beyond the statute (for example, expanding the statute's requirement for a 300-foot buffer zone between blasting operations and nearby dwellings to a 1,000-foot buffer zone).[51]

Growing State Opposition

The states acted as allies of the coal industry in many of these attacks on OSM, raising many of the same objections at congressional oversight hearings and joining the industry in at least some litigation. While opposition to federal intrusion was greatest among those states most heavily dependent upon coal, many states objected to what they saw as high-handed treatment by OSM. Throughout the period in which interim and permanent regulations were being written, OSM encouraged the states to take advantage of the "state window" provision, discussed above, to propose alternative means to comply with the statute. However, the agency remained deeply distrustful of both the coal industry and the states and also remained subject to counterpressures by environmental groups. As a result, state attempts to propose alternative approaches were typically rejected or significantly modified by OSM. OSM showed little flexibility in approving state programs until 1980 after a good deal of feedback from the OSM regional offices.[52]

In this regard, the experience of West Virginia is fairly typical. State officials welcomed the passage of the act initially. West Virginia's surface mining statute was considered to be quite strong, and the new federal law was expected to force other coal-producing states into similar programs, thus eliminating the cost advantage for coal producers in states with weaker regulations. Accordingly, administrators within the state's Department of Natural Resources looked forward to working with OSM to develop the new intergovernmental regulatory structure. At an early meeting between DNR and OSM officials in April 1978, OSM also paid lip service to the need for cooperation and consultation, acknowledging that West Virginia's program was a strong one and admitting that federal regulators did not have the resources or expertise to develop a program for West Virginia.[53]

Amicable relations between the two agencies did not last long, however. The emerging federal regulations were found to be unduly complex and often inappropriate for West Virginia mines. Federal inspections of local mines, mandated by the statute, were perceived as threatening by state inspectors.[54] Attempts by the Department of Natural Resources to obtain federal grants were held up by OSM:

> More than $27 million was awarded to 23 states in fiscal years 1978 and 1979. Ostensibly, these grants were intended to strengthen the management capacity of the states to administer the regulatory program and to offset expenses incurred for operating the interim program. Initially, OSM officials viewed the grants as important vehicles for influencing the states. As one OSM official put it, "we are blatantly coercive about state use of grants." This attitude encountered stiff resistance in some states, particularly West Virginia. . . .[55]

DNR officials became increasingly frustrated with OSM as the effort to secure the two federal grants continued over a period of several months. Eventually, the dispute attracted the attention of Gov. Jay Rockefeller, who delivered a speech critical of OSM at the National Governors' Conference in late August of 1978, and further criticized the agency before the Senate oversight committee. When the two grants were finally awarded by OSM in November 1978, the state refused to accept the smaller of the two grants in protest against the agency's handling of the proposals.[56]

More significant was Governor Rockefeller's call for legislation to nullify OSM's rule-making authority. West Virginia representatives introduced the so-called Rockefeller amendment in both houses of Congress; the amendment specified that state regulatory programs need be in conformity only with the original terms of the Surface Mining Control and Reclamation Act, and not with the ensuing regulations issued by OSM. Not surprisingly, the Rockefeller amendment was vigorously supported by various elements of the coal coalition, as well as by various state governments. The Rockefeller amendment passed the Senate in September of 1979. While the bill remained bottled up in the House committee, where Morris Udall's opposition virtually precluded its passage, the Senate's action got the attention of OSM's high officials, making it very clear that additional flexibility was needed in dealing with the states.[57]

The state of Kentucky sent a similar message to bureaucrats at OSM. When OSM rejected the state's proposed regulatory program. Kentucky refused to submit a revised program. State officials recognized, correctly, that OSM did not really want the responsibility of inspecting all its mines indefinitely. The disastrous potential inherent in the Kentucky precedent forced OSM officials to acknowledge the need for a negotiated compliance strategy.[58]

Accordingly, OSM adopted a more conciliatory posture toward the states. In a symbolic gesture, the associate solicitor for surface mining, who had become a lightning rod for state and industry attacks on OSM, was dismissed in 1979. In a more substantive vein, OSM became more receptive to state proposals under the state window provision. However, President Carter's defeat in the fall election ensured the advent of a new administration before a meaningful change in enforcement strategy could be established.[59]

DECENTRALIZATION OF ENFORCEMENT
UNDER THE REAGAN ADMINISTRATION

The election of 1980 gave the Republican party control of both the White House and the Senate for the first time since Dwight Eisenhower's first term. As noted in Chapter 6, the 1980 election is perhaps best understood as an instance of voters holding the incumbent party accountable for serious problems plaguing both domestic and foreign policy. While the two presidential candidates differed dramatically on environmental issues, the election cannot be interpreted as yielding a mandate on the strip mining issue. In fact, public opinion polls consistently found the American public to be much more supportive of strong environmental laws than their new president.[60]

Nevertheless, the 1980 election virtually guaranteed a dramatic shift in priorities on the strip mining issue. Restoration of a strong and growing economy was one of the president's major objectives in 1981, and he saw his objective as being in fundamental conflict with many of the environmental programs enacted in the 1970s. Furthermore, the president regarded the environmental movement as unduly alarmist on many points and felt federal standards could be relaxed without significant harm to the environment. Moreover, like presidents Nixon and Ford before him, President Reagan strongly believed in federalism. In distinct contrast both to President Carter and to bureaucratic officials within OSM, President Reagan strongly believed that the states should be given more autonomy in policy-making on most issues, including surface mining regulation.[61]

The new secretary of the interior, James B. Watt, was an ardent conservative with prior experience both as an undersecretary of the interior and as an attorney for the Mountain States Legal Foundation, a conservative public interest law firm that often opposed environmental groups in litigation.[62] Watt shared the president's desire to open up federal lands for the extraction of coal, oil, and gas.[63] The administration's general support for greater state autonomy and the elimination of major obstacles to mineral extraction would require a significant redirection of the surface mining act.

Shortly after taking office, Secretary Watt met with Department of Interior employees to lay out his vision of the future. As is customary, OSM's political appointees offered their resignations, which were accepted almost without exception. Within several months, top-level positions in the agency were filled with committed supporters of the Reagan agenda, including at least two individuals who were identified with state-level resistance to OSM in the Carter years.[64]

In late spring, Secretary Watt announced that OSM would undergo a fundamental reorganization. The five major units within OSM's Washington headquarters would be consolidated into three new units, each headed by an assistant director. The five existing regional offices would be abolished, to be replaced with fourteen state offices and seven field offices. The staff of OSM would decline from its current level of 1,000 to a total of 616 within twelve months.[65]

Not surprisingly, the proposed reorganization alarmed environmentalists and their allies in Congress. Reorganization of the agency stimulated Morris Udall to convene an oversight hearing of the energy and environment subcommittee of the House Interior and Insular Affairs Committee. In testimony before the subcommittee, Secretary Watt and his staff defended the reorganization plan. In effect, the dialogue between the subcommittee and the secretary took the form of a conflict over the definition of the situation, much as Schattschneider might have predicted. Where environmental groups characterized the reorganization as an attempt to cripple the federal agency and thus undermine enforcement, Secretary Watt pointed to the original statute's provision for eventual state primacy. Watt argued that OSM was obligated to give the states primary responsibility for enforcement; in this regard, eighteen of the twenty-five states with significant coal production had secured OSM approval for their regulatory programs and received primacy by January of 1981. While five states still had not submitted programs, only two states (Ohio and Pennsylvania) had had their programs rejected.[66] The proposed reorganization simply reflected a fully appropriate shift from a direct enforcement role to an oversight and assistance role as required by the act.[67] Finally, the secretary noted that plans to reorganize the agency were already in the works in the last year of the Carter administration; the Reagan administration's proposed reorganization merely built on these efforts.[68]

Secretary Watt was successful in redefining the issue to the administration's advantage, and the reorganization proceeded as planned. While members of the subcommittee were skeptical of the administration's motives, the secretary had strongly endorsed the act's objectives and presented the reorganization plan as being consistent with the act's requirement for eventual state primacy.[69] Moreover, Congress was receptive to major budget cuts in a wide array of programs in the wake of what was perceived as a conservative mandate in the 1980 election and the prospect of major budget deficits generated by the major tax cuts enacted that same year.[70] Finally, environmental issues (including strip mining) lacked salience for the mass public in 1981; while the public remained strongly supportive of environmental laws in general, the issue received little attention from most people.[71]

Following the reorganization of OSM, a number of important changes were made in the regulations flowing out of the surface mining act. In February of 1981, President Reagan issued an executive order requiring federal agencies to review and revise or eliminate all potentially counterproductive regulations. The new leadership within OSM responded to this order with real enthusiasm, proposing that 89 sections of existing OSM regulations be deleted and 329 more be significantly revised. More important, the old emphasis on enforced compliance would give way to a new approach stressing negotiated compliance. Wherever possible, design standards were replaced with performance standards, and the state window provision was eliminated. Where the wording of federal regulations had previously specified that state regulations must be "no less stringent" than federal regulations, new wording stipulated that state regulations need only be "no less effective" than federal rules.[72]

Moreover, the agency's enforcement style was significantly changed. The number of inspections peaked in 1980 under President Carter. The number of inspectors declined by roughly 25 percent from 1979 to 1981, from 204 to 156. Under the new administration, there would be a slight drop-off in the number of mines inspected and a significant decline in the number of citations issued for violations. While the decline in citations began in the waning days of the Carter administration, probably as a reflection of the agency's uncertainty as to how to proceed in the transition period, the pattern for the Reagan years appears to mark a genuine redirection; the monthly ratio of citations to inspections dropped off sharply in 1981 and remained stable at this new, lower level well into 1982.[73]

Reclamation efforts were characterized by a similar pattern. Under the terms of the statute, it will be recalled, old mines (i.e., those in existence prior to enactment of the surface mining law) would be reclaimed using revenues from an Abandoned Mine Land Fund, financed through a complicated tax on coal producers. To finance reclamation of new mines, operators would be required to post a performance bond in order to secure a permit to begin surface mining; civil penalties assessed against violators would go into this fund as well. A series of investigations by the House Committee on Government Operations discovered a pattern of lax enforcement of these provisions under the Reagan administration. Debts owed to the Abandoned Mine Land Fund went uncollected; in many instances, there was no attempt even to assess what was owed to the fund. Fines were not assessed for many violations; for those violations actually assessed civil penalties, the collection rate had fallen from approximately 8 percent at its peak to less than 1 percent in 1986.[74] Performance bonds (which are set by the states) have been found to be inadequate to fully fund reclamation in many instances. In one state, bond forfeitures accounted for only 12 percent of the ultimate costs of reclamation.[75]

It is unclear whether the Reagan administration sought to undermine the implementation of the surface mining act by these actions or merely sought more effective means to shared objectives. Representatives of the Reagan administration, including Secretary Watt, consistently endorsed the objectives of the act while pointing to the statutory requirements for eventual state primacy. Moreover, the findings of political science research on policy implementation strongly suggest that some form of negotiated compliance strategy is essential, particularly when dealing with state and local governments.[76] Thus the shift toward greater latitude for the states under Reagan can be defended as consistent both with the act and with sound principles of intergovernmental relations. What is clear is that implementation underwent a significant redirection under the Reagan administration, reversing attempts by Carter administration officials to achieve something approaching a nonincremental policy change. Regulations would henceforth be a good deal less stringent, and power would flow to that level of government where corporate counterpressures are strongest.

NOTES

1. For a concise discussion of the issues separating these groups, see Carol D. Rasnic, "Federally Required Restoration of Surface-Mined Property: Impasse Between the Coal Industry and the Environmentally Concerned," *Natural Resources Journal,* 23 (April 1983), pp. 335–349.
2. U.S. Department of Energy, Energy Information Administration, *Historical Plant Cost and Annual Production Expenses for Selected Electric Plants, 1982* (August 1984), pp. 9–10.
3. On the end of easy oil, see Robert Stobaugh and Daniel Yergin (eds.), *Energy Future,* 3d ed. rev. (New York: Random House, Vintage Books, 1983). On exponential growth in energy demands, see Albert A. Bartlett, "Forgotten Fundamentals of the Energy Crisis," *American Journal of Physics,* 46 (September 1978), pp. 876–888. On the limitations of various technological "fixes" to the energy crisis, and on the need for a much greater role for conservation in our energy policy, see Walter A. Rosenbaum, *Energy, Politics, and Public Policy,* 2d ed. (Washington, D.C.: Congressional Quarterly Press, 1987), as well as Stobaugh and Yergin.
4. Neil Shover, Donald A. Clelland, and John Lynxwiler, *Enforcement or Negotiation* (Albany: State University of New York Press, 1986), p. 17.
5. Shover, et al., p. 18.
6. Economists use the term *production possibility frontier* to refer to the outer limits of production for a particular technology (e.g., the set of maximally efficient combinations of various goods). Strip mining represents a radical improvement in the technology available for extraction of coal; the invention of strip mining has the effect of shifting the entire production possibility frontier outward. With the new technology, the outer limits of production are substantially expanded.
7. Shover, et al., pp. 17–18.
8. Walter A. Rosenbaum, *Environmental Politics and Policy* (Washington, D.C.: Congressional Quarterly Press, 1985), pp. 105–139.

9. On the environmental consequences of strip mining, see Shover, et al., pp. 17–23, and Richard H. K. Vietor, *Environmental Politics and the Coal Coalition* (College Station: Texas A&M University Press, 1980), pp. 237–244. For particularly evocative accounts, see two works by Harry M. Caudill: *Night Comes to the Cumberlands* (Boston: Little, Brown, 1962), pp. 219–248; and *My Land Is Dying* (New York: Dutton, 1971).

10. Vietor, pp. 240–241.

11. Caudill, *My Land Is Dying,* p. 106.

12. On the regulation of strip mining in Pennsylvania, see Vietor, Chapter 3, ''Sportsmen and Strip Mining in Pennsylvania: The Fight for Controls,'' pp. 58–84. On the relative performance of Ohio and Kentucky (and on Kentucky's poor performance generally), see Caudill, *My Land Is Dying,* and *Night Comes to the Cumberlands.*

13. Vietor, pp. 18–35.

14. Shover, et al., pp. 27–29.

15. Shover, et al., pp. 30–31.

16. Vietor, p. 87.

17. Quoted in Shover, et al., p. 31.

18. Vietor, pp. 90–95.

19. Vietor, pp. 95–96.

20. Shover, et al., pp. 31–33. See also Vietor, pp. 99–100.

21. Vietor, pp. 101–102.

22. See Joseph P. Kalt, ''The Costs and Benefits of Federal Regulation of Coal Strip Mining,'' *Natural Resources Journal,* 23 (October 1983), pp. 899–906.

23. Vietor, pp. 252–255.

24. Donald C. Menzel, ''Implementation of the Federal Surface Mining Control and Reclamation Act of 1977,'' *Public Administration Review,* 41, no. 2 (March/April 1981), p. 213. See also Shover, et al., pp. 37–39.

25. U.S. Congress, House of Representatives, Committee on Government Operations, ''Surface Mining Law: A Promise Yet to Be Fulfilled.'' Eleventh Report, 100th Congress, 1st Session, 1987. House Report 100–183, pp. 6–8; and Menzel, ''Implementation,'' p. 213.

26. For a full treatment of the various legislative proposals discussed below, see Vietor, pp. 88–92.

27. Shover, et al., p. 38.

28. Vietor, p. 109.

29. An alluvial valley is an area within an arid region that is underlain with an aquifer, thus permitting at least some agricultural use for the land. See Shover, et al., pp. 64–65.

30. Vietor, pp. 122–124.

31. This discussion of federal policy implementation draws heavily on a model of policy implementation developed by Carl Van Horn. See Carl E. Van Horn, *Policy Implementation in the Federal System* (Lexington, Mass.: Lexington Books, 1979). For a book-length application of the model to the CETA case, see Donald C. Baumer and Carl E. Van Horn, *The Politics of Unemployment* (Washington, D.C.: Congressional Quarterly Press, 1985).

32. See Jerome T. Murphy, ''The Education Bureaucracies Implement Novel Policy: The Politics of Title I of ESEA, 1965–1972,'' in Allan P. Sindler (ed.), *Policy and Politics in America* (Boston: Little, Brown, 1973), pp. 160–198.

33. Van Horn, pp. 130 and 146–150.

34. Shover, et al., p. 39.

35. Shover, et al., p. 11.

36. See Richard E. Neustadt, *Presidential Power,* rev. ed. (New York: Wiley, 1980); and Graham T. Allison, *Essence of Decision* (Boston: Little, Brown, 1971).

37. Shover, et al., p. 41.
38. Shover, et al., p. 45.
39. Shover et al., p. 46. On the tendency of new agencies to attract "zealots," see Anthony Downs, *Inside Bureaucracy* (Boston: Little, Brown, 1967); and Marver P. Bernstein, *Regulating Business by Independent Commission* (Princeton, N.J.: Princeton University Press, 1955).
40. Quoted in Shover, et al., p. 48. I have shortened and consolidated two short quotations from the same respondent here.
41. Shover, et al., p. 47.
42. Shover, et al., pp. 49–50.
43. Shover, et al., pp. 61–63; Menzel, pp. 214–215.
44. See Shover, et al., pp. 56–70, for a review of the evolution of several regulatory standards.
45. Shover, et al., p. 75.
46. Shover, et al., p. 75.
47. Shover, et al., p. 81.
48. Shover, et al., pp. 80–105.
49. Shover, et al., pp. 109–115.
50. Shover, et al., pp. 116–117.
51. Shover, et al., pp. 112–113. For a concise review of one of these cases, as it moved all the way to the Supreme Court, see Rasnic, pp. 336–342.
52. Shover, et al., pp. 61–64 and 121.
53. Menzel, "Implementation," pp. 213–214.
54. Menzel, "Implementation," p. 216.
55. Menzel, "Implementation," p. 214.
56. Menzel, "Implementation," p. 216.
57. Menzel, "Implementation," p. 216. See also Shover, et al., p. 121.
58. Shover, et al., p. 122.
59. Shover, et al., pp. 119–122.
60. Robert Cameron Mitchell, "Public Opinion and Environmental Politics in the 1970s and 1980s," in Norman J. Vig and Michael E. Krafts (eds.), *Environmental Policy in the 1980s* (Washington, D.C.: Congressional Quarterly Press, 1984), pp. 51–74.
61. Norman J. Vig, "The President and the Environment: Revolution or Retreat?" in Vig and Kraft, pp. 77–95.
62. Ron Arnold, *At the Eye of the Storm: James Watt and the Environmentalists* (Chicago: Regnery Gateway, 1982).
63. Regina S. Axelrod, "Energy Policy: Changing the Rules of the Game," in Vig and Kraft, pp. 203–225.
64. Shover, et al., pp. 150–151. See also Donald C. Menzel, "Redirecting the Implementation of a Law: The Reagan Administration and Coal Surface Mining Regulation," *Public Administration Review*, 43, no. 5 (September/October 1983), pp. 412–414.
65. Menzel, "Redirecting," pp. 412–414.
66. Menzel, "Redirecting," p. 412.
67. Menzel, "Redirecting," p. 414.
68. Menzel, "Redirecting," p. 414.
69. Menzel, "Redirecting," p. 414.
70. David A. Stockman, *The Triumph of Politics* (New York: Avon Books, 1987).
71. Mitchell, pp. 54–57.
72. Menzel, "Redirecting," pp. 414–415.
73. Menzel, "Redirecting," pp. 415–418.

74. "Surface Mining Law: A Promise Yet to Be Fulfilled," Eleventh Report by the Committee on Government Operations, U.S. House of Representatives, 100th Congress, 1st Session. House Report 100-183 (Washington, D.C.: U.S. Government Printing Office, 1987).

75. Wesley Marx, "Can Strip Mining Clean Up Its Act?" *Readers Digest,* March 1987, pp. 123–124.

76. See Martha Derthick, *The Influence of Federal Grants* (Cambridge, Mass.: Harvard University Press, 1970); Helen Ingram, "Policy Implementation Through Bargaining: The Case of Federal Grants-in-Aid," *Public Policy,* 25 (Fall 1977), pp. 499–526.

CHAPTER 8

The Policy Process:
Some Generalizations

The surface mining issue, reviewed in the previous chapter, provides a fairly typical case (if there is such a thing) of the constraints operating to prevent nonincremental policy outcomes under normal circumstances. While no single case study can illustrate all the aspects of each model, this chapter will identify generalizations derived from the models that apply to the strip mining case as it moved through the agenda-setting, policy adoption, and policy implementation stages. Generalizations regarding conditions for policy change will follow in Chapter 12.

PROBLEM IDENTIFICATION
AND AGENDA SETTING

Problem identification is not typically a rational process; there will typically be a struggle over the definition of the problem. According to the rational model, no important public problem would go unperceived for very long, and once perceived, public problems would be defined accurately and in the same way by all participants. While resource or time constraints might preclude dealing with all problems that might arise at any one time, the rational model would suggest that problems somehow be ranked in order of seriousness (with all participants agreeing on a ranking) and then dealt with until resources are exhausted, beginning with the most serious problems.

However, as we have seen, participants do not typically agree on how problems are to be defined, or even on whether a particular problem is legitimately public in nature or serious enough to warrant government action. In part, this is because different people make different trade-offs among conflicting values (energy vs. the environment, for example). Even more important, however, conflict over problem definition arises out of the fact that issues typically affect different groups in different ways, thus generating distinct interests. Where environmental and community groups stressed the environmental damage resulting from strip mining, coal producers fought to preserve the productivity gains yielded by surface mining techniques. As time went on, the interests of Eastern and Western coal interests diverged, reflecting the differential effect of the Clean Air Act of 1970 on their competitive position.

Problem definition and issue placement profoundly affect ultimate policy outcomes; these actions can never be neutral whenever politics involves a clash of interests. As Schattschneider observed, some groups will profit by keeping a given conflict "privatized" while others will seek to "socialize conflict" by bringing the issue to government for resolution. In much the same way, one group may be strongest at the national level while another has the advantage at the local level. This was very much the case on strip mining; environmental groups sought full federal preemption of regulatory authority because they were strongest at that level, while coal interests sought to retain as much authority as possible at the state level. It should be clear that arguments about whether a problem is public or private and whether it is properly a matter for state or federal resolution are really arguments about who is going to have a resource advantage in the contest over the substance of policy. The same is true of disputes over which federal agency should be given the responsibility for dealing with the problem. Coal interests fought hard to place the new agency within the Interior Department, which has historically favored extractive industries over environmental interests.

Put another way, most issues can be defined in more than one way simply because they involve a trade-off among conflicting values, and trade-offs can be made in different ways by different actors. While the regulation of strip mining internalizes a significant externality by forcing producers to bear the costs of reclamation, it is simultaneously an obstacle to expanded coal production, and thus to greater energy independence, and a serious threat to regional economies. To the extent that alternative definitions of the issue create very different cleavages within the polity (a phenomenon Schattschneider referred to as "the displacement of conflict"), the outcome of the struggle over problem definition is critically important to the subsequent struggle over policy substance.

All interests are not represented equally in this struggle; some issues are more likely than others to reach the agenda. There is little reason to believe that all problems will generate publics, to paraphrase Charles O. Jones.[1] To the contrary, there are systematic biases to the interest group universe produced by the free rider problem and the costs of mobilization. In general, small groups will be more likely to organize than large, diffuse interests, and affluent groups will be more likely to mobilize than the poor. Because the free rider problem never goes away for membership groups, institutions of all sorts (including corporations) will be more likely than mass membership groups to survive over the long term.

The surface mining issue posed the trade-off between energy and the environment in bold terms, making conflict over objectives and a struggle among contending interests inevitable. Where all Americans benefit from a stable and relatively inexpensive supply of energy, however, the direct environmental consequences of surface mining are localized. While this concentration of damages may be made for smaller affected publics with a correspondingly better chance of overcoming the free rider problem, it also made it difficult to socialize conflict to larger publics. As we saw in the previous chapter, strip mining was a serious problem long before it reached the federal agenda. Strip mining is only one of a whole cluster of issues, including air and water pollution, that were placed on the institutional agenda largely in response to the mobilization of the environmental movement in the late 1960s and early 1970s.

Our capitalistic system depends upon a high degree of business performance—performance that cannot be demanded but rather must somehow be induced. While the surface mining law was a response to serious environmental abuses, even Morris Udall acknowledged the need for expanded coal production in the wake of the energy crisis.[2] The legislation was carefully crafted (and repeatedly compromised) to permit surface mining to continue under a wide variety of circumstances. Coal interests were able to block legislation that would have abolished strip mining entirely as well as proposals to place regulatory responsibility in an agency with a strong environmental mission and the authority to bypass the states in dealing with the industry.

POLICY ADOPTION

For any given issue, the policy equilibrium will be a function of who participates (the configuration of demand), what resources each participant brings to bear, and how effectively each group translates its resources into influence. While Lindblom and the group theorists are correct in viewing the policy process as a group struggle under normal circumstances, there is no reason to believe that policy outcomes will result in the public interest. (More specifically, there is no reason to believe that the outcome of the group struggle will serve to identify a public interest that could not otherwise be defined.) To the contrary, many interests will be left out of the group struggle, and there is little reason to believe resources will be distributed evenly among those that show up.

The configuration of interests profoundly affects the pattern of politics for any given issue. There is a fundamental difference between consensual and conflictual issues, as we saw in Chapter 4. Where a multiplicity of groups are active on all sides of an issue, as with the strip mining issue, a pattern of atomistic competition is produced. (Short of this, enough interests may be represented to assure the political analogue of what economists term ''workable competition.'') This is the ideal case, according to both Lindblom and the group theorists: so many groups are active that no single group can wield political market power.

However, while the pattern of group pressures is one sided and overwhelming in the consensual case, the relative resources of various participants come into play where the configuration of interests is conflictual. In Chapter 4, we identified several resources of interest groups that can contribute to effective influence. While some of these resources (particularly money and manpower) are tangible in nature, on many issues the more important dimensions are intangible ones such as expertise, strategic position, and legitimacy.

Corporations possess significant resource advantages in the group struggle, making for a system of imperfect social competition on many issues. As suggested by Lindblom and Miliband, corporations occupy a privileged position within capitalistic societies. They are extraordinarily legitimate, to the point that policy makers often equate corporate interests with the public interest. They also occupy an unparalleled strategic position within our economic system that is reinforced by the effects of federalism and the pressures for localism operative within our political system. And on economic issues, business executives possess important expertise, which forces policy makers to seek their advice when other groups must compete to gain access to decision makers.

The coal coalition possessed a number of these advantages in lobbying on the surface mining issue. While coal producers do not dominate the national economy in the same way that they do some state economies, the coal coalition brought into play a wide array of industries with a common interest in blocking or weakening surface mining regulation. Taken together, these industries (which included both big banks and a number of major oil companies along with some smaller fry) played a significant role in the national economy. In addition, the various elements of the coal coalition possessed a major advantage over environmental groups in technical expertise, which came into play most forcefully at the critical committee markup stage. If these resources were insufficient to keep the issue from arising, they were more than sufficient to preclude a nonincremental outcome.

We saw in Chapter 5 that business involvement in national politics has tended to wax and wane in response to the ebb and flow of specific threats (e.g., labor unions, the rise of the consumer movement). The coal coalition conforms to this general pattern. The industry has been conspicuously unsuccessful in offensive lobbying. The fortunes of coal in this century have tended to wax and wane in response to developments in the oil economy. Early in the century, the rise of the automobile led to an oil boom at the expense of coal that has lasted several decades; the recent resurgence of interest in coal has had more to do with OPEC than the power of the coal lobby.[3] The surface mining issue was brought to the agenda by environmental interests over the objections of the coal industry. Attempts to suppress the issue by nondecision-making were ineffectual, and the coal coalition was forced to shift its strategy to one of nominal support for federal regulation coupled with a call for state primacy that would maximize industry influence over day-to-day regulatory decisions.

To the extent that policy outcomes are a function of what groups mobilize and what resources and skills they bring to bear, major policy change implies a major shift in the equilibrium of groups contending on any given issue—for example, the entry of new groups into the system and/or a significant shift in the balance of resources available to active groups. In general, the socialization of conflict for a previously privatized issue does not produce nonincremental change, at least in Lindblom's terms. Rather, it is better understood as transforming a one-sided (and thus incomplete) configuration of interests, creating in its place the kind of atomistic competition among interests idealized by both Lindblom and the group theorists. While the mobilization of new groups can produce a "preformed majority" for large change, as in the 1970 clear air case, in general the socialization of conflict makes for a broader configuration of interests. Although more balance is plainly desirable on prescriptive grounds, it can also make it more difficult to secure agreement on objectives, perhaps the most important precondition for large change.

As we have seen, the surface mining issue moved from the systemic agenda to the institutional agenda in the early 1970s with the mobilization at the national level of the environmental movement. This socialized a conflict that had previously been privatized at the state level. The end result was not a nonincremental change, however, but rather a long and difficult group struggle giving rise to a bill that was, in many respects, disappointing to environmentalists. The mobilization of the environmental movement (and the movement of environmentalists into key institutional positions in 1977) made it possible to pass a law involving the federal government in the regulation of surface mining for the first time, but it was insufficient to give the federal government primary enforcement authority or even to place the agency responsible for enforcement within the most sympathetic cabinet department.

As the sole elected official within our system with a national constituency, the president offers voters their one chance to control public policy through a system of majority rule. However, the weakness of the American parties and the fact that a failure to maintain party cohesion in Congress will not lead to a dissolution of the government means that the president will be forced to construct a new coalition for each issue. While the president's party in Congress may serve as the foundation for some of these coalitions, no president can count upon support in Congress for his program as a matter of course. That support must typically be bought on an individual basis through some form of quid pro quo.

The weak legislative parties within our system are best understood, in David Truman's terms, as potential groups. The congressional parties must thus compete with a variety of other groups in the struggle over policy, and in seeking to maintain cohesion, the party leaderships are confronted with a free rider problem no less serious than that facing organized interest groups. As noted in Chapter 6, both parties consist of like-minded individuals who would prefer, in the absence of countervailing pressures, to see their party triumph on most issues. However, legislators are accountable to local electorates rather than the national parties and thus find themselves tempted on many issues to defect from party positions in response to constituency or interest group pressures. Party leaders possess few resources for overcoming this free rider problem, and the development of a coherent party program is further impeded by a bicameral Congress, which makes for very different constituencies and institutional perspectives among legislative members of the same parties.

The Carter administration gave strong support to surface mining legislation where President Ford vetoed two different bills, and Democrats tended in general to be more favorable to federal regulation of strip mining than Republicans. Nevertheless, the coal coalition received vigorous support from various Democrats representing coal-producing states, who faced real cross-pressures on the issue. While the direct consequences of strip mining tend to be localized, the coal industry is critically important to these same local economies. Mountaintop removal was thus preserved through an amendment sponsored by Sen. Wendell Ford, a Democrat from Kentucky, for example. John Seiberling, author of the Seiberling amendment designed to protect the competitive position of Appalachian coal, was a Democrat from Ohio. Senators Robert Byrd of West Virginia and Harry Byrd of Virginia, both Democrats, were also reliable allies of the coal industry. By contrast, legislation that would have given enforcement authority to the EPA and provided for full federal preemption of regulatory authority was sponsored by three Democrats from states with little, if any, dependence on the coal industry: Gaylord Nelson of Wisconsin, Edward

Kennedy of Massachusetts, and George McGovern of South Dakota. An isolated (and politically courageous) exception to this general pattern would be Rep. Kenneth Hechler, a Democrat from West Virginia, who introduced the bill in the House to abolish strip mining entirely.

Divided government virtually guarantees stalemate between the parties on divisive issues and precludes the placing of blame on either party for resulting policy failures inasmuch as no one has been given effective control over the institutions of government. Since 1954, different parties have controlled the White House and at least one house of Congress for two-thirds of the time, leading James L. Sundquist to suggest that the United States has entered into a new era of coalition government. While some writers have suggested that the voters are deliberately choosing to balance conservative presidents with liberal congresses, the evidence suggests that this result has instead been produced by a minority of the electorate that engages in ticket splitting.[4]

John Kingdon has argued that a "policy window" is typically necessary to permit legislative action on an issue. Such windows close quickly, and failure to seize the moment may forfeit any real opportunity for action for years.[5] (Kingdon's model will be discussed in more detail in Chapters 9 and 10.) The most common policy windows are crises, focusing events that serve to arouse public opinion on an issue, or a change in presidential administrations. There was no crisis or focusing event to arouse public opinion in the strip mining case. Rather the issue remained on the systemic agenda for three decades before achieving institutional agenda status in the early 1970s with the mobilization of the environmental movement. The "window" that finally permitted passage of a bill in 1977 was the end of divided government.

While elections do not typically yield a clear mandate in the United States, they can shift the balance of forces for issues already on the institutional agenda. For an election to send a clear mandate to policy makers, the candidates must make issues the centerpiece of their campaigns, and the voters must decide on the basis of these issues and nothing else. These are very difficult conditions to satisfy, particularly in the American system. At the presidential level, as we saw in Chapter 7, candidate appeal is often more decisive than party stands on the issues. Moreover, presidential candidates face powerful incentives to minimize or obscure their differences on divisive issues. Even where the candidates contest the election over certain clear issues, there is no guarantee that the electorate will take an interest in these issues.[6]

Strip mining was not an issue in either the 1976 or 1980 presidential campaign, and it seems unlikely that very many (if any) voters made their choices on the basis of that issue. Nevertheless, as we saw in the previous chapter, the results of these two presidential elections virtually guaranteed sharp changes in direction with regard to surface mining regulation, which was already on the congressional agenda during this period. The election of Jimmy Carter made passage of a strip mining bill almost inevitable in 1977 by removing the prospect of a presidential veto. Similarly, presidents Carter and Reagan made the trade-off between energy needs and environmental concerns in very different ways. While the strip mining issue did not come up during the 1980 campaign, interest groups with a stake in the issue, who had been paying close attention to the campaign, had little difficulty predicting the sharp shift in priorities that occurred under the new administration.

POLICY IMPLEMENTATION

It is misleading to think of policy implementation as a struggle among contending groups with the agency at the center; rather, the agency must be viewed as one of many interests involved in a struggle with policy at the center. Seen in this light, the creation of a federal agency with the formal authority to issue regulations does not so much determine the final allocation of values for society as it injects into the group struggle a new entity with a good deal of legitimacy and a mission to represent the broader public interest. As the institutions formally charged with the responsibility for policy implementation, government agencies possess what Earl Latham termed "officiality": they have been given the authority to allocate important values for society. However, legislative outcomes are frequently incremental, leading to limited budgets and an incomplete arsenal of formal powers. As a result, for all their formal authority, agencies must often compete with a variety of other actors in an attempt to shape policy.

While the surface mining law did involve the federal government in regulation of the industry for the first time, the legislation had been significantly compromised in many respects, permitting surface mining to continue under a wide range of circumstances unacceptable to environmentalists. Moreover, the statute provided for an eventual assumption of regulatory authority by the states. Nevertheless, the new Office of Surface Mining vigorously pursued its vision of the public interest in writing the interim and permanent regulations, which would guide the states in developing their own implementation plans, and actually succeeded in reversing many of the defeats suffered by environmental groups at the policy adoption stage. In so doing, however, the agency exceeded both its statutory authority and its base of political support. Predictably, the agency was unable to sustain these stringent regulations in the face of a determined countermobilization by the states and the coal industry. The incremental legislative outcome reflected the real balance of forces active on the issue; the agency's attempt to move beyond this equilibrium to a stronger federal role was doomed to fail.

Federalism assures an ongoing tension between separate levels of government contending over shared powers and thus makes for a process of "due deliberation" in which a multiplicity of interests are almost sure to be represented. In distinct contrast to the agenda-setting and policy adoption stages, it simply makes no sense to speak of a "policy window" permitting successful policy implementation. The implementation stage is a protracted process with no clear resolution or end point. Moreover, while the participants in the agenda-setting and policy adoption stages overlap to some extent, policy implementation brings into play an entirely different group of actors who are spread over three levels of government. For most domestic issues, federal objectives are sought through grants-in-aid to the states and localities, and compliance with federal directives must be achieved through bargaining and inducements. State and local administrative agencies, like their federal counterparts, remain dependent upon state legislatures, city councils, and so on for budgetary resources and statutory authority. Thus, federal mandates inevitably come into conflict with the needs of various subnational actors, triggering a whole series of group struggles between federal implementors and a multiplicity of state and local authorities.

In the American system, the power of corporations to affect policy will be greatest at the implementation stage. The tremendous financial resources available to corporations make them better equipped than almost any other groups to bear the high costs of participation at this stage. Moreover, their high legitimacy and a near monopoly on vital expertise on technical matters of production virtually dictate that administrators will consult industry representatives in the drafting of regulations affecting them. Finally (and by no means least important), the strategic position of business within capitalist societies is reinforced by our system of federalism and the resulting tendency to implement policies intergovernmentally. While business groups must compete with a variety of other interests at the national level (including other business groups), individual corporations are often critically important to state and local economies.

This was very clearly illustrated in the strip mining case. The Office of Surface Mining distrusted both the coal industry and existing state agencies. The agency's resulting high-handed treatment of these groups led to the formation of a coalition between coal interests and many of these state governments. The extent to which this alliance reflected the strategic position of coal within state economies is well summarized by the authors of a book-length study of the passage and implementation of the surface mining law:

> There is a fundamental lesson here: local state agencies are more responsive to economic conditions than are federal-level state managers. In revolting against the OSM, local state managers were not acting as instruments of capital, they were simply doing their job, "steering" the local economy by providing a good business climate.[7]

The nature of the group struggle over policy implementation, like that at the policy adoption stage, will be profoundly affected by the configuration of active groups. OSM's regulatory zeal, as compared with the tendency of state regulatory agencies to succumb to the strategic position of coal interests within local economies, would seem to suggest that effective enforcement was virtually precluded by the statute's provisions for eventual state primacy. By contrast, a number of federal regulatory agencies (the Federal Communications Commission, for example) deal directly with the industries they regulate; intergovernmental implementation of domestic policies is a common pattern, but not inevitable. As we saw in the previous chapter, however, there was never anything approaching majority support in Congress for full federal preemption of surface mining regulation. This was doubtless due at least in part to the influence of the coal coalition on many legislators. It was probably due as well to the sheer magnitude of the task of regularly inspecting thousands of mines spread over thirty-eight states; at its peak, OSM never came close to inspecting all the nation's mines even twice a year, as mandated by the statute during the interim period.

Even if OSM had been given the full responsibility for enforcing the act, the record of federal regulation by independent commission provides few grounds for optimism. While agency "capture" is virtually precluded where numerous organized groups are mobilized (as, for example, with the Environmental Protection Agency), co-optation by clientele groups is much more likely where the configuration of attentive groups is one sided. This is most commonly the case where agencies, like OSM, regulate individual industries.

To a degree, the configuration of groups at this stage will reflect the configuration of demand at the policy adoption stage. Conflictual demand patterns in Congress tend to give rise to incremental outcomes and interest group liberalism, thus generating conflictual group patterns at the implementation stage. Similarly, consensual demand patterns in the policy adoption stage often yield distributive outcomes likely to be dominated by the same one-sided coalitions in the implementation stage.

This correlation, although strong, is imperfect, however; the question of who should participate is never neutral, and there is always a potential for the socialization or privatization of conflict. Privatization is perhaps the more common pattern, as many groups active in the policy adoption stage will tend to drop out here, making for a much narrower circle of players. The cost of participation increase for groups at each stage of the policy process. It is relatively inexpensive to call attention to an issue and place it on the institutional agenda. While it is considerably harder to secure adoption of legislation dealing with the issue, at least the costs of participation promise to stop with passage of a law. Policy implementation, by contrast, requires groups with a stake in this issue to monitor agency behavior at all times and for all time. Few groups have the financial resources and full-time staff to do this.[8]

In the strip mining case, reprivatization of the conflict was almost surely facilitated by the statutory provisions for state primacy. While OSM was charged with regulating a single industry, it was clearly not co-opted by mining interests. Environmental groups active at the policy adoption stage not only maintained their involvement in the administrative process of writing regulations, they largely dominated that process, turning an incremental legislative outcome into a strong vehicle for effective regulation. While the coal coalition had sought to avoid such an outcome by securing placement of the new agency within the Interior Department, rather than EPA (which coal interests saw as "captured" by environmental groups), the configuration of demand within the environment of OSM was sufficiently conflictual to offset the otherwise formidable resource advantages possessed by the coal coalition. By contrast, state regulatory agencies were highly responsive to industry concerns, if not fully captured by the industry. This was entirely predictable given the strategic position of coal within local economies combined with the failure of environmental interests to mobilize at this level.

HOW TO EXPLAIN NONINCREMENTAL CHANGE

The five models reviewed in this volume call our attention to distinct factors responsible for the prevalence of incrementalism in policy-making. While incremental outcomes are the norm within our political system, nonincremental policy change is more common than Lindblom's incremental model would predict. The remaining chapters shift our attention, therefore, to the preconditions for significant policy change.

NOTES

1. Charles O. Jones, *An Introduction to the Study of Public Policy*, 3d ed. (Monterey, Calif.: Brooks/Cole, 1984), p. 34.
2. Neal Shover, Donald A. Clelland, and John Lynxwiler, *Enforcement or Negotiation* (Albany: State University of New York Press, 1986), p. 36.

3. See David Howard Davis, *Energy Politics,* 2d ed. (New York: St. Martin's, 1978), pp. 19–47; and Duane Chapmen, *Energy Resources and Energy Corporations* (Ithaca, N.Y.: Cornell University Press, 1983), pp. 183–199.

4. James L. Sundquist, "Needed: A Political Theory for the New Era of Coalition Government in the United States," *Political Science Quarterly,* 103 (Winter 1988–89), pp. 633–634.

5. John W. Kingdon, *Agendas, Alternatives, and Public Policies* (Boston: Little, Brown, 1984).

6. In the 1968 presidential election, for example, many voters were prepared to vote on the Vietnam War issue; however, issue voting was precluded by the ambiguous stances adopted by the major party candidates, Richard Nixon and Vice President Humphrey. See Benjamin Page and Richard Brody, "Policy Voting and the Electoral Process: The Vietnam War Issue," *American Political Science Review,* 66 (September 1972), pp. 979–995. For an excellent example of an election in which the voters largely ignored the central issue differentiating the two major party candidates, see Leon D. Epstein, "Electoral Decision and Policy Mandate: An Empirical Example," *Public Opinion Quarterly,* 28 (Winter 1964), pp. 564–572.

7. Shover, et al., p. 122. This book is an attempt to test various conventional and neo-Marxist theories of economic regulation through a book-length study of the passage and implementation of the surface mining law. In the previous chapter, I made no attempt to introduce the reader to most of these theories. It should, therefore, be made clear that the authors employ some standard neo-Marxist terms in the quotation just cited. State managers are, essentially, elected officials and administrators with some responsibility for managing the economy and meeting certain requirements for the survival of capitalism. Local state managers are officials of various state governments. Federal-level state managers would include officials within OSM and the Interior Department, presidents Carter and Reagan, legislators, etc. *Capital* refers to business as a class, or in this quotation, the coal coalition.

8. Although probably less common, socialization of conflict can also occur at this stage of the policy process. The best example here, discussed in earlier chapters, is the case of nuclear power. Long dominated by a policy subsystem consisting of the reactor industry, the Atomic Energy Commission, and the congressional Joint Committee on Atomic Energy, a nuclear power policy-making has become much more pluralistic over the past ten to fifteen years. A variety of new environmental and antinuclear interests have penetrated the system, and Congress has dismantled both the Atomic Energy Commission and the Joint Committee on Atomic Energy. The end result is an "issue network" in which a much greater range of views is routinely represented, and that shows no signs of reprivatization for the foreseeable future.

PART II
Understanding Policy Change

CHAPTER 9

Rationality and Nonincremental Policy

We turn our attention in the remainder of this book to the prospects for nonincremental change within the American political system. This chapter will begin that analysis by re-examining Lindblom's analysis of the conditions giving rise to major policy changes. An alternative typology advanced here will expand upon Lindblom's original formulation in several respects, making clearer the circumstances under which rationalizing break-throughs are possible and pointing to some realms of decision making not identified by Lindblom.

TWO CASES OF NONINCREMENTAL CHANGE

Two instances of seemingly nonincremental policy-making have been subjected to de-tailed analysis by political scientists explicitly concerned with identifying the precon-ditions for major policy change. The first, which is fully compatible with Lindblom's theory, occurred during congressional consideration of the air pollution issue in 1970. As documented by Charles O. Jones, previous policy-making on the issue had conformed al-most perfectly to the incremental model, nibbling away at the problem and gradually ex-panding the scope of federal authority. In 1970, however, a dramatic increase in public awareness of the pollution problem, along with the rise of the environmental movement, forced policy makers to respond more boldly, resulting in a significant expansion of fed-eral regulatory authority, specific and technology-forcing air quality standards for several pollutants, and the creation of new line and staff institutions to deal with the problem. Jones characterized these outcomes as falling somewhere within Lindblom's quadrant D (large change/low understanding), thus shedding new light on how policies in that cell might arise.[1]

A second case, the lunar landing program, poses serious problems for Lindblom's theory, suggesting that the rational ideal may be operative even where dramatic departures from existing policy are envisioned. According to Paul R. Schulman, the commitment in 1961 to put a man on the moon clearly represented a nonincremental departure from previous policies.[2] The nature of the project dictated that decision makers could not let diminishing returns dictate resource commitments. As NASA administrator James E. Webb observed: "We could not stop with doing 80 or 90 or 99 per cent of what we needed to do and come out reasonably well . . . a partial success was likely to be a complete failure."[3]

At the same time, decision making approximated the rational ideal. While the problem was not entirely understood at the outset, research and testing were undertaken to gradually expand the available knowledge base. Spending on space exploration rose sharply, with more than 80 percent of NASA's initial outlays going into research and development. Contrary to Lindblom's theory, achieving an adequate knowledge base would have been impossible in this project without an attempt at nonincremental change. Large amounts of land and equipment had to be acquired. Interdisciplinary research teams had to be assembled, and extensive and time-consuming tests were necessary to prevent equipment malfunctions. The best available scientific and engineering talent was attracted both by the challenge inherent in the problem itself and by the very magnitude of the undertaking. By contrast, when NASA later came under political attack after the series of moon shots had been successfully completed, organizational decline set in rapidly. Cutbacks in staff and funding undermined organizational morale, and the best minds began to move on to more exciting challenges elsewhere.[4]

A REFORMULATION OF LINDBLOM'S TYPOLOGY

Lindblom characterized policy proposals as falling along two continuous dimensions. (See Figure 2.1 in Chapter 2.) The degree of proposed change from previous policies (ranging from incremental to nonincremental) was seen as dependent on the extent to which policy makers possess adequate understanding of the problem they confront. Lindblom believed departures from normal incrementalism will occur only under very special circumstances (e.g., within the realm of "wars, revolutions, and grand opportunities"). In his view, the rational-comprehensive method of decision making will be confined to technical problems of administration, which are relatively small and manageable. Large policy changes are never characterized by rational decision making inasmuch as "the information and comprehension requirements of synoptic problem-solving simply cannot be met for large-scale social change."[5]

Throughout Lindblom's various works on incrementalism, however, the need for agreement on objectives and value trade-offs is given equal weight as a precondition for rational decision making. It is the breakdown of both these conditions under normal conditions that makes the incremental model both normatively and descriptively superior to the rational ideal in his view. When the need for consensus on objectives is incorporated into Lindblom's typology, we begin to get a clearer picture of the circumstances under which large change may occur. In particular, we will see that rational policy-making is possible for a wider range of decisions than Lindblom would predict, including at least some instances of nonincremental change. The typology that follows also points to the existence of two important categories of decision making that Lindblom failed to recognize in his original formulation, even as it specifies more precisely the conditions making for disjointed incrementalism under normal circumstances.

Consensual Knowledge

The first dimension, measuring the extent to which decision makers understand the problem at hand, will be little changed from Lindblom's typology. Ordinarily, according to Lindblom, problems are complex, giving rise to a variety of alternative interpretations and severely taxing inherently limited human cognitive capacities. Information costs inevitably limit the analysis of options. Important consequences are all too often unknown, as a complete understanding of cause-and-effect relationships would require comprehensive theories that are "greedy for facts" and "constructed only through a great collection of observations."[6]

At the other end of this continuum, where problems are well understood, there will be agreement, at least among specialists in the area, regarding the relevant variables for analysis, the nature of important interrelationships among these variables, and the most appropriate questions for further research. In short, there is a common language and agreement on fundamentals as to how the world works. This is what Thomas Kuhn has termed a "paradigm."[7]

The history of scientific revolutions, as described by Kuhn, suggests caution in imputing a high degree of objective understanding of most problems. As noted in Chapter 1, all models of reality are inherently tentative and subject to replacement whenever they fail to explain observed events. It is worthwhile, however, to distinguish between subjects characterized by substantial agreement on how the world works and on basic facts regarding the problem at hand and those problems lacking such a paradigm. Robert Rothstein has termed such agreement on a common paradigm for understanding events "consensual knowledge:"

> . . . a body of belief about cause-effect and ends-means relationships among variables (activities, aspirations, values, demands) that is widely accepted by the relevant actors, irrespective of the absolute or final "truth" of these beliefs.[8]

It is critically important to understand how consensual knowledge is transmitted throughout the political system. For this purpose, following Rothstein, we can conceive of the political system as consisting of a series of concentric circles. (See Figure 9.1.) The innermost circle would consist of academic or technical experts possessing "narrow but deep knowledge and almost no political power."[9] Agreement on basic facts and important cause-and-effect relationships may not exist even at this level, as for example with the disagreement among scientists as to the feasibility and safety of increased reliance on nuclear power or on the prospects for breeder reactors or hydrogen fusion. However, when a genuine consensus develops, as was the case among economists on the issue of transportation regulation in the 1960s and 1970s, it can facilitate major policy change.[10]

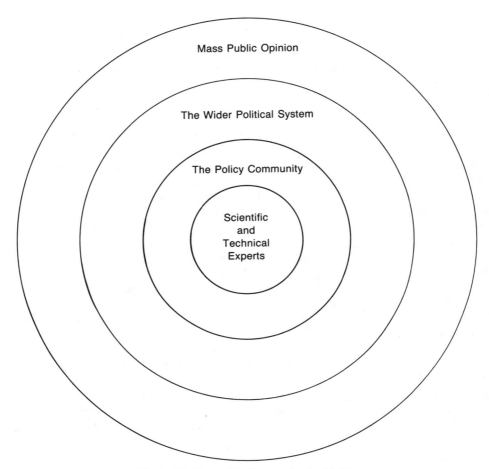

Figure 9.1 Concentric Circles of Policy-Making

The second circle would be composed of the "attentive public" with a specialized and ongoing stake in the problem area: government agencies with jurisdiction over the issue, members of legislative committees with oversight responsibility, affected interest groups, and so on. Such "policy communities," to borrow John Kingdon's term,[11] may either take the form of distributive policy subsystems or more pluralistic and conflictual issue networks, as described in Chapter 4. While agreement on basic facts is much more likely within distributive policy subsystems, Kingdon's analysis strongly suggests that the development of consensual knowledge within an issue network can be a catalyst for legislative action.[12]

A third circle, larger still, would consist of the wider political system: the president, the full House and Senate, the congressional party leadership groups, executive agencies and congressional committees normally unconcerned with the issue, and so on. While the policy community normally retains the primary responsibility for developing solutions to problems, policy makers within the second circle remain dependent upon this third circle for ratification or amendment of their decisions.

The outermost circle would consist of mass public opinion. For most issues, mass public attention is limited and supported by low levels of information. While mass public opinion may at times set distinct boundaries within which policy makers must operate, there is usually a great deal of latitude within these constraints as to what specific policies should be pursued. In the case of the Clean Air Amendments of 1970, for example, public opinion was unusually restrictive in demanding some form of stronger regulation of air pollution. Although mass public opinion was unusually aroused and directive on this issue, it did not force policy makers to pursue a specific solution to the pollution problem.

Consensual knowledge will tend to move outward from the inner circles, although the transmission of such a consensus from the innermost circle (academic or technical experts) to the policy community is by no means automatic.[13] The diffusion of consensual knowledge is unlikely to occur in the opposite direction, as the involvement of mass public opinon will seldom, if ever, be triggered by changes in the technical knowledge base. Thus consensual knowledge within the two innermost circles may be sufficient to permit action, at least where disagreements over problem definition or objectives have not socialized conflict to the outer circles.

Consensual Objectives

The second dimension centers around the degree of agreement on objectives among participants in the decision process. As noted in Chapter 2, rational decision making cannot function without consensus on objectives; where there is no agreement on ends, means-ends analysis breaks down. According to Lindblom, this requirement is almost never met, and this condition may indeed be even more difficult to satisfy than the need for consensual knowledge insofar as almost all values come into conflict with other important values at some point, forcing policy makers to make trade-offs. If nothing else, budget considerations will arise sooner or later, as all public expenditures have opportunity costs. At the same time, however, the lunar landing case suggests strongly that agreement on goals can occur, at least in the short run, and that such agreement on objectives can permit rational action and even nonincremental change where public support is stable enough to permit the development of an adequate knowledge base.

Here again, the question of diffusion arises, and the same set of concentric circles can be employed to aid our analysis. If consensual knowledge tends to be transmitted from the inside out, as suggested above, political accountability clearly operates from the outside in. While legislators need reliable information on the consequences of alternative policies, which draws them to the inner circle of technical experts, as elected officials they are ultimately accountable to voters and draw political support from organized interests. If forced to make a choice, most legislators will respond to discontent in the outermost circle, which can threaten their survival, before they will respond to a consensus among experts, which may in any case be too complex to explain to the voters back home.

Thus the diffusion of consensual objectives (or, at the other extreme, the socialization of conflict over objectives) can occur in either direction. Where an issue lacks salience, or where potential opponents fail to mobilize, consensus on objectives may be unnecessary beyond the two innermost circles. The formulation of policy proposals will be left to a distributive policy subsystem, with the wider political system becoming involved chiefly to ratify proposals emanating from congressional committees. Where the policy community consists of a more pluralistic "issue network," as identified by Heclo, consensus on objectives will be more problematic.[14] Within such an issue network, the development of consensual objectives (and thus shared criteria for evaluating policy proposals) marks the achievement of what Kingdon termed an "integrated" policy community, thus facilitating the development in turn of consensual knowledge.[15]

By contrast, where an aroused mass public demands strong action to solve a problem (like air pollution) a strong consensus on objectives can be communicated quite rapidly from the outside in as well. Similarly, where the public loses confidence in a policy subsystem due to dramatic or highly publicized performance failures, no amount of consensus within the inner circles can prevent the intrusion of the wider political system. The decline of nuclear power in recent years provides a good illustration here, as increasing concerns over reactor safety and excessive secrecy led Congress to abolish the Atomic Energy Commission in 1974 and the Joint Committee on Atomic Energy in 1977. The AEC's responsibilities were given to two new agencies, the Nuclear Regulatory Commission and the Energy Research and Development Administration. The Joint Committee's oversight responsibilities were parcelled out to eight different standing committees in the House and Senate.[16] With the mobilization of various interest groups in opposition to nuclear power and the collapse of public confidence in the wake of nuclear accidents at Three Mile Island and Chernobyl, the breakdown of the once autonomous nuclear subsystem would seem to be irreversible.

POLICY-MAKING IN THE FOUR QUADRANTS

Combining these two continua produces a revised typology of decision-making conditions, as shown in Figure 9.2. Following Lindblom, I will treat these two dimensions as continuous rather than dichotomous. It is thus misleading to speak of a single policy process for each quadrant, as if all issues falling within a given quadrant possessed identical characteristics. It is nevertheless instructive to consider the pure, or polar, cases within each quadrant as ideal types.

It should also be understood at the outset that initial placement of a particular issue into one of the four quadrants in no way precludes its movement into one of the other quadrants over time. The categorization of issues is properly determined by their placement on the two underlying dimensions. Thus issues will move whenever change occurs along one or both dimensions: for example, whenever agreement on values or the available knowledge base is affected by events.

Quadrant A is clearly the realm of *rational decision making*, combining as it does

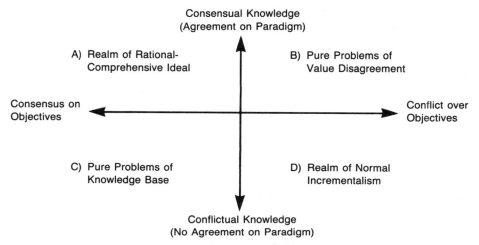

Figure 9.2 Lindblom's Typology Reformulated

agreement on values with consensual knowledge regarding basic facts and cause-and-effect relationships. As Lindblom suggested, relatively small, technical problems may fall here. However, policies involving significant policy change may also occur here, as with the program to put a man on the moon. Large change will not always be value maximizing, but it is at least possible in this cell.

According to Lindblom, a strict application of the rational method would require a comprehensive examination of all alternative definitions of the problem as well as all alternative value mixes (or "social welfare functions"). The extraordinary demands for time and information imposed by such an exhaustive analysis preclude a realiance on the rational method in its pure form.[17] In this sense, then, Lindblom is certainly correct in saying that decision making is almost never rational.

However, for our purposes, agreement on values in no way requires policy makers to systematically examine alternative value mixes or definitions of the problem. Thus, as Lindblom and Miliband suggest, apparent agreement on objectives may merely reflect an incapacity to conceive of alternatives to the prevailing social or economic order. To say that policy-making is "rational" in quadrant A is merely to say that agreement on ends is combined with consensual knowledge on cause-and-effect relationships. Just as consensual knowledge does not presume an objectively comprehensive and accurate understanding of the problem, agreement on values does not necessarily imply that the agreed upon objectives are necessarily the best available, or that *any* alternative goals have even been considered. Such a consensus is important for our purposes, whether or not alternative values or definitions of the problem have been explored. It is worth distinguishing between policies that result from an equilibrium process (as most no doubt do) and those that emerge from a conscious process of analysis and decision, however constrained and incomplete.

Moreover, as we saw in Chapter 4, agreement on objectives can be a function of a restricted circle of decision makers. Whenever the configuration of demand is consensual, either through the failure of some affected groups to mobilize or through successful efforts to privatize conflict, a form of rational policy-making can result. Value-maximizing policies (albeit operating at the expense of unrepresented interests) are made possible to the extent that the active groups share common objectives.

Quadrant D is just as clearly the realm of *normal incrementalism*. As Lindblom observed, problems are typically complex and poorly understood. Conflict over important values or trade-offs among values necessitates majority-building through a process of partisan mutual adjustment. In the language of the group struggle model, there is no agreement on any clearly defined conception of the public interest; rather, politics must necessarily involve a clash of interests. Outcomes in this quadrant are typically incremental. While nonincremental options may well receive consideration, contrary to Lindblom's theory, the necessity for compromise typically produces incremental outcomes. This is reinforced in the American system by the need to build a series of concurrent majorities at different decision points.

The energy issue, which occupied so much time from 1973 to 1979, provides an almost classic example here. As noted in Chapter 2, the issue was forced on the agenda by the Arab oil embargo of 1973 and stayed there, off and on, for the next seven years. Progress in developing a national energy policy was limited at best, and many of the programs enacted during that period to encourage the development of alternative sources of energy were discontinued under the Reagan administration, leaving the United States arguably more vulnerable to a new oil shock in 1990, when Iraq invaded Kuwait, than we were in 1973.

While there is no question that both our constitutional system and the privileged position of the major oil companies and other corporate interests played a role in preventing a more satisfactory response to the energy crisis, the really debilitating problem here was the breakdown of the underlying conditions necessary for rational policy-making. There was never any agreement, either among policy makers or the general public, on the proper definition of the problem or even on whether the ''crisis'' was real or contrived (whether by the Arabs or the major oil companies). Nor was there any consensus on the proper trade-offs among conflicting values, in particular regarding the environmental consequences of various alternatives to imported oil. This lack of agreement was reinforced by a clear absence of consensual knowledge on almost all points, even within the innermost circle of technical and scientific experts: how much domestic oil remained to be discovered, whether or not that oil could be extracted without significant damage to the environment, whether or not nuclear power could be operated in a ''safe'' manner, whether nuclear wastes could be disposed of (or even transported) without appreciable damage to the environment or the public health, whether a continued reliance on coal contributed to acid rain and/or a gradual global warming, and so on. At no time were policy makers ever able to agree upon an alternative source of energy, or even a mix of sources, adequate to replace our reliance on petroleum when existing supplies run out. In short, the rational-comprehensive ideal broke down on all points.

Quadrant C consists of what might be termed *pure problems of knowledge base*. Here, substantial consensus on values exists, and complete agreement as to a desired course of action is precluded only by an inadequate understanding of the problem. Within this quadrant, policy-making can be characterized as purposeful, although of necessity not fully rational; in other words, policy makers will be goal seeking, but subject to incomplete or misleading information. Cybernetic models of decision making would seem to apply best to cases in this quadrant. Such models emphasize the capacity for systems with stable goals to monitor information from the environment and thus adapt to changing circumstances through an ongoing process of feedback and adjustment. Under such circumstances, "it might be profitable to look upon government somewhat less as a problem of power and somewhat more as a problem of steering."[18]

The management of fiscal policy provides a good illustration here, as this policy area is noteworthy for both the clarity and stability of its policy objectives. Policy makers of all parties and ideological persuasion accept the twin goals of full employment and price stability. Inability to attain both these goals creates some ground for disagreement, forcing policy makers to emphasize one desired good over another. However, the two objectives are not generally perceived as being in fundamental conflict; rather, the operative constraint is thought to be a limited knowledge base in the face of complex and rapidly changing circumstances that prevents their simultaneous attainment.[19]

The Clean Air case of 1970 provides a very different kind of example in this cell, inasmuch as the consensus on values that gave rise to this technology-forcing legislation was extremely superficial and temporary. With the inevitable decline in public attention to the issue (and the onset of the energy crisis), pollution politics settled back into a pattern of normal incrementalism in the mid-1970s, albeit one characterized by a much more balanced group struggle than before.[20] In effect, air pollution was always a classically incremental issue in Lindblom's terms, characterized by conflicts over problem definition and value trade-offs as well as by a lack of consensual knowledge. Unique circumstances in 1970 combined to create a situation of high salience and apparent consensus that could not persist in the long term.

By contrast, quadrant B consists of what might be termed *pure problems of value disagreement*. Here problems are well understood, either because they are relatively straightforward or because the participants have acquired long experience with the issues through repeated policy cycles. To the extent that the issues are clearly understood by all involved, conflict can be particularly intense within this cell. Where problems are poorly understood, as in the realm of normal incrementalism, conflict will often be tempered by what Bauer, Pool, and Dexter termed "complexity of self-interest."[21] Under such circumstances, problems are subject to alternative definitions and, what is more important, the consequences of various policies for affected groups cannot be known with certainty. This complexity of self-interest is what gave legislators such surprising latitude in the tariff case studied by Bauer, et al. Most constituents were not following the issue at all, and organized groups with a greater stake in the issue were vulnerable to obfuscation through vague statutes granting ambiguous delegations of discretion to administrators.

By contrast, within the realm of pure value disagreement, constituents with a stake in the issue can more easily understand and remember what they see. Lowi's category of "redistributive" issues will tend to fit here, as potential winners and losers from proposed policies are acutely aware of their stake in alternative outcomes.[22] An excellent example of such an issue is provided by recent efforts to reform Social Security financing. Social Security is a vexing issue for policy makers precisely because the underlying problem is so well understood, and because any solution to it must have almost immediate redistributive consequences.

This issue is often portrayed as being more technical than it really is. For example, reform efforts in 1978 failed to provide a long-term solution due to alleged errors in estimating trends in the number of eligible recipients and the likely rate of inflation in subsequent years. However tenuous the art of forecasting in such matters (and the difficulties involved are very real), it is more likely that policy makers recognized that these estimates were unrealistic at the time they were made. Any serious attempt to reform Social Security must impose hardships on some politically aware groups; it is essentially an issue of whose ox will be gored. Politicians are understandably reluctant to impose costs that will be readily perceived by the groups involved. Fudging the anticipated rate of inflation downward made for a lower estimate of cost-of-living adjustments. Similarly, understating the number of future beneficiaries would reduce the apparent need for payroll tax increases, benefit reductions, cost-of-living formula adjustments, or increases in the retirement age. If such a reform package failed to guarantee long-term solvency, another administration could decide how to deal with the next crisis.[23]

The contemporary abortion issue provides a similar problem for policy makers. While scientists remain unable to say precisely when life begins, a great deal is in fact known about the evolution of the fetus from conception to birth. The intense conflicts aroused by this issue are rooted in fundamental conflicts over values: at what point does a fetus become a life, and what protections (if any) is it entitled to prior to that point? Such conflicts will not likely be resolved by new additions to the available scientific knowledge base.

NONINCREMENTAL CHANGE AND THE FOUR QUADRANTS

Lindblom saw few prospects for intelligent decision making whenever the policies under consideration involved large change. Where problems are poorly understood, which is usually the case in his view, even small changes will be better pursued through the strategy of incrementalism outlined in Chapter 2: remediality, adjustment of objectives to policies, partisan mutual adjustment, seriality, and so on. Large policy changes are poorly understood almost by definition, and they will occur, if at all, through a process of revolutionary change or crisis decision making that can hardly be characterized as rational.

The analysis advanced here suggests somewhat different conclusions, while at the same time pointing to two classes of problems not addressed by Lindblom. Where problems are poorly understood and substantial disagreement over values prevails, the rational-comprehensive ideal is undermined on all points. Some form of group struggle is virtually inevitable, and the prospects for significant departures from existing policies are understandably bleak. Much of the time, these conditions do in fact apply, making incrementalism a valuable descriptive model.

However, conflict over objectives and a lack of consensual knowledge are not necessarily characteristic of the policy process, nor do these two pathologies necessarily have to occur together. Where agreement on values is combined with an adequate knowledge base, the conditions for the rational ideal are met, and nonincremental change is possible. Thus, the rational model need not be limited to technical problems, as Lindblom suggests. The lunar landing program demonstrates that where public support is sufficiently broad and relatively stable, efforts to effect large change can overcome initial threshold problems and sustain ample levels of funding and personnel over long periods.

Large changes are clearly problematic where agreement on values is combined with an inadequate knowledge base. Initial commitments to large policy change are likely to go unfulfilled in the long run unless expansions in the available knowledge base follow in due course, permitting the development of consensual knowledge and a genuine consensus on objectives. In the clean air case, for example, the tenuous consensus on values that developed between 1967 and 1970 was not matched by any corresponding increase in the scientific knowledge base available to policy makers. As Jones observed:

> Given existing technology, organization, and resources in federal air pollution control, the bold new authority in the Clean Air Amendments of 1970 had to be based in large measure on *speculation* that capabilities would improve to meet the demands of the law.[24]

This decision to "legislate beyond capability" would later cause great problems in policy implementation. Obtaining even partial compliance with federal directives is problematic at best under normal circumstances, as discussed in Chapter 3. National administrators are outside actors intervening in ongoing state and local political systems. The tools available for influencing the local policy environment, particularly the threat of withholding federal funds, are blunt instruments of dubious credibility. Inevitably, a process of negotiation takes place between different levels of government, in which the statute serves as a baseline that all involved recognize as being flexible.[25]

Charged with implementing an unusually specific and stringent statute, and lacking the knowledge base necessary to develop regulations eliciting broad public support, administrators in the clean air case soon found themselves armed only with a law widely understood to be unrealistic and unenforceable. In time, the inevitable "issue attention cycle" produced a decline in the salience of the issue to the mass public and a resurgence of value disagreement among organized groups active on the issue. Industries sought relief at state and local levels, where their strategic position in maximized. The onset of the "energy crisis" in the mid-seventies brought an abrupt end to what was to have been "the environmental decade." As a result, the ultimate outcome, both nationwide and in Pittsburgh, which Jones examined in depth, was an incremental improvement at best in air quality.[26]

Large policy changes are likewise problematic for pure problems of value disagreement. Here, progress is not dependent upon an expansion of the available knowledge base. The problem under consideration is well understood, and complexity of self-interest does not plague the constituencies involved in the issue. Policy makers have correspondingly little room for maneuver, as obfuscation is rendered almost impossible. In 1982, for example, almost no policy makers wanted to deal with the Social Security issue. It was placed on the agenda by an action-forcing crisis: the imminent bankruptcy of the Social Security trust fund. In view of the political awareness of the groups directly affected, nonincremental change was out of the question, and even incremental change—in this case, a complicated mix of tax increases and benefit reductions that left the basic structure of the system unchanged—was so difficult as to necessitate the creation of a bipartisan, blue ribbon panel to reach some kind of agreement on how to deal with the issue.[27]

Nonincremental policy change will tend to occur for such quintessential "whose ox is gored" issues only where there is a dramatic shift in the balance of forces, giving rise to a substantial change in the group equilibrium. Such alterations in the group equilibrium will be extremely rare and subject in turn to subsequent shifts in the balance of forces. Deregulation of the airlines in 1978 (an instance of major decremental change) would appear to be just such a case. The major airlines clearly understood the threat to their interests posed by deregulation; none of the major carriers favored deregulation initially, and only United Airlines ever reversed its opposition to deregulation.[28] Contrary to existing theories of regulation, these organized interests in opposition to procompetitive reform were defeated by a coalition of actors acting on behalf of an ostensibly general interest in improved economic efficiency.[29]

This surprising result was made possible by a convergence of elite opinion behind the desirability of deregulation. Economists had long viewed airline regulation as shoring up an industry cartel. While a full account of the motives of various actors is beyond the scope of this chapter, suffice it to say that consensual knowledge within the innermost circle (economists engaged in research on regulation of public utilities) eventually gave rise to a convergence of opinion within the second and third circles (successive CAB chairmen, presidents Ford and Carter, senators Kennedy and Cannon, and so on), that effectively isolated the airlines and made deregulation possible. In effect, the issue had shifted from Quadrant B (pure problems of value agreement) to Quadrant A (rational decision making).[30]

To conclude, rational decision making is possible only where two certain very restrictive preconditions are met: agreement on objectives and a clear understanding of how to achieve them. Where these conditions are met, rational policy-making may well result in nonincremental policy departures. Where either of these conditions is lacking, however, rational decision making is precluded and the prospects for nonincremental change are severely limited. Where both conditions are unmet, incremental policy-making becomes virtually inescapable. Moreover, to the extent that incrementalism results from constraints on rational decision making, it may well be the best way to formulate policies, as Lindblom suggested. To move ahead without a firm consensus on objectives or to attempt large change where the knowledge base is inadequate is to risk the eventual collapse of public support. In either case, a return to normal incrementalism is likely over the long term.

NOTES

1. Charles O. Jones, "Speculative Augmentation in Federal Air Pollution Policy-Making," *Journal of Politics,* 36 (May 1974), pp. 438–464; and Jones, *Clean Air* (Pittsburgh: University of Pittsburgh Press, 1975).
2. Paul R. Schulman, "Nonincremental Policy Making: Notes Toward an Alternative Paradigm," *American Political Science Review,* 69 (December 1975), pp. 1354–1370. In the wake of the Sputnik launch by the Soviets in 1957, policy makers recognized an urgent need to upgrade existing scientific capabilities. An immediate, albeit indirect, response was the passage of the National Defense Education Act of 1958, the first major program of federal aid to education, fueled almost entirely by fears that the United States had fallen behind in the space race. However, the limited capacities and institutional rigidities of existing space agencies prevented any direct action to close this perceived gap for almost four years, until President Kennedy's call in May 1961 for a massive ten-year project to put a man on the moon.
3. Quoted in Schulman, p. 1362.
4. Schulman, pp. 1256–1357.
5. David Braybrooke and Charles E. Lindblom, *A Strategy of Decision* (New York: Free Press, 1963), pp. 78–79.
6. Charles E. Lindblom, "The Science of 'Muddling Through,' " *Public Administration Review,* 19 (Spring 1959), p. 87. On these points, Lindblom's argument finds further support in the writings of Herbert Simon and Anthony Downs on information costs and bounded rationality. See Herbert A. Simon, *Models of Man* (New York: Wiley, 1957); and Anthony Downs, *An Economic Theory of Democracy* (New York: Harper and Row, 1957). See also Jones, *Clean Air,* on the importance of an adequate knowledge base.
7. Thomas S. Kuhn, *The Structure of Scientific Revolutions,* 2d ed. (Chicago: University of Chicago Press, 1970).
8. Robert L. Rothstein, "Consensual Knowledge and International Collaboration: Some Lessons from the Commodity Negotiations," *International Organization,* 38 (1984), p. 736. Rothstein takes this definition without change from Ernst Haas's guidelines for a panel at the APSA meetings in Chicago, Illinois, in September 1983.
9. Rothstein, p. 736. For a concentric circle model of foreign policy-making, see Roger Hilsman, *To Move a Nation* (New York: Delta Books, 1967).
10. Martha Derthick and Paul J. Quirk, *The Politics of Regulation* (Washington, D.C.: Brookings Institution, 1985).
11. John W. Kingdon, *Agendas, Alternatives, and Public Policies* (Boston: Little, Brown, 1984), pp. 123 ff. The term *attentive public* is taken from Gabriel Almond's classic work, *the American People and Foreign Policy* (New York: Praeger, 1965).
12. Kingdon (pp. 146–151) refers to this phenomenon as "tipping"—e.g., the development of a consensus within the policy community around a single solution to a problem.
13. For example, the economic case for airline deregulation was made more compelling to the

extent that it pointed to a problem (a regulated cartel contributing to inflation and allocative inefficiency) with a relatively clear and simple solution (deregulation) that could be readily implemented and easily understood by all involved. See Derthick and Quirk, pp. 246–252.

14. Hugh Heclo, "Issue Networks and the Executive Establishment," in Anthony King (ed.), *The New American Political System* (Washington, D.C.: American Enterprise Institute, 1978), pp. 87–124.

15. See Kingdon, pp. 123–128 and 140–145. Within the social welfare policy community, for example, policy analysts of various disciplines and ideologies would all employ the criteria of horizontal and vertical equity (among others) to evaluate alternative proposals for welfare reform.

16. Walter A. Rosenbaum, *Energy, Politics, and Public Policy*, 2d ed. (Washington, D.C.: Congressional Quarterly Press, 1987), p. 143.

17. Braybrooke and Lindblom, pp. 6–23.

18. See Karl W. Deutsch, *The Nerves of Government* (New York: Free Press, 1966), p. xxvii. See also John D. Steinbruner, *The Cybernetic Theory of Decision* (Princeton, N.J.: Princeton University Press, 1974).

19. Fiscal policy provides a particularly interesting case of inadequate knowledge inasmuch as macroeconomic theory is characterized by a variety of competing schools of thought: Keynesians, post-Keynesians, monetarists, rational expectations theorists, supply-siders, and so on. These alternative schools would all qualify as paradigms, in Kuhn's terms. Each has its own vocabulary, emphasizes a different set of variables, and thus points to very different "puzzles" to be solved, thus serving as a reminder that the lack of consensual knowledge within a given problem area is not necessarily a function of primitive or "preparadigmatic" analysis. This clash of rival paradigms within macroeconomic theory does not carry over into microeconomic theory, however. At the micro level, economic theory is characterized by consensus on a common paradigm—a body of theory widely perceived to be perhaps the most elegant and powerful in the social sciences.

20. On air pollution policy-making after 1970, see Richard H. K. Vietor, *Environmental Politics and the Coal Coalition* (College Station: Texas A&M University Press, 1980), pp. 194–226; R. Shep Melnick, *Regulation and the Courts* (Washington, D.C.: Brookings Institution, 1983); and Norman J. Vig and Michael E. Kraft (eds.), *Environmental Policy in the 1980s* (Washington, D.C.: Congressional Quarterly Press, 1984).

21. Raymond A. Bauer, Ithiel de Sola Pool, and Lewis Anthony Dexter, *American Business and Public Policy*, 2d ed. (Chicago: Aldine-Atherton, 1972). On the use of legislative delegation by legislators to obfuscate issues, see Michael T. Hayes, "The Semi-Sovereign Pressure Groups: A Critique of Current Theory and an Alternative Typology," *Journal of Politics*, 40 (February 1978), pp. 134–161.

22. Theodore J. Lowi, "American Business, Public Policy, Case Studies, and Political Theory," *World Politics*, 16 (July 1964), pp. 677–715.

23. On the difficulties facing policy makers in formulating the 1978 reforms, see Joseph A. Califano, Jr., *Governing America* (New York: Simon and Schuster, 1981), pp. 368–401.

24. Jones, "Speculative Augmentation," pp. 449 and 458–459.

25. Martha Derthick, *The Influence of Federal Grants* (Cambridge, Mass.: Harvard University Press, 1970).

26. On the issue attention cycle, see Anthony Downs, "Up and Down with Ecology—the Issue Attention Cycle," *The Public Interest*, 28 (Summer 1972), pp. 38–50. On implementing the Clean Air Amendments of 1970, see Jones, *Clean Air*, pp. 211–292.

27. See Paul Light, *Artful Work* (New York: Random House, 1985).

28. Derthick and Quirk, pp. 20–27.
29. On the difficulties in securing deregulation, see especially Roger G. Noll and Bruce M. Owen, *The Political Economy of Deregulation* (Washington, D.C.: American Enterprise Institute, 1983).
30. Equally important, the extremely broad grant of legislative authority under which the CAB operated permitted proreform chairmen (like Alfred Kahn) to substantially deregulate the industry without enacting formal legislation. Procompetitive actions by the agency in 1977 created a situation of considerable fluidity and uncertainty for the airlines in which the passage of some legislation—even legislation establishing full deregulation—was seen as preferable to continued uncertainty. See Derthick and Quirk, p. 245.

CHAPTER 10

When Is Policy Change Nonincremental?

In the previous chapter we saw that nonincremental change is unlikely to occur or to endure where the conditions for rational decision making are not met. This chapter will take that analysis one step further, differentiating between familiar and unfamiliar issues and arguing that the conditions for rational decision making may in fact emerge over time as policy makers gain valuable experience with policies.

DEFINING NONINCREMENTAL CHANGE

Before we can undertake that analysis, we must first come to grips with a hard question we have avoided up to now: when does a policy change properly qualify as nonincremental? If nonincremental changes are "major" changes in policy, when is a policy change properly classified as major?

We saw in Chapter 2 that Lindblom treated this distinction as a continuous rather than a dichotomous variable. Nonincremental change was merely one of the two endpoints on a continuum, with no clear threshhold point at which policy change properly became characterized as nonincremental. Beyond this, we saw in Chapter 5 that Lindblom has in recent years equated nonincremental policy change with systemic transformation. In particular, Lindblom (along with Ralph Miliband) would characterize as incremental any policy changes that fail to pose a fundamental challenge to capitalism as a form of economic organization.

Significant problems of classification arise, however, when all policy outcomes falling short of systemic transformation are lumped together under the single heading of incremental policy change. By this definition, a great many initiatives that most people would characterize as "large" or "significant"—the 1964 Civil Rights Act, Medicare, the 1986 Tax Reform Act, or airline deregulation, for example—would constitute, at best, "large increments" in Lindblom's terms.[1] To the extent that different observers have different values, and thus different policy priorities, comparative judgments as to the larger social or economic significance of various policy changes are bound to be highly subjective at best. What appears to be a major change to one observer may be classified as incremental by another. Even if we accept Lindblom's definition, we are still left with the task of explaining why the policy process sometimes gives rise to outcomes that are properly characterized as large increments rather than small ones.

A more promising foundation for a definition of nonincremental change is Lawrence D. Brown's distinction between "breakthrough" and "rationalizing" policies. A breakthrough policy, according to Brown, is essentially an effort to get government involved in a new activity. These are termed "breakthrough" policies because it is typically so difficult to win majority support for new federal activities within the American political system. Such issues generate intense conflict, both between political parties and across major social interests, resulting in a pattern of deadlock that can persist for years. A breakthrough thus typically requires a major change in public attitudes toward governmental action, usually stemming from a depression or war and expressed by means of election results.[2] Medicare, which took the better part of two decades of struggle to enact, would constitute one obvious example. The Civil Rights Act of 1964 would be another.[3]

However, to the extent that problems are poorly understood or prove less tractable than first thought, new programs produce new problems as well as new accomplishments. Rationalizing policies are thus attempts made by government "to solve evident problems of existing government programs."[4] The negative income tax constituted a classic example of a rationalizing policy, inasmuch as it promised to reform a welfare system of overlapping and uncoordinated benefits in such a way as to stop punishing work. With the major expansions in the scope and scale of government in the New Deal and again in the 1960s and 1970s, policy-making at the national level consists more and more of rationalizing politics and less and less of breakthrough politics.[5]

We cannot simply equate breakthrough policies with nonincremental change, however.[6] As the case of strip mining regulation in the previous chapter clearly demonstrates, breakthrough policies are subject to the normal erosion of policy proposals as they move through the legislative process, as outlined in the first seven chapters of this volume. Proposals for nonincremental policy change usually emerge from Congress with inadequate budgetary and staff resources and ambiguous and incomplete statutory mandates.

A TYPOLOGY OF POLICY CHANGE

John Kingdon has drawn an important distinction between what he terms the *agenda* and the *alternatives*. The agenda consists of the set of public problems receiving serious attention from policy makers at any given time. The alternatives, by contrast, consist of the short list of possible *solutions* receiving attention from policy makers at any given point in time.[7] While my purposes are very different from Kingdon's, the typology of policy change outlined below builds on this important distinction.

The first dimension differentiates between policies establishing a new federal responsibility (and thus focusing on a new problem) and those building on a previously established federal role (familiar problems). This distinction is important for a variety of reasons. As we will see in a later section of this chapter, policy-making tends to take on very different patterns for familiar and unfamiliar problems. Familiar problems tend to be much better understood by policy makers and face a much easier path to the agenda than new problems, inasmuch as they tend to be "recurring items" that come up naturally when authorizing legislation expires.[8] Finally, and most important for our present purpose, new problems tend to give rise to "breakthrough policies," in Brown's terms, while old problems tend to produce "rationalizing policies."

The second dimension focuses on alternatives: in particular, whether policy makers have acquired a clear understanding of the problem and agree on a workable solution to it. At times, Congress adopts a clear-cut strategy for dealing with a problem that has become fairly well defined over time, as with the negative income tax approach to welfare reform. Kingdon terms this phenomenon "tipping" toward a solution; a precondition for the emergence of consensus around a single solution is the development of an integrated policy community, as discussed in the previous chapter.

More often, however, Congress responds to a pressing social or economic problem with a vague law consisting of little more than "a set of rhetorical goals which represent no more than estimates of what the public wants to hear, presumably in functional terms, as a test for defining the real limits of policy application."[9] As Murray Edelman has observed, such legislation is often symbolic, destined to reassure an aroused mass public that its interests are being protected.[10] Even where legislators genuinely want to address an urgent problem, they may lack the scientific, technological, or organizational knowledge base for solving it. Under such circumstances, statutes serve to establish a particular problem as an important federal priority and assign responsibility for deciding how to respond to it to one or more federal agencies. They say little or nothing about the means through which the problem is to be solved. As E. E. Schattschneider observed:

> Every statute is an experiment in learning. When Congress attempts to deal with a new problem it is likely to pass an act establishing an agency with vague powers to do something about it. The new agency makes an investigation, it issues some literature about its functions, invites comments by interested parties, assembles a library of information, tries to find some experts, tries to get people to do something about the problem, and eventually reports back to Congress recommending some revisions of its statute. Thereafter the problem is passed back and forth between Congress, the President, the agency, interested people, the public. It is debated, criticized, reviewed, investigations are made, the statute is revised, over and over again, sometimes for years before a policy is evolved.[11]

There would thus seem to be a worthwhile distinction between statutes that do little more than commit the federal government to deal with a problem (an approach Theodore J. Lowi has aptly termed "policy-without-law") and those going further to identify some specific means for dealing with the problem, even if those means turn out in the long run to be misguided.[12] This parallels the distinction drawn in the previous chapter between policy outcomes that represent the equilibrium of a group struggle and those that are the product of a more conscious process of analysis and decision, however constrained and incomplete.

Combining these two dimensions yields four distinct categories of policy change. As we shall see, this classification clarifies the meaning of the two polar categories of incremental and nonincremental change. At the same time, it points to the existence of two distinct forms of breakthrough policies that account for the bulk of the policy changes most observers would tend to classify as nonincremental. (See Table 10.1.)

As Lindblom would suggest, many (and probably most) public policies build on a previously established federal role and make changes by small increments. Policies falling within this cell, which Lindblom would thus characterize as normal incrementalism, also constitute a significant portion of what Brown would term "rationalizing policies," inasmuch as they deal, through trial and error and feedback, with problems arising out of government programs. Accordingly, I will term policies within this category *incremental rationalizing policies.* For example, the 1967 public welfare amendments left the basic structure of AFDC intact but sought to increase work incentives under the program by reducing the 100 percent marginal tax rate on earned income for AFDC recipients.[13]

By contrast, unambiguously nonincremental policies would involve both the creation of a new federal responsibility for dealing with a particular problem and the formulation of a coherent strategy for solving the problem. I will suggest below that very few policies fall within this cell, which I will term the realm of *nonincremental innovations.*

It is much more common for breakthrough policies to establish a new federal activity without really providing any specific solution to the problem. For example, while the Elementary and Secondary Education Act of 1965 created a major new federal role in education, it was by no means clear how federal involvement was supposed to improve the quality of education at the local level, beyond the injection of substantial new money into the system. Similarly, the open housing law passed in 1968 symbolically outlawed discrimination in the sale or rental of housing while withholding important enforcement powers and failing to assign clear responsibility for enforcement to any single agency.[14] Each of these statutes gave the federal government important new responsibilities, but ultimately failed to specify a concrete strategy for attaining federal objectives. I will term these policies *federal role breakthroughs* to distinguish them from a second kind of breakthrough policy to be discussed below.

The Clean Air Act of 1970 provides a particularly clear illustration of a federal role

TABLE 10.1. A TYPOLOGY OF POLICY CHANGE

	Policy Establishes a New Federal Role (Breakthrough Policy)	Policy Builds on Established Federal Role (Rationalizing Policy)
Inadequate Knowledge Base— Policy-Without-Law	Federal Role Breakthroughs	Incremental Rationalizing Policies
Consensual Knowledge— "Tipping" toward a single solution	Nonincremental Innovations	Rationalizing Breakthroughs

breakthrough. Federal involvement began tentatively with the Clean Air Act of 1963, which provided categorical grants to states and localities to encourage research on the effects of air pollution.[15] The federal role breakthrough took place in two parts. The Air Quality Act of 1967 required the secretary of Health, Education, and Welfare to designate a series of "air quality control regions" and issue "criteria" for ambient air quality sufficient to protect public health and welfare after studying variations in pollution problems in different atmospheric areas of the country. The states would retain the formal authority to set air quality standards subject to these federal "criteria."[16]

This mandate left the actual responsibility for standard setting ambiguous, creating in effect an "elaborate and time-consuming process . . . whereby the federal government would set and enforce standards *without appearing to do so.*"[17] [Emphasis in original.] When the federal government failed to meet its statutory deadline for establishing air quality control regions and setting air quality criteria, the states were understandably reluctant to set standards that might later be found in violation of the federal criteria. As a result, the three-year authorization period for the Air Quality Act expired in 1970 with no state having completed all the requirements for setting and enforcing air quality standards.[18]

By contrast, the 1970 act clearly placed standard-setting responsibility at the federal level. Between 1967 and 1970, public opinion polls registered a dramatic increase in public concern over pollution. At the same time, there was a veritable explosion in the number of mobilized environmental groups. Potential oponents were thrown off balance by the breadth and intensity of support for pollution control, finding it difficult to oppose stronger regulation without seeming to be in favor of air pollution. The result was a kind of bandwagon effect that Jones termed "policy escalation," in which elected officials sought to outdo one another in proposing strong provisions to deal with the problem. The Clean Air Act of 1970 not only gave the federal government the clear authority to set ambient air quality standards, but also set technology-forcing standards for several of the most serious sources, requiring, for example, a 90 percent reduction in various automobile emissions within five years when no known technology existed for achieving this objective.[19]

While the 1970 act clearly established a federal role in air pollution standard setting and enforcement, it did not go beyond the sweeping declaration of objectives to establish a workable strategy for achieving its goals. Rather, the states would be left responsible for formulating a strategy for attaining federal air quality goals. These state implementation plans (or SIPs, as they are commonly known) would be submitted to EPA for review and approval or rejection.

In fact, as Jones emphasizes, the statute was an instance of "legislating beyond capability." The dramatic expansion of federal authority was not a response to any increase in the scientific or administrative knowledge base (e.g., there was no tipping toward a solution, in Kingdon's terms) but rather represented an attempt to appease an aroused mass public through symbolic reassurances.[20] Serious research on the effects of emissions on public health had begun in response to the Clean Air Act of 1963, and much remained to be learned. The technology for reducing emissions was nonexistent or unproven in many instances. Equally important, no one knew how to set up a bureaucracy that would interact with industry and state and local governments to make progress toward attainment of the air quality standards. Elected officials put the best face on these inadequacies by characterizing the legislation as ''technology forcing,'' but in reality there was little the federal government could do to force the attainment of air quality goals. As noted in Chapter 3, threats to cut off federal funds are blunt instruments at best, and federal bureaucrats must typically bargain with state and local actors in implementing federal mandates. Variations in the magnitude of the problem from one place to another, as well as variations in the local political environment, force acceptance of a wide variety of levels of performance as being in compliance with the act. For all its grandiose declarations of technology-forcing objectives, the Clean Air Act of 1970 still faced all the normal problems of intergovernmental implementation.[21]

The final category consists of policies that significantly expand federal capacity for effective action in a policy area where a federal role has previously been established. I will term these policies *rationalizing breakthroughs.* Brown's analysis suggests that rationalizing policies may establish a new (and, we hope, more effective) way to attack an old problem. He lists a number of possibilities, including deregulation, alteration of incentive structures, reorganization, decentralization, or even disengagement from the policy area altogether. Thus, in contrast to the pattern for incremental rationalizing policies, a rationalizing breakthrough requires the emergence—from any of a wide variety of sources— of an apparent solution to a problem already plaguing the federal government in carrying out a previously established role.[22]

A particularly good example of such an innovation is provided by the creation of health maintenance organizations in an attempt to control escalating medical costs by introducing a degree of competition into a policy area characterized by a variety of serious market failures.[23] A subsequent effort at cost containment during the 1980s involved the federal adoption of DRG (diagnostic related groupings) billing for Medicare reimbursements.[24] Both of these would fall under Brown's general heading of altering incentive structures within a policy area.

The Voting Rights Act of 1965 provides another example of a rationalizing breakthrough. The federal role breakthrough here occurred in the earlier civil rights acts of 1957 and 1960, which allowed citizens alleging a deprivation of voting rights to bring civil actions against local officials and authorized the federal government to go to court on behalf of disenfranchised blacks.[25] At best, these litigative strategies were cumbersome and prone to delay. Moreover, initiation of a civil suit carried with it the real risk of economic or physical reprisals, with no guarantee that the district courts (inevitably consisting of white, Southern judges) would ultimately render a favorable verdict.[26]

The rationalizing breakthrough in 1965 circumvented the litigative strategy by triggering direct federal intervention to register minority voters in states where literacy tests were employed as a registration requirement and less than 50 percent of the voting age population voted in the previous election. While progress in increasing black registration rates had been negligible under the 1957 and 1960 acts, the mere threat of direct federal intervention in voter registration was sufficient to produce a dramatic expansion in the black electorate within most Southern states—a development that has profoundly altered the patterns of party competition in the South, as noted in Chapter 6.[27]

The Clean Air Amendments of 1977 illustrate a somewhat different kind of rationalizing breakthrough on the issue of prevention of significant deterioration in air quality

(PSD).[28] Both the 1967 Air Quality Act and the 1970 Clean Air Act included language explicitly committing the federal government not just to improve air quality in polluted areas but also to protect and enhance the quality of air in areas (like national parks and wilderness areas) currently in compliance with the government's air quality standards. In both cases, these provisions amounted to little more than verbal pledges with no real program or enforcement powers, and EPA attempts to strengthen these provisions were thwarted within the Nixon administration. In 1972, the Sierra Club brought suit in the federal district court in Washington, D.C., to force EPA to reject state implementation plans permitting clean air to deteriorate significantly. The court ruled in favor of the environmental group in a landmark case, *Sierra Club v. Ruckleshaus,* which was later upheld by the Supreme Court.[29]

As a result, over the next several years EPA was forced to develop a workable PSD program. The PSD issue fostered intense regional conflicts, ultimately leading to a very strange coalition of environmentalists and Eastern coal interests. Legislators from Sunbelt states tended to oppose PSD because a stringent ceiling on allowable emissions in these states made it almost impossible to encourage economic development. Representatives from heavily industrialized Northeastern states tended to favor PSD for precisely this reason, inasmuch as an effective PSD program would make it difficult for industry to relocate in the Southwest. Western coal interests benefited from stringent air quality standards because Western coal tends to be lower in sulfur content than Midwestern and Appalachian coal. Not surprisingly, Eastern and Midwestern coal producers opposed any policy that put high-sulfur coal at a competitive disadvantage. Environmental groups favored PSD, of course, but also strongly opposed strip mining of coal. Because Western coal is extracted almost entirely through strip mining, while much Eastern coal is not, environmental groups faced a real dilemma.

The way out of the dilemma—and a policy deadlock extending over almost five years—lay in mandating a specific control technology for stationary sources of sulfur emissions (primarily coal-burning electric utilities). Prior to the 1977 Clean Air Amendments, a plant could meet emissions requirements either by using low-sulfur coal or by installing a "scrubber" on its smokestacks that would substantially reduce the sulfur content of its emissions. While utilities in the West would most likely use nearby coal in any event, Midwestern and Eastern utilities would calculate whether it was cheaper to install and maintain a scrubber or to ship low-sulfur Western coal hundreds of miles at a significant expense. If all utilities could be forced to install scrubbers on their smokestacks, there would no longer be any economic advantage to using low-sulfur Western coal.

Thus the 1977 Clean Air Amendments went beyond the 1970 Clean Air Act to mandate specific means to attain the emissions standards for stationary sources. Scrubbers would be required on all new plants, giving Eastern coal interests a competitive advantage over Western coal. At the same time, environmentalists put a damper on what would have been a significant increase in demand for strip mined coal. Finally, pristine air would be preserved for wilderness areas, which tended to be located in Western states, where nearby low-sulfur Western coal would have a competitive advantage. The combination of low-sulfur coal with scrubber technology would lead to the lowest possible sulfur emissions.

Mandating the use of scrubbers was a political solution to a political deadlock among contending interest groups. In many ways, mandating the use of scrubbers makes for dubious public policy: subsidizing some coal producers over others and encouraging utilities to postpone building new plants subject to the scrubbing requirements, and thus indirectly leading to higher levels of pollution in the short run.[30] Scrubbers thus provided a rationalizing breakthrough in the limited sense that this political compromise broke a deadlock over an important area of air pollution policy that would otherwise have prevented any action from being taken on PSD. With the resolution of the scrubber issue, Congress was able to ratify in the 1977 Clean Air Amendments the EPA's highly controversial PSD program.[31]

FAMILIAR POLICIES, POLICY COMMUNITIES, AND NONINCREMENTAL CHANGE

Not surprisingly, very few policy *outcomes* involve nonincremental change, by Lindblom's definition, inasmuch as they fall short of systemic transformation. As we saw in Chapter 5, the evolution of our capitalistic economic system into a mixed economy characterized by a substantial degree of government intervention probably constitutes a systemic transformation; however, it has occurred gradually, precisely as predicted by the incremental model. But fundamental changes occurring in a single, large step—what I have termed nonincremental innovations—are extremely rare. Innovations of this magnitude are occasionally proposed (national health insurance, for example), but they are highly unlikely to emerge from the legislative obstacle course unscathed. Perestroika and the recent events in the Soviet Union would probably qualify. Within the United States the New Deal might also. These examples would suggest that a systemic crisis is required to produce nonincremental innovations—one that threatens the very survival of the existing political or economic order. As Lindblom suggested, such changes would seem to fall within the realm of "wars, revolutions, and grand opportunities."[32]

This is not to say that policy makers necessarily confine themselves to analysis of incremental alternatives. To the contrary, major new federal activities (federal role breakthroughs) as well as major expansions of federal capacity to deal with previously established federal activities are routinely considered at the agenda-setting and policy adoption stages. This section will explore at length the distinctive sets of circumstances contributing to the adoption of such policies, which would likely comprise the universe of policy changes most observers would classify as nonincremental.

The Life Cycle of Issues

Brown argued that policy-making will differ significantly for breakthrough and rationalizing policies. For example, once a breakthrough is achieved within a given policy area, partisan and ideological conflict should decrease. "While liberals contemplate the need for repairs on their handiwork, conservatives, who earlier fought to keep the new commitment off the federal agenda altogether, come to recognize that the program they failed to block is here to stay."[33] This process of "agenda convergence" is further characterized by a growing emphasis on effective management of ongoing programs. Both congressional staffs and the institutionalized presidency expand in an effort to gain control of a growing bureaucracy, and reform of budgetary institutions is necessitated by rapid growth of federal expenditures. Conflicts between parties and among contending groups shift from symbolic and emotional debates over basic values to technocratic debates over the best means to ends that are now widely shared.[34]

While Brown points to a number of additional differences between breakthrough and rationalizing policies, for our purposes a more important difference may be identified between problems that are genuinely new or unprecedented and those that have gone through one or more policy cycles, thus becoming at least somewhat familiar to policy makers. In this vein, all problems may be viewed as going through a predictable life cycle. In particular, new problems will lack definition and will almost inevitably be characterized by low levels of understanding of cause-and-effect relationships among critical variables. However, a good deal of learning will normally take place as any issue moves through one or more policy cycles. While Lindblom did not specifically allow for the possibility of rational-comprehensive decision making on issues that have gone through several policy cycles, he did anticipate a good deal of learning through experience with policies, a process he termed "seriality" in the incremental model (see Chapter 2).

It would thus seem reasonable to expect the level of information available to policy makers to increase substantially over time. Moreover, if Brown is correct in predicting a high degree of agenda convergence for rationalizing policies, a consensus on objectives should also emerge over time. In terms of the analysis of the previous chapter, issues originating in quadrant D (normal incrementalism) can move through agenda convergence to quadrant C (pure problems of knowledge base) and eventually into quadrant A (rational decision making). While there is certainly no guarantee that the conditions for rational decision making will ever be fully satisfied, policy-making will change in important ways as policy makers learn more and more about an issue.

Policy-making on Unfamiliar Issues

Perhaps the most important difference between familiar and unfamiliar issues concerns the development of what John Kingdon has termed "policy communities." As we saw in the previous chapter, a policy community consists of elected officials, bureaucrats, congressional staffers, interest groups, academics, and other participants having a specialized and ongoing interest in a given issue; in short, it constitutes the "attentive public" for the issue.[35] Where these experts speak a common language, share a common view of what variables are important for their policy area and how they fit together, and agree on the criteria by which to judge policy proposals, the policy community is "integrated," in Kingdon's terms. Where participants lack such a common worldview, the policy community may be described as "fragmented."[36]

Ordinarily, according to Kingdon, for any issue to reach the agenda (he makes no distinction between familiar and unfamiliar issues), a "solution" must already have been identified within the policy community when a "window" of opportunity opens for legislative action, either through presidential leadership, legislative entrepreneurship, or a crisis or focusing event of some sort.[37] In his view, the process by which a problem reaches the agenda is largely independent of the process by which it is analyzed and a solution formulated.[38] Once an issue is addressed by the political system, however incompletely, it loses its salience for most people and recedes from the agenda. Efforts to solve it do not necessarily stop with a single piece of legislation, however. An attentive public, or policy community, will develop through subsequent policy cycles. Where members of this attentive public manage to achieve agreement on a workable solution to a problem, they will typically be powerless to place their proposals on the agenda until the issue somehow regains its salience for politicians and/or the public—a development that typically owes a great deal to chance.[39]

Contrary to Kingdon's analysis, however, many problems are forced on the institutional agenda by events that no one has a good idea how to solve. The imminent bankruptcy of the Social Security trust fund in 1982 provides a good case in point. No one had a magic solution for solving the funding crisis, and elected officials were extremely reluctant to deal with the issue inasmuch as any solution to it was bound to impose readily visible costs on politically aware constituencies. Public opinion polls pointed to a clear demand for strong action to save the Social Security system even as large majorities opposed virtually all available alternatives. The issue nevertheless reached the institutional agenda and stayed there until a workable compromise was found because the problem was extremely significant to a large number of people and inaction was simply unacceptable to everyone involved.[40] To the extent that a new problem is action-forcing or promises to get worse until it is effectively dealt with (like the more recent savings and loan bailout), policy makers will be compelled to deal with the issue whether they want to or not.

Policy communities take time to develop and thus will not exist for genuinely new problems. More specifically, those policy communities in existence when a new problem emerges will be centered on old problems. The onset of the energy crisis in 1973 provides a good case in point. Prior to the Arab oil embargo, energy policy-making was characterized by separate policy communities for different fuels; oil, natural gas, coal, and nuclear power each fell under the jurisdiction of different congressional committees and executive agencies. There was little coordination of policies across these policy areas; in the language of Chapter 4, these were essentially distributive subgovernments, concerned primarily with promoting stable profits for producers within each arena. As Congress attempted to deal with the issue in the mid-1970s, more than thirty-eight separate committees and subcomittees touched on various aspects of energy policy within the House of Representatives, and at least ten major committees and several dozen subcommittees claimed some jurisdiction in the Senate.[41] A similar pattern of institutional fragmentation characterized the executive branch.

Policy communities (like any rational decision maker confronted with an overwhelming mass of information) will strive to minimize information costs by filtering out seemingly irrelevant data. Indeed, as noted in Chapter 1, one of the primary purposes of all analysis is to filter out what is irrelevant in order to focus on what is relevant. Ordinarily, this is done by building upon the past and making minor changes in previous policies. Problems are not analyzed in a vacuum, but rather are defined through the search for relevant analogies (e.g., U.S. military assistance to El Salvador risks getting us involved in another "Vietnam"), and potential solutions are identified by examining relevant precedents for appropriate lessons: What did we do the last time we faced this problem? What solutions have other countries employed?[42]

This process of analagous formulation will be slow to recognize fundamentally new problems, however. Policy makers must determine for themselves that the world has changed in important ways, making what used to be relevant information increasingly irrelevant. The Social Security case shows how familiar problems can change their fundamental character over time. For about forty years, benefits were provided to a relatively small percentage of the population while costs were spread over the entire work force. This made for a benefits pie that appeared infinitely expandable, leading politicians to increase benefit levels, add new constituencies, protect benefits against inflation, lower the retirement age, and otherwise dispense largesse to potential voters, particularly in election years. By 1978 (and again in 1982), the ratio of taxpayers to current beneficiaries had declined significantly, necessitating much higher payroll taxes to sustain legislated benefit levels and thus making for a much more conflictual, zero-sum pattern of politics. However, the profound transformation of the issue was not immediately apparent to many policy makers, who still clung to the old distributive conception of the problem until imminent bankruptcy forced them to redefine the problem.[43]

In short, new problems will tend to be ignored or misperceived until they are forced on the agenda by dramatic performance failures (crises or focusing events) that cannot be ignored.[44] In the case of energy, for example, it took the Arab oil embargo in October 1973 to force the issue on the agenda, despite a wealth of statistical indicators of our steadily increasing dependence on imported oil.[45]

Once on the agenda, there is no guarantee that policy communities devoted to solving old problems will readily grasp the new realities facing them. Fifteen years after the Arab oil embargo there is still a good deal of reluctance to accept the fact that American oil supplies will be effectively exhausted by the end of this decade. President Carter's efforts to move away from excessive reliance on oil through various taxes on consumption were largely thwarted in the Senate, and the Reagan administration drastically curtailed funding for research on alternative sources of energy that had been initiated in the previous decade.[46]

Ready-made solutions will not exist for brand new problems that are forced on the agenda by events. Indeed, policy communities do not even exist for such problems. The development of policy communities for such issues will require the creation of new institutions (new congressional committees and new executive departments or agencies) and the redistribution of power from existing institutions to new ones. Such changes will tend to encounter stiff resistance from established institutions and thus will occur very slowly, if at all. It took a full four years after the onset of the energy crisis to create a cabinet-level Department of Energy. Similarly, although both the House and Senate have now granted primary responsibility for energy issues to specific committees (the Energy and Commerce Committee in the House and the Energy and Natural Resources Committee in the Senate), in reality, the pattern of institutional fragmentation—multiple committees and subcommittees contending over jurisdiction—continues on pretty much as before.[47]

Majority building will tend to be extraordinarily difficult for newly emerging issues, given both the lack of any apparent solutions and the severe institutional fragmentation resulting from the lack of a policy community appropriate to these issues. Ordinarily, as with the energy issue, the new problem will fall within the jurisdiction of several existing policy communities, making for a legislative obstacle course that is even longer than usual. While nonincremental change may be warranted by the situation (e.g., a major shift away from a reliance on fossil fuels and toward nuclear power and/or renewable sources of energy), incrementalism is almost guaranteed by the limited capacity of the system to even consider, let alone produce, large change when faced with an unfamiliar problem.

To the extent that existing policy communities are irrelevant to the new problem and resistant to change, ad hoc institutional arrangements may have to be developed to deal with the short-term crisis. The House of Representatives created an Ad Hoc Select Committee on Energy in 1977 to facilitate handling of President Carter's comprehensive energy proposals.[48] Similarly, the recurring deadlocks on Social Security reform in 1982 were eventually broken by various devices to circumvent normal institutional arrangements, beginning with the President's Blue Ribbon Commission on Social Security, and culminating with various informal bargaining sessions among major congressional and executive branch participants.[49]

Policy-making for Familiar Issues

Policy-making is much easier for familiar issues. Where the conditions for rational decision making remain unmet, at least a well-developed (and possibly even integrated) policy community will typically exist. Statistical indicators and feedback from the operation of ongoing government programs will thus be routinely monitored for signs of emerging problems or new threats, and policy proposals may at least begin to move forward without the need for an additional push from crises or focusing events.[50]

However, legitimation remains a difficult process—albeit not as difficult as that for brand new problems—due to the presence of multiple congressional committees, a bicameral Congress, the possibility of a Senate filibuster, weak legislative parties, and so on. Bargaining and compromise will typically be required to construct the necessary concurrent majorities, as discussed in Chapter 3. Passage of legislation is always problematical, and incremental outcomes are by far the normal occurrence.

Conflict may be socialized at any point, however, by a focusing event or a crisis. While this can occur early, thrusting an issue on the institutional agenda that would otherwise not have received serious consideration, it may also occur late in the legislative process, improving the chances of passage for a bill already in the works or permitting the passage of a strong bill where a weak one was likely before. In this vein, it is worth recalling that their pollution issue was not forced on the agenda in 1970 by the arousal of mass-public opinion. Rather, the issue was foreordained to come up with the expiration of the 1967 Air Quality Act; air pollution was now a "recurring item." The effect of the aroused mass public opinion was to facilitate passage of a stronger bill than would have passed otherwise.[51]

Federal Role and Rationalizing Breakthroughs

Plainly, the emergence of workable solutions to problems is much more likely to occur for familiar issues, where a federal role has already been established. The development of policy communities over time tends to produce an expansion in the available knowledge base combined with agenda convergence, which can facilitate both rational decision making and large changes in policy.

The 1986 reform of the federal income tax provides a case in point. Tax reform was a process of nonincremental change from beginning to end; at every stage of congressional consideration, the proposals receiving serious consideration would all have abolished the existing tax code and replaced it with a coherent alternative constructed from the ground up. But tax reform constituted a rationalizing breakthrough for a familiar problem. The federal income tax was first authorized in 1913 and has been revised many times since then. An integrated policy community exists for the issue, consisting of the Treasury Department, the House Ways and Means Committee, the Senate Finance Committee, a plethora of corporate lobbyists, and academic economists taking an interest in tax reform issues. The members of this attentive public had many years of experience with the policy area, understood all the issues involved, and agreed on the major problems plaguing the tax code. By the mid-1980s, a consensus had developed on the basic elements of a comprehensive approach to tax reform. To be acceptable to the tax policy community, a comprehensive tax reform proposal would have to close most (if not all) loopholes in order to broaden the tax base, reduce the number of tax brackets sharply, and lower the maximum rate on earned income. At least two distinct approaches satisfied these criteria already when President Reagan entered the lists in 1986: in the House, Jack Kemp's flat tax proposal helped to create a constituency for tax reform among Republican members, while in the Senate, the Bradley-Gephart ''fair tax'' plan (which was a more conventional approach retaining several tax brackets and thus some progressivity) attracted the support of many Democrats. When President Reagan also took up the issue, passage became almost inevitable, although the process of working out the details of a compromise acceptable to the various groups was by no means automatic.[52]

By contrast, the identification of workable solutions is almost precluded for genuinely new and unfamiliar issues. Understanding of the problem is limited, conflict over values is often intense, and deadlock is common. Where a breakthrough occurs, the outcome is almost sure to be what I have termed a federal role breakthrough involving an incremental expansion at best in federal capabilities. However, the newly identified problem will typically recede from the congressional agenda once a federal role has been established, only to recur later on as a familiar problem, subject to at least some degree of analagous formulation. Ideally, a consensus will eventually develop around a potential solution to the problem, thus permitting a rationalizing breakthrough in a subsequent policy cycle. But if the policy community is slow to develop—or if a budding policy community is dismantled, as was the case for energy policy during the Reagan era—the problem may simply recur as an unfamiliar problem once again, subject to all the difficulties just outlined.

A TYPOLOGY OF POLICY CONTRACTION

The analysis advanced thus far has treated policy change exclusively in terms of the expansion of governmental activities and federal capabilities. However, attempts at major policy change in recent decades have increasingly focused on the contraction of federal responsibility. If the politics of the New Deal/Great Society era were predominantly incremental, the politics of the past two decades are better characterized as predominantly decremental.[53] Beginning in the Nixon and Ford years with efforts to decentralize the administration of federal grant programs through revenue sharing and block grants, this trend continued with the Carter administration's efforts to deregulate various industries. The pace of policy contraction clearly accelerated during the Reagan years, as President Reagan's ideological opposition to most domestic programs combined with the need to confront massive and enduring deficits resulting from the 1981 tax cuts. Indeed, attempts to assess the significance of the so-called Reagan revolution inevitably focus on the degree to which President Reagan's assault on federal programs has succeeded in reducing the range of federal activities and reducing federal capacities for action.[54]

In general, decremental policies tend to be rationalizing policies inasmuch as they operate to reform or contract existing federal programs. In this regard, Brown identified seven rationalizing strategies as being of major analytic significance. Of these seven, three can be characterized as inherently decremental: decisions by the federal government to decentralize by delegating important federal responsibilities to state or local governments, to foster competition among private actors by deregulation of previously regulated industries, or to disengage from a policy commitment "on the grounds that the program in question was a mistake in the first place, has outlived its usefulness, has been poorly administered, is otherwise inefficient, or is simply too expensive. The extreme form of disengagement is to abolish a program, that is, to strike it from the agenda altogether."[55]

In terms of the analysis developed in the previous section, decremental policies by their very nature involve familiar problems. Moving away from a federal presence and toward a greater role for private actors or state and local governments is to return to a situation that existed prior to federal involvement.[56] The concept of a "breakthrough policy" necessarily takes on a very different meaning in this context; it will be used here to refer to major reductions (e.g., by large decrements) in contractionary rationalizing policies. Where decremental rationalizing policies reduce federal commitments or capabilities by small decrements, decremental rationalizing breakthroughs do so through large decrements or by establishing an innovative approach to an old policy area that significantly reduces the federal government's role. Brown's three rationalizing strategies of decentralization, deregulation, and disengagement can thus fall within either category. Much as is the case for other kinds of familiar problems, the final extent of the policy contraction will be a function of a confluence of political circumstances—in particular, whether a "solution" is in place within the policy commmunity when events conspire to make a particular rationalizing problem salient.

Decentralization policies. The decremental policy era began in the early 1970s with efforts to delegate increased responsibility for federally mandated activities to state and local levels. As Paul R. Dommel noted in his study of general revenue sharing:

> Decrementalism, while having budgetary implications for individual programs, is not basically a budgetary policy. Increases in total federal aid to state and local governments (due to growth in income support programs) may coexist with it. Fundamentally, it is a policy whereby the federal government gradually reduces its own policy role of defining and overseeing the resolution of particular social and economic problems and turns more and more decision-making over to state and local officials, who use federal money as they see fit. Within this context, revenue sharing, as implemented by the Nixon administration, is seen by some of its opponents as the cutting edge of a new process not of incremental policy making, but of incremental policy unmaking.[57]

As noted in Chapter 3, categorical grants offer federal assistance to states and localities for narrowly defined purposes (e.g., aid to female-headed families with dependent children) that generally come with a large number of federal strings attached (for example, a requirement that welfare administration take place through a single state agency and that state administrators possess advanced degrees and be appointed through merit systems).[58] With the proliferation of federal grant programs over the years, a consensus gradually developed that overlapping federal programs all too often imposed burdensome and at times even contradictory requirements on state and local implementors. (The evolution of revenue sharing and block grants thus provides a classic instance of a familiar problem; policy makers had acquired a high degree of understanding of the federal grants system through repeated policy cycles for a variety of programs.) Both liberals and conservatives in Congress came to believe a great degree of latitude was warranted for state and local officials. Moreover, while conservatives found the idea of strenghthening state and local governments appealing, liberals liked the idea of apportioning federal revenues to states and localities in proportion to need, thus ameliorating major resource disparities across states and localities.

President Nixon sought to do this primarily through a program of general revenue sharing, which would provide states and localities with complete discretion in allocating funds. The president's plan encountered opposition in Congress, both from liberals who wanted to retain some federal controls over spending of federal grants and from conservatives who objected to any program separating the authority for spending money from the responsibility for raising it. The end result was a political compromise in which the president won passage of a much reduced general revenue sharing program, along with a series of a new block grant programs that provided federal aid with a minimum of strings for broad purposes (e.g., law enforcement, community development), thus retaining some federal control over state and local spending decisions at the same time it gave state and local actors more latitude then they had possessed under categorical programs. While general revenue sharing may be characterized as a decremental rationalizing breakthrough, inasmuch as it sharply reduced federal control over what happened to federal money, block grants are better described as decremental rationalizing policies.

These decentralizing initiatives originated in a bygone era of chronic federal budgetary surplus (the so-called "fiscal dividend" resulting from economic growth pushing taxpayers into higher brackets in a progressive tax system). It is hardly surprising that general revenue sharing was one of the earliest casualties of the need to cut federal spending to reduce federal deficits during the 1980s. As noted in Chapter 3, however, block grants have proliferated during this same period, less because the Reagan administration liked states and localities than because the increased latitude to states and localities resulting from consolidation of categorical programs into block grants helped to sweeten substantial reductions in federal spending on these same grant programs. Thus in the austere budgetary climate of the 1980s, federal aid to subnational units of government became a luxury that could no longer be afforded, and the expansion of block grants into new areas served both to reduce federal spending and to increase state and local responsibility for action on many fronts.

A significant reduction of federal control over policy outcomes may instead be achieved without any formal statutory decentralization of authority. Management of EPA under Anne Gorsuch Burford in the early days of the Reagan administration provides one good illustration. Thwarted by Congress in its attempts to weaken the Clean Air Act, the Reagan administration employed administrative discretion to achieve its purposes. While the EPA retained nominal authority to reject state implementation plans under the Clean Air Act, Burford made it a practice to routinely approve SIPs, thus effectively decentralizing much of the effective responsibility for administration of the air pollution laws.[59] Similarly, the Reagan administration's disinclination to enforce many of the provisions of the Surface Mining and Reclamation Act led to devolution of effective responsibility for enforcement within this policy area as well, as we saw in the previous chapter.

Deregulation policies. The deregulation of surface and air transportation in the late 1970s further illustrates this contrast between decremental rationalizing and breakthrough policies. President Carter's efforts to deregulate surface transportation (trucks and trains) would provide an example of a decremental rationalizing policy aimed at fostering greater competition among private actors. In distinct contrast to the results for airline deregulation, to be discussed below, the Interstate Commerce Commission was left in existence with the nominal authority to regulate rates and entry for motor carriers and railroads, subject to new requirements that it substantially liberalize competition among carriers.

Where surface transportation deregulation preserved a nominal federal role in economic regulation, airline deregulation abolished the Civil Aeronautics Board entirely. Elimination of the agency's role in economic regulation did not occur in a single step, however. Serious consideration of airline deregulation began under the Ford administration in 1974. Carter appointees interpreted the CAB's existing statutory mandate (which was highly ambiguous) to permit a policy of encouraging liberalized competition, much as had been the case with the ICC. Increased competition led to lower prices, greater passenger volume, and higher profits—thus undermining airline industry opposition to reform. The ensuing Airline Deregulation Act of 1978—a decremental rationalizing breakthrough—deregulated airline traffic through a series of planned reductions in agency authority, culminating with the demise of the CAB in 1981.

Disengagement policies. As noted by Brown, the extreme case of disengagement would be the abolition of a federal program.[60] During the 1980s, a variety of programs were subjected to draconian budget cuts in the Reagan administration's relentless quest for deficit reductions, and a few were eliminated altogether. Most of the abolished programs, like the Carter administration's Synthetic Fuels Corporation or the general revenue sharing program, were eliminated through a series of severe cuts imposed over a two- or three-year period.

By contrast, most of the Reagan administration's budget cuts left in place at least some nominal federal responsibility while sharply reducing federal capacity. Dommel contrasted the new era of decrementalism with the previous era of incrementalism:

> This policy operates in a reverse fashion from incrementalism. The latter is the process of expanding policy at the margins enough (either in additional money or in new programs) to keep most concerned groups reasonably satisfied. Decrementalism turns this around, shrinking selected policies at the margins by impoundments, phase outs, and terminations just enough to keep people from becoming outraged.[61]

Even as a gradual series of incremental policy changes can add up to a major transformation in policy, a series of decremental budget cuts can produce a significant reduction in federal capacity to pursue legislated policy objectives. With both the defense budget and major entitlements programs largely off limits during the Reagan years, federal discretionary spending programs were subjected to repeated budget cuts in order to meet the annual Gramm-Rudman deficit reduction targets. The Federal Aviation Administration provides but one example here among many. The effects of repeated budget cuts combined with a sharp increase in air traffic stemming from the elimination of entry barriers under deregulation have made it impossible for the agency to inspect more than a fraction of all planes currently in operation.[62] Similarly, the neglect of safety and environmental considerations at nuclear weapons plants over the past decade has recently forced several of these plants to shut down, cutting off supplies of tritium that are critical in the detonation of atomic weapons.[63]

CONCLUSION

This chapter has attempted to define what constitutes nonincremental change and to identify the circumstances giving rise to various forms of nonincremental change. In so doing, we have found it useful to distinguish both federal role breakthroughs and federal capacity breakthroughs from the more common incremental rationalizing policies that Lindblom regarded as almost universal, and to make an additional distinction between expansionary and contractionary policy changes. In general, major increases in federal capability—as well as innovative contractions in federal responsibility—are most likely to occur for relatively familiar issues for which a policy community has been developed. Unfamiliar issues, by contrast, tend to permit federal role breakthroughs at best.

NOTES

1. Professor Lindblom used the term *large increments* to characterize many of these same policies in a critique of an earlier draft of this volume.
2. Lawrence D. Brown, *New Policies, New Politics* (Washington, D.C.: Brookings Institution, 1983), pp. 7–11.

3. On Medicare, see Theodore R. Marmor, *The Politics of Medicare* (Chicago: Aldine, 1973). On the Civil Rights Act of 1964, see Charles and Barbara Whalen, *The Longest Debate* (New York: New American Library, 1985).

4. Brown, p. 7.

5. For a similar argument, see Brian Hogwood and B. Guy Peters, *Policy Dynamics* (New York: St. Martin's, 1983).

6. Brown himself would reject such a conclusion. He introduces the terms *breakthrough* and *rationalizing policies* as an improvement over Lindblom's terminology, which he regards as too broad to be of much use. See Brown, footnote 14 on pp. 7–8.

7. John W. Kingdon, *Agendas, Alternatives, and Public Policies* (Boston: Little, Brown, 1984), pp. 3–4.

8. The term *recurring items* is taken from Jack L. Walker, "Setting the Agenda in the U.S. Senate," *British Journal of Political Science,* 7 (October 1977), pp. 423–445.

9. Charles O. Jones, *Clean Air* (Pittsburgh: University of Pittsburgh Press, 1975, p. 295).

10. Murray Edelman, *The Symbolic Uses of Politics* (Urbana: University of Illinois Press, 1964).

11. E. E. Schattschneider, *Two Hundred Million People in Search of a Government* (New York: Holt, Rinehart, and Winston, 1969), p. 89.

12. Theodore J. Lowi, *The End of Liberalism* (New York: Norton, 1969). While the terminology is different here, this distinction is essentially equivalent to one I have drawn elsewhere between delegative and allocative outcomes. See Michael T. Hayes, *Lobbyists and Legislators* (New Brunswick, N.J.: Rutgers University Press, 1981), pp. 25–39.

   Lowi's term, *policy-without-law,* is an apt description of incrementalism. One of the virtues of incrementalism, according to Aaron Wildavsky (one of its cofounders), is its capacity to reduce political conflict by deflecting attention away from program objectives and how resources contribute toward achievement of those objectives. Rather, the focus is on increments, and how increments compare with one another across programs. In incremental budgeting, the budget is taken apart and dealt with in pieces and then put back together again. Total expenditures are not a planned amount but rather sum up to whatever the pieces total. To be precise, incrementalism might better be described as "policy-without-programs" or "policy-without-purpose." See Aaron Wildavsky, *The Politics of the Budgetary Process,* 4th ed. (Boston: Little, Brown, 1984).

13. Vincent and Vee Burke, *Nixon's Good Deed* (New York: Columbia University Press, 1974), pp. 25–26. The marginal tax rate was lowered only slightly, from 100 percent to 67 percent, and recipients were allowed to "disregard" the first $30 in monthly earnings to offset work-related expenses.

14. On the Elementary and Secondary Education Act, see Eugene Eidenberg and Roy D. Morey, *An Act of Congress* (New York: Norton, 1969), and Stephen K. Bailey and Edith K. Mosher, *ESEA: The Office of Education Administers a Law* (Syracuse, N.Y.: Syracuse University Press, 1968). On open housing enforcement, see Charles M. Lamb, "Equal Housing Opportunity," in Charles S. Bullock III and Charles M. Lamb (eds.), *Implementation of Civil Rights Policy* (Monterey, Calif.: Brooks/Cole, 1984), pp. 148–183.

15. Jones, *Clean Air,* pp. 74–76. The 1963 act also provided a cumbersome and largely ineffectual process by which the federal government could become involved in pollution abatement.

16. Jones, *Clean Air,* p. 83.

17. Jones, *Clean Air,* p. 83.

18. Jones, *Clean Air,* pp. 126–129.

19. Jones, *Clean Air,* pp. 137–210.

20. Jones, *Clean Air,* pp. 272–275.

21. Robert W. Crandall, *Controlling Industrial Pollution* (Washington, D.C.: Brookings Institution, 1983), p. 11.

22. In his attempt to develop a general theory of the agenda-setting process, John Kingdon asserts that the development of a consensus within the relevant policy community in support of a single solution to a problem (a phenomenon he terms "tipping") is necessary for any issue to move toward an imminent decision. See John W. Kingdon, *Agendas, Alternatives, and Public Policies* (Boston: Little, Brown, 1984), pp. 147–151. The analysis of this chapter would suggest that tipping is a necessary precondition for rationalizing breakthroughs but not for what I have termed incremental rationalizing policies, which involve only minor modification of existing policies rather than the development of an innovative strategy.

23. Brown, p. 14.

24. Under this system, the federal government agreed, essentially, to reimburse hospitals and physicians for the average cost of treating a given illness, as computed from population experience, rather than for the specific costs associated with treating a given individual. On DRGs, see Louise B. Russell, *Medicare's New Hospital Payment System* (Washington, D.C.: Brookings Institution, 1989).

25. On the 1957 and 1960 civil rights acts, see Daniel M. Berman, *A Bill Becomes a Law*, 2d. ed. rev. (New York: Mcmillan, 1966).

26. Howard Ball, Dale Krane, and Thomas P. Lauth, *Compromised Compliance* (Westport, Conn.: Greenwood, 1982), pp. 40–44.

27. Ball, Kane, and Lauth, pp. 44–58. See also Richard Scher and James Button, "Voting Rights Act: Implementation and Impact," in Bullock and Lamb, pp. 20–54. On the events leading up to the Voting Rights Act, see David J. Garrow, *Protest at Selma* (New Haven, Conn.: Yale University Press, 1978).

28. The 1977 Clean Air Amendments are long and complicated, and the issues involved are highly technical. I have tried here to present an accurate, albeit highly simplified account of the big picture. For a more detailed analysis of the 1977 act, see the following sources: Richard H. K. Vietor, *Environmental Politics and the Coal Coalition* (College Station: Texas A&M University Press, 1980); Peter Navarro, "The Politics of Air Pollution," *The Public Interest* (Spring 1980), pp. 36–44; Bruce A. Ackerman and William T. Hassler, *Clean Coal/Dirty Air* (New Haven, Conn.: Yale University Press, 1981); and R. Shep Melnick, *Regulation and the Courts* (Washington, D.C.: Brookings Institution, 1983), pp. 71–112.

29. See Melnick, pp. 71–86.

30. Mandatory scrubbing leads to a variety of additional negative effects. See Navarro, pp. 42–43.

31. The PSD program divided the country into three categories based on air quality: Class I areas (like national parks and wilderness areas) would not be permitted any deterioration in air quality; Class II areas (which included much of the rest of the country) would be permitted moderate economic growth; while Class III areas would face few restrictions on economic growth. See Navarro, p. 40, and Melnick, pp. 86–103.

32. In this vein, James MacGregor Burns has suggested that the transformation of the presidency and the executive branch under Roosevelt really took place in Roosevelt's third term, in response to the needs of the war, rather than in the earlier New Deal years. See James MacGregor Burns, *Roosevelt: Soldier of Freedom* (New York: Harcourt, Brace, Jovanovich, 1970). pp. vii–viii and 331–355. See also Robert Higgs, *Crisis and Leviathan* (New York: Oxford University Press, 1987).

33. Brown, p. 12.

34. Brown, pp. 18–34.

35. Gabriel Almond, *Public Opinion and Foreign Policy* (New York: Praeger, 1965).

36. John W. Kingdon, *Agendas, Alternatives, and Public Policies* (Boston: Little, Brown, 1984), Chapter 6, "The Policy Primeval Soup," pp. 122–151.

37. See Kingdon, p. 150, on the importance of an available solution. Jack L. Walker makes a similar point in "Setting the Agenda in the U.S. Senate," *British Journal of Political Science,* 7 (October 1977), pp. 423–445. On the importance of chance events and rational factors in thrusting problems on the agenda, see Kingdon, pp. 95–108.

38. Here Kingdon distinguishes between what he terms "the agenda" and "the alternatives" and between a "visible cluster" of participants (including the president, Congress, and cabinet secretaries) and an "invisible cluster" of executive branch officials, congressional staffers, bureaucrats, etc. In general, the agenda (the short list of problems receiving serious attention) is set by the visible cluster, while the alternatives (the short list of solutions receiving serious attention) is determined by the invisible cluster. See Kingdon, pp. 23–74.

39. Actually, these two processes, which Kingdon refers to as the problem and policy streams, do not constitute the whole of Kingdon's model. A third stream, which he terms the political stream, must also be activated for most issues to reach the agenda. The political stream is essentially a majority-building or legitimation stream. Kingdon departs from conventional treatments of the policy process by treating agenda setting, policy formulation, and legitimation as independent streams rather than sequential stages. It should also be noted that Kingdon is not trying to explain how issues reach the institutional agenda, as we defined that term in Chapter 1 (e.g., the short list of issues receiving serious attention from policy makers). Rather, he is concerned with what he calls the "decision agenda," or the list of subjects within the institutional agenda that are up for imminent decision. (See Kingdon, p. 4.) Inasmuch as most students of the agenda-setting process use the term *agenda setting* to refer to attaining a place on the institutional agenda (or, in Kingdon's terminology, the governmental agenda), some confusion can result. In particular, it is much easier to get on the insitutional agenda than Kingdon's analysis makes it sound; what Kingdon is saying is that three streams must be activated for an issue to move toward an imminent decision. He comes very close to offering a theory of why some issues pass and others do not.

40. See Paul Light, *Artful Work* (New York: Random House, 1985).

41. See Walter A. Rosenbaum, *Energy, Politics and Public Policy* (Washington, D.C.: Congressional Quarterly Press, 1981), pp. 72-76.

42. See Charles O. Jones, *An Introduction to the Study of Public Policy,* 3d ed. (Monterey,Calif.: Brooks/Cole, 1984), p. 88. Jones makes an important distinction between analagous formulation as I have just described it and what he terms "creative formulation," in which new problems are treated as being essentially unprecedented. It should be stressed that analagous formulation is both inevitable and efficient most of the time. A political system that treated all issues as unprecedented might qualify as "creative," but it would also be incapable of learning from past experience.

    The near inevitability of analogous formulation is also acknowledged by Kingdon in his discussion of what he terms "spillovers." Once a principle is established by a particular piece of legislation (e.g., auto safety), a whole host of other issues may be recast in the same terms and dealt with analogously (e.g., follow-up legislation on flammable children's clothes, coal mines, etc., culminating with passage of the Occupational Safety and Health Act). See Kingdon, pp. 201–203. See also Jack L. Walker's discussion of "reform cycles" in "Setting the Agenda in the U.S. Senate."

43. See Light, pp. 33–44, and Martha Derthick, *Policy-Making for Social Security* (Washington, D.C.: Brookings Institution, 1979).

44. As I tell my students, policy-making is a lot like video games. When playing a video game, you are forced to react quickly to threats as you move along a path toward a predetermined objective. You possess an instruction book that tells you who the villains are, what they can do to

you, what you can do to them, and what winning involves. You also have a reservoir of experience you can draw on in the form of friends who have played the game before you. In real life, similar conditions often apply; foreign policy-making under the containment doctrine provided a good example for almost four decades, with particular events (Vietnam, for example) readily interpreted in terms of the overarching conflict between Communism and the West.

However, in distinct contrast to video games, real life often confronts policy makers with major changes in the parameters of the game, and at times even with a fundamental transformation in the nature of the game, without any instruction book or on-screen indications that the game has changed. The identities and/or the resources of the villains may have changed completely, along with your own capabilities, and the very nature of the game and the definition of what constitutes winning may have changed as well. What is important to understand is that no instruction booklet or reservoir of experience is available to tell policy makers that they are now playing an entirely different game. They must figure this out for themselves, while reacting to a flow of events and threats that often occur at high speed. In short, they must figure out that they are playing a brand new game while the game is still in progress with no time out for reflection.

The apparent end of the Cold War over the past two years is a good case in point. Although it is increasingly clear that the game has changed, and that containment is no longer an adequate guiding objective, it remains unclear exactly what the new game is in all respects. It is not clear whether the bad guys have become good guys, or whether they are just going through a period of weakness. Nor is it clear that new villains may not have emerged, more dangerous, albeit in different ways, than the old ones. And it is not clear at all what winning involves in this new age.

45. The most prescient prophet, of course, was M. King Hubbert, whose research on consumption patterns of various natural resources enabled him to predict with great accuracy when U.S. oil reserves would peak and begin to decline. Scorned at the time, Hubbert was vindicated by events, eventually winning almost every honor available to petroleum geologists. See M. King Hubbert, *Energy Resources,* A Report to the Committee on Natural Resources of the National Academy of Sciences and National Research Council (Washington, D.C.: National Academy of Sciences Publication 1000-D, 1962); and Hubbert, "Industrial Energy Resources," in Harry Foreman (ed.), *Nuclear Power and the Public* (Garden City, N.Y.: Anchor Books, 1972). For a discussion of Hubbert's research, see Duane Chapman, *Energy Resources and Energy Corporations* (Ithaca, N.Y.: Cornell University Press, 1983), pp. 90–91.

46. Don E. Kash and Robert W. Rycroft, "Energy Policy: How Failure Was Snatched from the Jaws of Success." Paper delivered at the 1983 annual meeting of the American Political Science Association, Chicago, Illinois, September 1–4, 1983.

47. See Walter A. Rosenbaum, *Energy, Politics and Public Policy,* 2d ed. (Washington, D.C.: Congressional Quarterly, Inc., 1987), pp. 50–51.

48. Bruce I. Oppenheimer, "Policy Effects of U.S. House Reforms: Decentralization and the Capacity to Resolve Energy Issues," in James E. Anderson (ed.), *Cases in Public Policy-Making,* 2d ed. (New York: Holt, Rinehart, and Winston, 1982), pp. 116–138.

49. Light, especially pp. 139–238. To circumvent at least some of the veto points in the legislative process, an initial group, termed the Gang of Seventeen, was established, consisting of five senators, seven representatives, and five members of the executive branch with access to the president. When this group was found to be too unwieldy and prone to leaks to the press, a smaller Gang of Nine was established. Both groups bargained in absolute secrecy, and the details of the ultimate agreement were attributed (falsely) to the bipartisan Social Security Commission to shield legislators from political repercussions in their districts.

50. On statistical indicators and feedback, see Kingdon, pp. 95–99 and 106–108.

51. Close readers of Kingdon's work will see that I am modifying his model here by developing slightly different variations of it for familiar and unfamiliar issues. I am suggesting, to use his vocabulary, that unfamiliar issues will often reach the agenda through an action-forcing crisis or focusing event in the problem stream, thus avoiding the need for a convergence of all three of Kingdon's streams. On such issues, one stream (if sufficiently powerful) can be enough. At the same time, crises and focusing events are much less important in placing familiar issues on the agenda. These issues may very well arise through presidential or legislative entrepreneurship as rationalizing policies. On familiar issues, crises or focusing events are more important as catalysts for passage or strengthening of proposals already in the works.
52. For an excellent case study of this act, see Jeffrey H. Birnbaum and Alan S. Murray, *Showdown at Gucci Gulch* (New York: Random House, 1987).
53. See Paul R. Dommel, *The Politics of Revenue Sharing* (Bloomington: Indiana University Press, 1974), p. 192.
54. See, for example, John L. Palmer and Isabel V. Sawhill, *The Reagan Experiment* (Washington, D.C.: Urban Institute, 1982); and Lester M. Salamon and Michael S. Lund (eds.), *The Reagan Presidency and the Governing of America* (Washington, D.C.: Urban Institute, 1984). A typology of policy contraction could be developed by simply making appropriate changes in the two defining dimensions of the typology of policy change developed above. The first dimension would distinguish proposals eliminating a federal role altogether from those leaving in place at least a nominal federal responsibility to act in the policy area. The second dimension would distinguish between policies reducing federal capacity by small and large decrements. The result would be a four-cell typology of contractionary policies that provides a mirror image of the typology of policy change developed earlier in this chapter. It is somewhat confusing to approach the problem in this way, however, since virtually all decremental policies are rationalizing policies, as discussed below.
55. Brown, pp. 15–16. Hogwood and Peters develop a typology of policy change, ranging from policy innovation at one end to policy termination at the other, with policy maintenance in the center. They identify a series of increasingly severe policy contractions, which they term exogenous decline, dilution and deterioration, removal of a category of clientele, elimination of a program element, and elimination of the program. See Hogwood and Peters, pp. 26–50.
56. In the case of airline deregulation, to be discussed below, regulation was originally imposed during the industry's infancy, when few people were brave enough to travel by plane and carriers offering passenger service had to be subsidized with federal air mail contracts. Thus, a move toward an unregulated market was not a return to anything like the previous experience with unregulated airlines. If it had been, there would have been little support for deregulation. On the failure of competition in the airline industry prior to the onset of regulation in the 1930s, see Gilbert Goodwin, *Government Policy Toward Commercial Aviation* (New York: King''s Crown Press, 1944).
57. Dommel, p. 193.
58. Martha Derthick, *The Influence of Federal Grants* (Cambridge, Mass.: Harvard University Press, 1970).
59. Anne M. Burford with John Greenyea, *Are You Tough Enough?* (New York: McGraw-Hill, 1986); and Richard A. Harris and Sidney M. Milkis, *The Politics of Regulatory Change* (New York: Oxford University Press, 1989), Chapter 6, ''Regulation and Deregulation at the Environmental Protection Agency,'' pp. 225–277.
60. Plainly, airline regulation would also qualify as an example of disengagement. Not all instances of disengagment involve purposeful efforts to stimulate increased competition among private actors, however.
61. Dommel, p. 192.

62. John H. Cushman, Jr., "F.A.A. Staggers Under Task of Monitoring Airline Safety," *The New York Times,* February 13, 1990, p. A1, col. 5.

63. Keith Schneider, "Defects in Arms Industry Minimized in Early Reagan Years," *The New York Times,* November 7, 1988, p. A1, col. 1; Kenneth R. Noble, "After 40 Years, the Silence is Broken on a Troubled Nuclear Arms Industry," *The New York Times,* Sunday, October 16, 1988, p. E4, col. 1.

CHAPTER 11

Welfare Reform:
Obstacles to Nonincremental Change

In 1970, Richard Nixon became the first president to propose a form of guaranteed annual income for people living below the poverty line. In 1977, President Carter made a similar proposal part of his ambitious domestic agenda. While both these proposals were widely perceived by the participants involved to be comprehensive reforms of the welfare system,[1] various constraints operated to preclude genuinely nonincremental change. Ultimately, as this chapter will show, both initiatives were destined to fail precisely because they failed to propose genuinely nonincremental change.

This chapter will examine these attempts at comprehensive welfare reform. All five of the models reviewed in this volume have something to contribute to our understanding of these outcomes. What follows is less a case study in the traditional sense than an issue analysis. There is no real attempt to provide a complete chronological account of events or a survey of all the key players. Rather, the central purpose is to show how each of the five models contributes to an understanding of the policy process on these two abortive attempts at nonincremental policy change.

AFDC AND THE WELFARE CRISIS

When President Nixon took office in 1969, more than 24 million people, or 12 percent of the nation's population, lived on incomes below the federal government's official poverty line, which stood at a little more than $3,700 for a family of four. This represented a decline from the 19 percent of the population living below the poverty line in 1964, when the government first developed an official definition of a poverty-level income. The percentage living in poverty had stabilized at this new level, however; it would hover between 11 and 13 percent for the next decade.[2]

By providing a guaranteed minimum income in cash to all citizens, whether they worked or not, a negative income tax would have marked a sharp departure from existing welfare policy. Existing cash assistance programs were (and still are) restricted to segments of the poverty population that can be classified as deserving. The Social Security Act of 1935 created the Aid to Dependent Children program (now known as Aid to Families with Dependent Children, or AFDC), which was originally confined to widows, along with separate programs to aid the blind and the elderly poor. The act was amended in 1950 to add a third program of aid for the permanently and totally disabled.[3]

In general, the only means-tested programs that are available to all poor are in-kind programs, like Food Stamps or Medicaid, which provide benefits to the poor without giving them cash. (The Food Stamps program provides recipients with coupons that can be spent only for approved food items; through Medicaid, the federal government pays medical bills for the indigent.) While these two programs have grown over the years to become comparable in size and expense to AFDC, both were relatively small in 1969. The Medicaid program was only four years old at that time, having been enacted along with Medicare in 1965. Food Stamps was only a pilot program until political pressures forced President Nixon to nationalize the program in 1970, during the debate over his negative income tax proposals.

Pressures for welfare reform when President Nixon took office were primarily stimulated by serious problems plaguing the Aid to Families with Dependent Children program. As noted above, this program was originally intended to aid widows with small children—families that had lost their primary breadwinner. Over the years, that program had evolved into something very different, and much larger, than originally envisioned. By the time President Nixon took office, it had turned into our nation's largest simple welfare program and our biggest welfare problem. Perverse incentives built into AFDC created a whole host of problems that eventually gave rise to demands for comprehensive welfare reform.

As the analysis in Chapter 3 would predict, AFDC failed to produce anything remotely approximating a uniform welfare policy for women with dependent children. Rather, AFDC is really a very different program for each state, with different benefit levels and very different eligibility standards. As with all categorical grant programs, AFDC is administered intergovernmentally. While the federal government provides money to the states according to a matching funds formula (e.g., the more the state puts up, the more federal money it gets), there is no mandatory minimum benefit level.[4] Each state determines a ''standard of need,'' which is typically set below the federal poverty line, and then decides what percentage of that needs standard it will pay in welfare benefits. Many states set welfare benefits well below their needs standards.[5] The end result is a vast disparity in benefit levels across states. In 1969, a family of four on AFDC in New Jersey would receive $263 a month; in Mississippi, an identical family would receive only $39 a month.[6]

To a very large degree, the states are also free under AFDC to set their own eligibility standards. Federal law requires that recipients' gross income (after exclusions) not exceed 150 percent of the state's need standard. Because the states have complete latitude in setting their own needs standards, they can restrict or expand eligibility as much as they want.[7] Moreover, states possess complete autonomy in establishing and enforcing application procedures. Cost-conscious agencies often fail to publicize benefit programs and may create layers of red tape to deter potential applicants.[8] Until recently, eligibility requirements were applied differently to blacks and whites, particularly in the rural South. Black women applying for AFDC were much more likely to be kept off the rolls and to receive lower benefit levels than whites if they did qualify for the program. They were also more likely to be subjected to work requirements.[9]

Discretion to the states in determining eligibility led to the transformation of AFDC over the years, particularly in urban, industrialized states. Persons falling outside the categories established by the Social Security Act are covered (if at all) by General Assistance, which is funded entirely by the states. For a variety of reasons, heavily urbanized and industrial states tend to be much more liberal than others on welfare spending.[10] Because recipients failing to qualify for AFDC remain the financial responsibility of the state, states with generous General Assistance programs have a strong incentive to redefine eligibility standards in order to transfer recipients to AFDC, which provides federal matching funds. (By contrast, in low-benefit states, particularly in the South, General Assistance is a much smaller program and this transformation has not occurred. In these states, welfare payments tend to be set below prevailing wage levels in order to encourage acceptance of jobs at low wages.)[11]

In Massachusetts, a typical liberal state, this was accomplished by relaxing the so-called fit parent clause. Where mothers of illegitimate children were previously denied General Assistance under this rule, federal regulations governing eligibility for AFDC were silent on the subject. By dropping the fit parent requirement, Massachusetts could switch large numbers of female-headed households to AFDC. This same phenomenon was repeated in most urban, Northeastern states, gradually transforming AFDC from a program of aid to widows to a program of aid to women with illegitimate children. In Massachusetts, the percentage of AFDC recipients who were widows stood at 70 percent in 1935, at the outset of the program. The fit parent rule was relaxed in 1937. By 1942, the percentage of recipients who were widows had fallen below 50 percent, and by 1956 it had fallen to 10 percent.[12]

A serious inequity arises from the exclusion of able-bodied males from the program. Less than half of all states participate in AFDC-UF, an optional program providing AFDC to households headed by able-bodied males. In order to qualify for that program, heads of households must work less than 100 hours per month.[13] Inasmuch as full-time jobs at the minimum wage can provide an income below the federal poverty level depending on family size, it is clear that the 100 hours per month requirement leaves many men with an unpleasant choice: either take a job, and provide inadequately for their families, or desert their families, thus rendering them eligible for AFDC, which often offers a higher monthly income. AFDC thus creates a real incentive for the breakup of families.[14]

AFDC also creates significant disincentives to work. Prior to 1967, AFDC recipients who took a job would have their benefits reduced on a dollar-for-dollar basis. When the costs of working were factored in (e.g., transportation to and from work, child care expenses, and so on), individuals would actually be losing money by taking a job. In 1967, Congress sought to remedy this disincentive to work by permitting recipients to keep one dollar out of every three dollars earned (or, to put it another way, by reducing benefit levels by only two dollars for every three dollars earned, rather than dollar for dollar, as had been the case before), and by permitting recipients to "disregard" the first $30 per month in earnings to offset the costs of working.[15] While this represented an improvement over the previous system, it only reduced the marginal tax rate on earned income from 100 percent to 67 percent.

Welfare rolls skyrocketed in the decade of the sixties, increasing by 100 percent or more over the latter half of the decade in many cities.[16] The reasons for this dramatic rise in the welfare rolls was not well understood at the time. By the mid-1970s, the worst would be over; welfare rolls would stabilize, albeit at a higher level than before. But policy makers in 1969 had no way of knowing when (if ever) the escalation of program costs would stop. What was known at the time was that 93 percent of the rise in AFDC cases between 1961 and 1967 involved absent fathers, the number of illegitimate births during that period had risen by 42 percent, and somewhere between 70 and 75 percent of the unmarried mothers on AFDC were black.[17]

THE CASE FOR A NEGATIVE INCOME TAX

Even as our welfare system cried out for a rational solution, support was steadily growing within the academic community for some form of negative income tax to replace existing cash and in-kind assistance programs. Credit for originating this idea is usually given to two famous economists, Milton Friedman and Robert J. Lampman, who developed the concept independently.[18] The basic idea behind the scheme is to extend the income tax system into the lowest income brackets, with individuals falling below a specified income level *receiving* payments from the government (rather than paying taxes) in inverse proportion to their income. To work properly, according to Friedman, the negative income tax must replace all existing welfare programs and be paid for and administered by the federal government to eliminate cross-state disparities in payment levels.[19]

While many variations on this basic idea have been offered by different authors, all negative income tax plans contain the same three core elements. All begin by setting a *guaranteed minimum income* that varies with family size. However, recipients are also allowed to keep some percentage of any income they earn; this percentage is the *negative tax rate*. (It is often useful to refer to the corresponding rate at which benefits are reduced for each dollar earned, which may be termed the *marginal tax rate*.) Together, the guaranteed minimum income and the negative tax rate combine to determine a *break-even level of income*, the point at which welfare payments from the government shrink to zero and the individual passes out of the negative income tax system. In theory, the guaranteed minimum income can be set at any level you want, and the negative tax rate can range from 0–100 percent. By varying one or both of these variables, an infinite number of negative income tax plans can be devised.

Friedman's proposal (which is the most popular of several variants on the scheme) set the guaranteed minimum income at one-half the federal poverty level and the negative tax rate at 50 percent. This results in a break-even point at the federal poverty line, as shown in Table 11.1. For purposes of illustration, I have assumed a federal poverty level

TABLE 11.1. GUARANTEED INCOME IS $6,000   MARGINAL TAX RATE IS 50%

Earnings	After Plan Income	Net Federal Payment
$ 0	$ 6,000	$6,000
2,000	7,000	5,000
4,000	8,000	4,000
6,000	9,000	3,000
8,000	10,000	2,000
10,000	11,000	1,000
12,000	12,000	0

NOTE: After Plan Income = $6,000 + 50% Earnings
Net Federal Payment = After Plan Income − Earnings

of $12,000 per year for a family of four (a nice, round number that closely approximates the current figure). Thus the plan guarantees an income of $6,000 per year. With a 50 percent negative tax rate, the break-even level of income is thus $12,000, or the poverty line.

The negative income tax has great appeal to students of social welfare policy because it does a better job than the existing system of meeting four basic tests of a good welfare policy. First, it alleviates poverty (policy analysts term this the adequacy criterion). Second, it improves the overall operation of the economy by creating a positive incentive to work (the efficiency criterion).[20] Third, it treats like cases alike (the principle of horizontal equity). Finally, it gives aid in proportion to need (the principle of vertical equity).

By these four criteria, the AFDC program was an abject failure. Benefit levels were inadequate to raise beneficiaries out of poverty in most states and were extremely low in some states. The significant disparity in benefit levels across states led to striking horizontal and vertical inequities. Arguably the most significant inequity centered around the exclusion of able-bodied males from the program. Finally, the program generated significant inefficiencies by discouraging work and by encouraging family dissolution; not surprisingly, the costs of the AFDC program were skyrocketing, and there was every reason to believe they would continue to do so.

By contrast, the Friedman plan was an improvement on all counts. The principle of horizontal equity was satisfied because the plan assured that identical families with identical incomes would always receive identical welfare payments. Moreover, families headed by able-bodied males would be eligible for aid under the plan, thus removing the largest single horizontal inequity. The negative income tax likewise satisfied the criterion of vertical equity by paying higher benefit levels to families with lower incomes. To see this, look at the final column in Table 11.1, which gives the net governmental payment for each income level. The net governmental payment is that portion of the recipient's total disposable income that does not come from work. As the level of earnings increase, the size of the government's payment gradually decreases, until it finally reaches zero at the break-even point.

Moreover, the Friedman plan would be relatively inexpensive. It is very hard to say with any real precision just how much any welfare reform would actually cost, inasmuch as program costs depend upon how many people ultimately end up in different income brackets, which in turn depends upon how people actually respond to the 50 percent negative tax rate. However, the Friedman plan kept program costs down relative to the alternative plans I will be presenting later by setting a fairly low guaranteed income (at only one-half the poverty level) and by setting a fairly low negative tax rate. However, this 50 percent marginal tax rate would still represent a considerable improvement over the 67 percent benefit reduction rate then operating under AFDC.

THE BREAKDOWN OF RATIONALITY

While the negative income tax would seem to provide a workable solution to the nation's welfare problems, the central requirements for rational-comprehensive decision making were lacking in 1969, when the Nixon administration took up the issue of welfare reform. Conflict over objectives was combined with an inadequate knowledge base on important questions. The Nixon administration would attempt to fashion a nonincremental departure in welfare policy when the circumstances dictated a reliance on normal incrementalism.

Conflicting Definitions of the Problem

If welfare reform was forced on the agenda by events and almost universally accepted as desirable, it nevertheless meant very different things to different people. Liberals wanted to raise benefit levels and fill in the gaps in coverage, which would inevitably cost more money. By contrast, conservatives wanted to stop the escalation in program costs by reducing fraud and by making work more attractive than welfare. While a negative income tax could be made appealing to some conservatives by emphasizing the built-in incentives to work, most found the prospect of a guaranteed income in any form profoundly disturbing.

Similarly, governors and mayors wanted federal relief from rising welfare burdens. However, full federalization of the program would add billions to the federal budget at a time when inflationary pressures were building up. The federal government was unlikely to take on any additional costs without making significant reforms in the program to put an end to its escalating costs. While a negative income tax along the lines of the Friedman plan might seem to offer something to all these groups, ultimately it would prove impossible to devise a plan that reconciled these conflicting objectives.

Dilemmas Inherent in the Negative Income Tax Approach

As noted earlier, the guaranteed income, negative tax rate, and break-even points can each be set at a wide variety of levels. Thus an infinite number of different negative income tax plans can potentially be devised. This created the false impression among policy makers that adjustments could be made in any negative income tax plan to overcome whatever shortcomings might arise.

To the contrary, there is a mathematical interrelationship among the three basic elements of any negative income tax plan. If you raise the guaranteed income level while leaving the negative tax rate the same, the break-even point must rise, and vice versa.

Similarly, if you let recipients keep a greater percentage of their income, the break-even point must rise. And so on. The fundamental objectives of adequate benefit levels, strong work incentives, and reasonable program costs are in conflict; some compromise must be made among these competing objectives. This should have been understood by all the participants involved from the outset, but it was not.[21]

For example, there is no escaping the fact that the Friedman proposal plainly fails to lift people out of poverty. By setting the break-even level at the federal poverty line, the plan guarantees at the outset that all recipients will end up with incomes at or below the poverty line. In fact, only those people earning enough money on their own to reach the break-even point (and thus reduce their welfare payment to zero) actually reach the poverty line. Those who remain unemployed or work part-time will fall significantly below the federal poverty line. At the same time, however, a negative income tax would aid families headed by able-bodied males for the first time, substantially supplementing their incomes.

The obvious way to satisfy the adequacy criterion is by raising the guaranteed minimum income. For purposes of illustration, I have set the guaranteed minimum income at $12,000 in Table 11.2 while retaining the 50 percent negative tax rate. Like the Friedman plan, the revised plan in Table 11.2 is efficient and both horizontally and vertically equitable. Because the guranteed minimum income is set at the federal poverty level, the plan now lifts *all* recipients out of poverty while at the same time preserving at least some work incentive by keeping the marginal tax rate at 50 percent. There is a price for doing this, however. Under the new plan, the break-even point is now $24,000—which means, in short, that the plan will be a *lot* more expensive. Not surprisingly, a much higher percentage of the population will now be receiving welfare payments, although many of these new recipients will be receiving relatively small amounts of money. (It should be readily apparent that the break-even point would be raised even further—with corresponding implications for the cost of the plan—if work incentives were improved by letting people keep significantly more than 50 percent of earned income.)

The only way to raise people out of poverty while keeping the break-even point relatively low is to raise the marginal tax rate on earned income. If people are allowed to keep, say, one-third of their earned income, the result is the plan in Table 11.3. As before, we will set the guranteed minimum income at the poverty level. With a negative tax rate

TABLE 11.2. GUARANTEED INCOME IS $12,000   MARGINAL TAX RATE IS 50%

Earnings	After Plan Income	Net Federal Payment
$ 0	$12,000	$12,000
4,000	14,000	10,000
8,000	16,000	8,000
12,000	18,000	6,000
16,000	20,000	4,000
20,000	22,000	2,000
24,000	24,000	0

NOTE: After Plan Income = $12,000 + 50% Earnings
Net Federal Payment = After Plan Income − Earnings

TABLE 11.3. GUARANTEED INCOME IS $12,000 MARGINAL TAX RATE IS 66⅔%

Earnings	After Plan Income	Net Federal Payment
$ 0	$12,000	$12,000
3,000	13,000	10,000
6,000	14,000	8,000
9,000	15,000	6,000
12,000	16,000	4,000
15,000	17,000	2,000
18,000	18,000	0

NOTE: After Plan Income = $12,000 + 33⅓% Earnings
Net Federal Payment = After Plan Income − Earnings

of 33 percent (or a marginal tax rate on earned income of 67 percent), the break-even point is now $18,000.

Ironically, it is not clear that we have significantly reduced the cost of the program by making this change in the negative tax rate. There is little incentive to work in the new program, with recipients allowed to keep only one dollar out of every three earned. (Attentive readers will recognize this plan as the work incentive reforms passed in the 1967 public welfare amendments, minus the $30 per month disregard feature. The 1967 reforms in effect established a negative income tax for the limited population of AFDC recipients.) As work incentives are reduced, one has to assume that rational individuals will work less, leading to a greater concentration of people in the lower income brackets, where the net government payment is higher. While it is again almost impossible to forecast exactly how much such a program would actually cost, it is clear that we are not saving money by raising the marginal tax rate in a misguided effort to lower the break-even point.

A guaranteed income plan, as distinct from a negative income tax, merely takes the above illustration one step further, raising the marginal tax rate on earned income to 100 percent. Under such a plan, the guaranteed minimum income would be equal to the break-even point—in our plan, $12,000. This would raise all recipients out of poverty while destroying any incentive to work, as individuals would now receive $12,000 per year whether they worked fifty-two weeks a year to earn it or sat home watching soap operas. What is worse, individuals earning more than $12,000 (and thus outside the negative income tax system) would now ask themselves whether it is worth working hard all year for, say, $15,000 when you could get $12,000 for doing absolutely nothing.

Unfortunately, this provides a good description of how AFDC actually worked before the 1967 work incentive reforms, and how it works again today in the wake of President Reagan's abolition of the 1967 work incentive reforms. A guaranteed income is just a negative income tax with a 100 percent marginal tax rate on earned income; AFDC provides such a guaranteed income (albeit one that varies by state and is set far below the federal poverty level) for female heads of households.

There is no escaping this trade-off between keeping costs down, providing work incentives, and providing benefits high enough to lift recipients out of poverty. To get more of one value, you must give up something else. Providing generous benefits while maintaining adequate work incentives (even at the 50 percent level) is very expensive and puts a lot of people on welfare. In fact, there is no way to create adequate work incentives without aiding a lot of people who are outside the system now. Raising the marginal tax rate lowers the break-even point, but ultimately raises the costs of the program by effectively undermining work incentives. Lowering the guranteed income significantly (say, to one-half the poverty level) allows you to hold down program costs while maintaining at least some work incentives. Although such a plan would improve the economic welfare of most current recipients while reaching for the first time households headed by males holding down low-wage jobs, the plan fails to fully raise recipients above the poverty line and appears to leave many people very poor, making the proposal potentially vulnerable to political attack.

Inadequate Knowledge Base

Moreover, much of the normative case for the negative income tax remained speculative at best. One could be sure of the horizontal and vertical equity inherent in the benefit structure. However, no one could be certain of the effects of a 50 percent negative tax rate on work effort. While a reduction in the marginal tax rate on earned income from 67 percent to 50 percent would represent a clear improvement, no one knew for sure whether that improvement would produce a significant increase in work among welfare recipients. After all, a 50 percent marginal tax rate means that individuals get to keep only fifty cents out of each dollar earned, hardly a rich inducement to work. (The 1986 Tax Reform Act lowered the top rate on earned income to 28 percent largely for this reason.) Moreover, no one knew for sure that a negative income tax would enhance marital stability among welfare recipients. It seemed likely to, inasmuch as it made aid available to able-bodied males and thus eliminated the need to desert one's family to qualify for aid. But no one could be certain.

To answer these questions, a controlled experiment had been initiated by the Johnson administration in 1967. An experimental group of welfare recipients would be given a negative income tax in place of traditional welfare programs; a control group (identical in every other respect) would receive existing welfare programs. The effects of a negative income tax on work and family stability could then be specified by comparing the experiences of the two groups over time. Ultimately, the results were profoundly discouraging on both counts. The negative income tax seemed to discourage work rather than encourage it, particularly among secondary wage earners (spouses and older children), and marital breakup was even greater among the experimental group receiving the negative income tax. But this information was not yet available when the debate over President Nixon's proposal took place; to the contrary, partial data (which seemed on all points to favor the negative income tax) was invoked by proponents of the plan.[22]

INCREMENTALISM AND WELFARE REFORM IN THE NIXON ADMINISTRATION

Whether or not conditions were ripe for nonincremental change, the new president would be forced to confront this steadily worsening problem, and the negative income tax would almost surely be included among the options he would consider. In the waning days of the Johnson administration, policy analysts at the Department of Health, Education, and Welfare developed a negative income tax plan and tried to convince Wilbur Cohen, then secretary of HEW, to propose it to President Johnson. Cohen dismissed their plan, partly because he believed programs targeted at the poor had less political appeal than social insurance programs benefiting the middle class, and partly because the president had recently rejected a less radical proposal to make participation in the AFDC-UF program mandatory for all states. During the transition period, and into the first year of his administration, President Nixon would be forced to turn for advice to holdovers from the Johnson administration. Ironically, these policy analysts would find the new and ostensibly conservative administration more receptive to their proposals.[23]

Shortly after his election, President-elect Nixon created a task force, headed by Richard Nathan, to make policy recommendations on welfare reform. A research associate at the Brookings Institution, Nathan was a young, liberal Republican who had previously distinguished himself as chair of a preelection Nixon task force on intergovernmental fiscal relations. For expert advice, Nathan turned to various members of the welfare policy establishment, virtually assuring that the recommendations ultimately emanating from the task force would propose at best incremental changes in existing programs.[24]

The Nathan task force gave primary emphasis to the wide disparities in AFDC benefits across states. To get at this problem, the group called for a federal floor under AFDC. The federal government would set a mandatory nationwide minimum benefit level, to be paid for by the federal government. The states would continue to administer welfare, but the federal government would now pay the full federal floor, plus one-half of any additional payments by which a state chose to supplement the basic benefit. The Nathan plan (as it came to be called) would thus simultaneously achieve two important goals, dramatically raising benefit levels in low-benefit states (which tended to be concentrated in the South), while at the same time providing fiscal relief to states currently paying generous benefits.

The primary alternative to the Nathan plan within the administration was a negative income tax proposal along the lines of the Friedman plan. The plan eventually proposed by the president set the guaranteed income at about 45 percent of the poverty level and the negative tax rate at 50 percent. However, recipients would pay no tax on the first $720 a year in earned income in order to offset the costs of work. A "work requirement" was included to make the plan more attractive to conservatives, but in reality an individual refusing to accept employment or job training would forfeit only his or her share of the total benefits—about $300 in most cases. The plan departed significantly from Friedman's in limiting eligibility to families with children; single individuals and childless couples would not be covered under the plan.[25]

Incremental Analysis

Not surprisingly, given the breakdown of the rational model, decision making on the issue conformed to many of the tenets of disjointed incrementalism. For example, according to Lindblom, the policy process is typically *remedial*. Utopian ideals (like the optimal distribution of income) are too abstract to serve as precise guides to policy; as a result, policy makers tend to move away from problems in need of alleviation rather than toward intangible objectives. The welfare reform issue in President Nixon's first term is no exception to this generalization. AFDC had become a serious problem by the time President Nixon took office in 1969. It discouraged recipients from working and encouraged the dissolution of intact families. There were major disparities in benefit levels across states. Even more important, the vast majority of families headed by able-bodied males—particularly those who succeeded in finding full-time but low-paying employment—were simply ineligible for the program. Finally, the program increasingly provided aid to unwed mothers rather than widows, and costs were escalating rapidly.

Within the executive branch, at least, the decision process was characterized by *adjustment of objectives to policies*. Participants did not examine alternatives in an effort to maximize values that had been agreed upon at the outset. Rather, the Nathan plan and the negative income tax would achieve very different objectives; to choose one plan over the other was thus to choose one set of objectives over the other. Where the Nathan plan would reduce cross-state benefit inequities and provide fiscal relief for states, it would do nothing to end the exclusion of able-bodied males from the program. Nor would it do anything to alter the pathological incentives regarding work and family breakup that characterized the status quo. By contrast, the negative income tax would significantly improve work incentives and eliminate the most serious horizontal inequity in AFDC, the exclusion of families headed by able-bodied males. However, it would provide less fiscal relief for states than the Nathan plan, and to the extent that generous states continued to supplement the basic federal payment, it would still leave a significant variation in payment levels across states.

Moreover, *analysis was confined to incremental alternatives*. The Nathan plan was perceived by all involved to be a significant, but nevertheless incremental, reform of AFDC. By contrast, the negative income tax appeared to be a major structural reform of AFDC, inasmuch as it expanded coverage to include families headed by able-bodied males and substantially improved the work incentives facing recipients. For these reasons (among others), the president ultimately chose the negative income tax plan over the Nathan plan, even though it appeared to be more expensive in the short run.

Properly understood, however, the proposal (which was ultimately titled the Family Assistance Plan, or FAP) represented at best an incremental improvement over previous policy. First and foremost, it would not eliminate any existing welfare programs. In fact, the president proposed through separate legislation to nationalize the Food Stamps program (which at that time was a small, pilot program unavailable in much of the country) even as he was introducing his negative income tax. While the administration would have preferred to "cash out" in-kind programs, including Food Stamps, considerations of political feasibility precluded an assault on the plethora of welfare programs spread across several cabinet departments and within the domain of several different congressional committees. Moreover, skillful political maneuvering by Sen. George McGovern, among others, forced the president to nationalize the Food Stamps program at a time when he would have preferred to focus congressional attention on FAP.[26]

With the decision to leave existing welfare programs in place, the president's proposal became little more than an incremental reform in AFDC. The 1967 public welfare amendments had already transformed the program into a negative income tax, albeit one with a 67 percent marginal tax rate. By reducing this tax rate to 50 percent and opening the program to families headed by able-bodied males, FAP was improving the program in significant ways, but the plan could hardly be characterized as nonincremental. In fact, when the complexities of combining FAP with Food Stamps and state supplementation of the federal benefit were taken into account, the marginal tax rate under FAP approached 67 percent.[27]

Similarly, FAP did nothing to alter the intergovernmental administration of AFDC, with the result that benefit levels would still differ significantly across states. This cross-state disparity would be reduced, but not eliminated, under FAP; while increased federal payments under the plan would raise benefit levels in the low-payment states, financial inducements were included in the bill to encourage high-payment states to continue supplementing federal payments at current levels.[28]

Partisan Mutual Adjustment and Group Struggle

With the breakdown of the rational model, policy-making would inevitably take on the form of a struggle among contending interests. Interest groups were active on all sides of the issue, making for a highly conflictual configuration of demand. The lineup of groups did not bode well for passage, however. Beyond the administration (which was itself internally divided on the merits of the proposal) there were few consistent proponents of the bill. The most persistent supporters were the nation's governors and county officials, who desperately wanted the fiscal relief promised by the bill. However, when that fiscal relief was later provided in a different form through the passage of President Nixon's revenue sharing initiative, the case for FAP became much less urgent to this group.[29]

Probably the most significant group mobilized in opposition to the president's proposal, inasmuch as its leadership ostensibly spoke for the poor, was the National Welfare Rights Organization. As we saw in Chapter 4, the potential costs of group membership weigh more heavily on the poor, making it almost impossible to mobilize the economically disadvantaged.[30] Founded in the early 1960s, the NWRO was an organization of AFDC recipients almost exclusively confined to the high-benefit states of the urban, industrialized states of the Northeast.[31] AFDC was treating this group well already; under FAP, their benefit levels would actually be reduced. Indeed, the only way to avoid hurting this group under any negative income tax proposal would be to set the income guarantee at a level equal to that in the highest paying state. The effect of such an increase in the guaranteed income is inevitably to raise the break-even point, the number of people on welfare, and the costs of the program to politically unacceptable levels.

At least two more distinct constituencies can be identified within the poverty population on the FAP issue, however. The first group, able-bodied males, would clearly benefit from FAP, inasmuch as AFDC provided them with no assistance whatever. A second group, beneficiaries living in low-payment states, particularly in the South, would also benefit through the significantly higher benefit levels FAP offered. Unfortunately, neither of these groups succeeded in mobilizing; the poor would be represented on this issue by a highly militant and vocal group that stood to lose from welfare reform.[32]

The NWRO went beyond mere opposition to FAP to charge that the measure was both punitive and racist (most of the group's members were black welfare mothers). NWRO's militant opposition to FAP reinforced the tendency among congressional liberals to distrust the president's motives and to oppose the bill as providing an inadequate guaranteed income level. The NWRO's proposal for a guaranteed income almost double that in the president's initiative—widely regarded as utopian and given no serious consideration by policy makers in the executive branch or on the congressional committees with jurisdiction over the issue—was nevertheless endorsed by numerous congressional liberals.[33]

The interests of the unorganized poor might have received at least some support from professional social workers or from representatives of organized religious groups. However, the National Association of Social Workers feared that FAP would eventually eliminate the need for social workers by providing the poor with cash rather than services. Ultimately the NASW joined with the NWRO in condemning FAP as both inadequate and racist.[34] Much the same thing could be said for the mainline Protestant groups. Although the Catholic Conference remained firm in support of FAP, Protestant groups developed serious doubts in the wake of the NWRO's militant opposition to the bill; in general, the Protestant position was one of damning with faint praise: support the principle of a guaranteed income while condemning the benefit levels as inadequate and calling for utopian reforms in the plan.[35]

Corporate Power and Welfare Reform

We saw in Chapter 5 that while corporations possess considerable potential power within any capitalistic society, business groups do not always act cohesively to pursue shared class interests. Welfare reform illustrates this phenomenon inasmuch as the major business groups were divided on the proposal. The National Chamber of Commerce worked to defeat the bill because it would add millions to the welfare rolls (and billions of dollars to the federal budget), and because its income guarantee would offer an alternative to low-wage employment, thus forcing up wages throughout the economy. At the same time, both the National Association of Manufacturers and the more liberal Committee for Economic Development endorsed the plan.[36]

Where the Chamber of Commerce was adamant in its opposition and mobilized effectively to undermine the bill at various stages along the way, support from the NAM and the CED was lukewarm. In Moynihan's words:

> Advanced opinion had come to look with favor on the notion of a guaranteed income to deal with problems of poverty and dependency. On the other hand, there were not many men with fire in their belly on the subject. One was simply in favor of it.[37]

Ultimately, welfare reform may be better understood as an instance of nondecision-making, as described in Chapter 5. Overt lobbying over the negative income tax—and apparent business divisions on the issue—would thus be less important than business control over the agenda. Seen in this perspective, FAP is less important for what it was—an incremental reform of AFDC—than for what it was not.

The chief proponents of this view are Frances Fox Piven and Richard Cloward. They see welfare as performing critical stablizing functions within any capitalistic economy:

> Historical evidence suggests that relief arrangements are initiated or expanded during the occasional outbreaks of civil disorder produced by mass unemployment, and are then abolished or contracted when political stability is restored. We shall argue that expansive relief policies are designed to mute civil disorder, and restrictive ones to reinforce work norms. In other words, relief policies are cyclical—liberal or restrictive depending on the problems of regulation in the larger society with which government must contend.[38]

By this reasoning, the welfare measures enacted in the New Deal period—including not only the various provisions of the Social Security Act but also direct programs of work relief—were a response to electoral instability and growing disorder generated by the Great Depression. With the return of high employment in the postwar years, relief was contracted through a variety of measures designed to make low-wage employment more attractive than welfare. Similarly, the urban riots of the 1960s, combined with the development of the welfare rights movement (in which the authors participated), led to a liberalization and expansion of welfare during that decade, which in effect produced the skyrocketing rolls facing the Nixon administration in 1969.[39]

Piven and Cloward thus rejected the Family Assistance Plan as being simply another in a long line of work-enforcing contractions of relief. In so doing, they gave more emphasis than most contemporary observers to the work requirements built into the program. As noted earlier, to qualify for FAP, a head of household would have to accept a job or job training. If he or she refused, however, only that individual's share of the total benefit—about $300 for most families—would be forfeited. Conservatives quickly dismissed this work requirement as inadequate, emphasizing that the plan still provided a substantial guaranteed income to families whether or not the primary wage earner worked at all. By contrast, Piven and Cloward saw this provision as inherently punitive, particularly when combined with a guaranteed income set at only 45 percent of the poverty level. On this point, Piven and Cloward are correct; proponents of the Friedman plan saw a low basic benefit as reinforcing the work incentives built into a negative income tax.

Seen in this light, welfare reform is a quintessential secondary issue; the grand issue of private control over labor market decisions was never raised. An ideal market presumes perfect factor mobility—the ability to shift resources instantly and costlessly from one line of commerce to another in response to changing prices. Inasmuch as few resources—least of all labor—are perfectly mobile, national and international economic events can severely disrupt local economies. At their worst, the dynamics of the free market can depress an entire region of the country (as with Appalachia in the middle part of this century and the industrialized Northeast more recently). Even individuals of strong character can do little to insulate themselves from these economic tides.[40] Seen in this light, the negative income tax was a conservative reform, designed to preserve the capitalistic economic system by mitigating the effects of economic downturns on workers and by rewarding low-wage employment.

A genuinely nonincremental change, in their view, would have involved a commitment by the federal government to guarantee full employment at "decent" wages through some combination of private investments and public service jobs. This had been the original aim of the Full Employment Act of 1946, which was vehemently opposed by business groups. The end result of that struggle was a much-weakened bill that identified full employment and price stability as coequal goals of economic policy and created the Council of Economic Advisers; provisions making the federal government the employer of last resort and establishing mandatory full employment targets were eliminated along the way.[41] Proponents of the Humphrey-Hawkins bill would mount a second campaign for these same reforms in the mid-1970s, again with disappointing results.[42] No such proposals would be forthcoming from the Nixon administration, however. FAP would encourage work and require heads of households to look for work, but it would do nothing to provide new jobs.

Effects of the Constitution on Policy-making

The constraints on rational decision making already operative on this issue were reinforced by the effects of the Constitution to virtually preclude a nonincremental outcome. We have already seen the contribution of federalism to the substantial problems plaguing the AFDC program; we have also observed that all of the alternatives receiving serious consideration within the Nixon administration would have preserved a significant role for the states in administering the program, thus accepting as inevitable a certain degree of cross-state variation in eligibility standards and benefit levels.

Moreover, the nation was in a period of divided government. President Nixon faced a Congress in which both houses were controlled by the Democratic party. As we saw in Chapter 3, however, the president is free in the American system of government to move beyond his party to construct a different coalition for every issue, and Democrats in Congress are much more supportive of higher spending and expanded coverage than are Republicans.

Unfortunately, the president's welfare reform proposal tended to divide both parties. Whenever social welfare initiatives have been proposed by Democratic presidents, the resulting congressional debate has tended to take on party lines; Northern liberal Democrats support such initiatives with enthusiasm while party pressures compel potential conservative defectors to support their president's program. At the same time, Republicans in Congress (with a small number of liberal exceptions) have been most comfortable in opposition both to new initiatives and to higher welfare spending.

With a Republican president proposing a major expansion of the welfare state, Republican conservatives were forced to choose between their principles and their president, while Southern Democrats were now free to engage in opposition.[43] At the same time, liberal Democrats, who might have supported the bill if it had been introduced by a Democratic president, were protective of their party's historical monopoly on the initiative in the policy area and, in any case, tended to despise and distrust President Nixon for his highly partisan attacks on various liberals in election campaigns dating back over two decades. A pathological form of party competition ensued, in which President Nixon sought to upstage the Democrats by proposing an initiative much bolder than any Democratic predecessor had seen fit to endorse, while Democrats responded by characterizing the plan as inadequate and ungenerous.

The president could not point to an electoral mandate for welfare reform to hold his party together and appeal to the opposition. In view of the consistent positions taken by the two parties on welfare issues over the years, few voters could have suspected that a Republican would become the first American president to propose a form of guaranteed minimum income, and there was no hint that this would be the case in the 1968 campaign. While Nixon had called for greater standardization of welfare benefits across states and emphasized the need to create new incentives for welfare recipients to move off welfare and onto private payrolls, he made no specific mention of a negative income tax.[44]

To become law, the Family Assistance Plan would have to pass both the House and the Senate before returning to President Nixon for his signature. Within the House, the bill would be referred to the Ways and Means Committee, chaired by Wilbur Mills, a powerful and highly effective chairman whose reputation for expertise on tax, trade, and welfare matters preserved a good deal of autonomy for the committee. With bipartisan support on the Ways and Means Committee (including both Mills and the senior Republican on the committee, John Byrnes of Wisconsin), FAP would pass the House in both 1970 and 1971.[45]

Within the Senate, however, the bill would face rougher sledding. Jurisdiction fell to the Finance Committee, which was almost devoid of potential supporters of welfare reform. The chairman, Russell Long of Louisiana, declared his opposition to FAP early on. The committee's seven Republicans were all conservatives, six from sparsely populated Western states with no real welfare problem. Six of the Democratic members were from the South or from border states, and three were deep Southerners who feared that FAP would undermine the caste system then operating in the South:

> Many white Southerners feared that FAP's guaranteed income would shrink the supply of cheap labor, bankrupt marginal industry, boost the cost of locally produced goods and services, increase taxes, and put more blacks into political office.[46]

With the lone exception of Sen. Abraham Ribicoff of Connecticut, who tried repeatedly (and unsuccessfully) to forge a compromise bill acceptable to the administration and a majority of the Senate, there were no members from urban constituencies with a real stake in welfare reform.

Opposition to the bill within the Finance Committee came from both the left and the right. The committee's liberals (with the important exception of Ribicoff, who knew something of the welfare problem from his days as governor of Connecticut and later as secretary of HEW) joined with the NWRO, NASW, and the mainline Protestant groups in denouncing the president's plan as inadequate and calling for a vastly more generous plan that had no real hope of passage.[47] The committee's conservatives were even more devastating in their attacks on the bill, pointing to the many ways in which work incentives built in to the negative income tax would interact with cutoff points for eligibility for in-kind programs to create disincentives to work for any individuals. (These were termed "notch effects.") While individuals were ostensibly made better off by working under a straight negative income tax, under FAP increased earnings would at some point forfeit eligibility for Medicaid, subsidized housing, or other in-kind benefits, thus making the individual much worse off than before.[48]

The Final Outcome

The various notch effects identified by the Finance Committee were sufficient to kill the bill in both 1970 and 1971, thus demonstrating the accuracy of Milton Friedman's thesis that a negative income tax must replace all existing welfare programs to work properly. If a genuinely nonincremental bill was precluded by political conditions, nothing less would stand a realistic chance of passage. However, even a fully federalized negative income tax that replaced all existing welfare programs, as called for by Friedman and others, would have been subject to the inherent trade-offs among conflicting objectives discussed earlier in this chapter.

One significant reform did emerge from the welfare policy debates of 1969 to 1971. Even as FAP was going down to defeat for the second time in 1971, Congress voted to consolidate the categorical assistance programs for the aged, blind, and disabled into a single program. The new program, Supplemental Security Income (or SSI), would be fully funded by the federal government and would provide a guaranteed income to members of these three previously distinct categories. In contrast to FAP, SSI passed easily, receiving almost no scrutiny from Congress, perhaps because it was perceived as an incremental reform of a set of programs aiding beneficiaries widely acclaimed as deserving.[49]

With the second defeat of FAP in 1971, President Nixon began to distance himself from the issue. George McGovern proposed a variation on the negative income tax in the 1972 primaries; Hubert Humphrey's attacks on that plan (which was poorly articulated and much more expensive than President Nixon's proposal) hurt McGovern in the later primaries. This convinced the president that it made little sense to continue spending scarce political capital on an idea with little popular support.[50] While variations on the negative income tax idea gained considerable support at HEW in the Ford years, they were forced off the agenda by Watergate and the energy crisis in 1974–1975.[51]

COMPREHENSIVE WELFARE REFORM
UNDER PRESIDENT CARTER

The welfare reform issue would resurface with the election of Jimmy Carter in 1976. In distinct contrast with the Family Assistance Plan, President Carter's attempt at welfare reform would consolidate existing welfare programs into a single, coherent plan. In instructing the Departments of Labor and Health, Education, and Welfare to work together in developing a reform proposal for submission to Congress, President Carter set important constraints on the internal debate over welfare reform. All proposals were to start off with the assumption that the existing welfare system would be abolished in its entirety, and that money currently going to those programs would be available instead for comprehensive reform initiatives. However, that sum would be the total available for welfare reform; the bureaucaracy was charged with finding a way to solve the welfare mess without spending any new money. This was referred to over the next three years as the ''zero cost requirement.''[52]

Another important lesson had been learned from the mistakes of the Nixon administration. Some distinction would have to be made between employables and unemployables. While it is very difficult to make this distinction in practice (particularly where mothers with small children are concerned), public opinion polls reveal an enduring support for making such a distinction. Moreover, as we saw earlier in this chapter, there is an inherent trade-off between adequacy and program costs in all negative income tax plans. Lifting recipients out of poverty by setting a high guaranteed income significantly raises the break-even point, adds millions to the welfare rolls, and significantly expands the costs of the program. By contrast, setting an income guarantee significantly below the poverty line lowers program costs, but it also makes the program vulnerable to attack as being "inadequate" for people with no other source of income.

Restricting coverage of the negative income tax to employables would avoid this problem. Unemployables could be given a straight guaranteed income (e.g., a negative income tax with a 100 percent marginal tax rate) set somewhere around the poverty line. With unemployables thus provided for, the guaranteed minimum income for employables could be set somewhere around half the poverty level, as with the Friedman plan, without invoking charges of benefit inadequacy for those with no other source of income. Indeed, a fairly low income floor would serve as an additional work incentive under the negative income tax.

Constraints on Comprehensive-Rationality

Despite these promising signs, there remained significant obstacles to a comprehensive overhaul of the welfare system in 1977. First of all, the case for welfare reform was much less urgent than had been the case in the early Nixon years. By 1977, welfare rolls were no longer skyrocketing; the number of beneficiaries had leveled off, albeit at a much higher level than ten years before. Moreover, the nationalization of the Food Stamps program had done much to ease the horizontal and vertical inequities of the AFDC program. The amount of food stamps one received was inversely proportional to cash income (including income from AFDC and other welfare programs): the lower the income, the higher the amount of food stamps received. Moreover, food stamps were available to male-headed households. While significant disparities in AFDC benefits persisted across states, the disparity in combined AFDC–food stamp benefits was not nearly so great, and no significant portion of the poverty population was excluded.[53]

If the tide for reform had ebbed, the welfare system was, if anything, even more irrational and incoherent than it had been when Nixon tackled the problem, however. With the dramatic expansion of both Food Stamps and Medicaid in the first half of the decade, the American "welfare state" consisted of a large number of poorly coordinated programs embodying very different approaches to the problem. According to Joseph Califano, secretary of HEW in 1977, at least twelve different cabinet departments administered welfare programs of one sort or another, falling within the jurisdiction of more than three hundred congressional committees or subcommittees.[54]

In short, President Carter's approach, in distinct contrast to Nixon's, was more utopian than remedial. With the major inequities largely ameliorated by the nationalization of the Food Stamps program, the major welfare program remaining was an untidy and uncoordinated patchwork of programs that was almost surely inefficient. A comprehensive overhaul of welfare might make this system more coherent, but it would do little to improve the lives of welfare recipients unless significantly higher amounts of money were devoted to attacking poverty, and the president's zero cost constraint (which was in turn a reflection of the political realities) ruled this out.

As we saw earlier, there is an inherent trade-off between adequacy and costs in any negative income tax plan. While this dilemma is reduced by separating out unemployables from the plan, the Carter initiative could not escape one problem Nixon faced. Setting the guaranteed income anywhere near the level of current benefits in the most generous states would protect current beneficiaries from harm under the program, but would also raise the program's costs well beyond the zero cost level. Keeping costs at or below the zero cost level necessitated a reduction of the income guarantee to somewhere around the middle of the range of state benefit levels; an early version of the plan was estimated to make more than nine million current recipients worse off while moving almost two million people below the poverty line.[55] Doing this immediately generated militant opposition from welfare rights organizations and their various advocates in Congress. There was simply no way out of this dilemma.

To get around the president's zero cost constraint, participants in the internal struggle within the executive branch began to expand the number of programs that were arguably part of the current welfare system and thus subject to abolition. If the pot of money available for welfare reform could be sufficiently enlarged, a workable compromise of these conflicting principles might still be possible. The reclassification of programs as poverty programs eventually went so far as to include legislative proposals by the administration to expand the CETA program or to buffer the poor from gasoline taxes in the president's energy package that had not yet been enacted into law. Ultimately, these phony ''offsets'' failed to fool key policy makers in Congress; the plan was widely understood as requiring substantial new revenues.

The primary political conditions for incremental policy-making still applied in 1977: conflict over objectives and an inadequate knowledge base. Welfare reform still meant different things to different people. At the same time, the consequences of various proposals remained unclear. The results of the negative income tax experiments were now in but were not encouraging. If anything, the negative income tax seemed to discourage work, only marginally in primary earners but more significantly among secondary earners (e.g., wives and older children). Even more important, the negative income tax was associated with *higher* levels of marital instability, contrary to all expectations. While no one had any good explanation of these findings, they called into serious question one of the most significant advantages claimed for the negative income tax over the existing AFDC program.[56] In short, nothing had happened between 1970 and 1977 to facilitate rational decision making on this troubled issue.

Checks and Balances

With the election of a Democratic president in 1976, divided government would no longer be an obstacle. The same party would control both ends of Pennsylvania Avenue for the first time in eight years. However, the welfare issue continued to divide Democrats in Congress. Comprehensive reform was favored by James Corman, chair of the House

Ways and Means Subcommittee on Unemployment Compensation and Public Assistance, and Sen. Daniel P. Moynihan, chair of the Senate Finance Subcommittee on Public Assistance. However, the chair of Ways and Means, Al Ullman, was adamantly opposed to the principle of a guaranteed income and favored incremental reform at best. Sen. Russell Long, still chair of the Senate Finance Committee, remained opposed to any form of guaranteed income and sought instead to devise ways to encourage welfare mothers to work.[57]

While President Nixon's decision to leave existing welfare programs intact may well have doomed welfare reform in 1970 and 1971, President Carter's decision to eliminate these programs would vastly expand the number of hostile committees through which a comprehensive reform package would have to pass. To make matters worse, the House committee reforms of the mid-1970s created a plethora of new subcommittees with overlapping jurisdiction over many policy areas, including welfare. Ultimately, President Carter abandoned efforts to abolish all existing welfare programs (which would have brought into play more than three hundred congressional committees and subcommittees, as noted above), choosing instead merely to cash out Food Stamps and to consolidate AFDC, Food Stamps, and the SSI program. Even this limited consolidation of benefit programs would have to clear six different congressional committees in addition to the House Rules Committee in order to reach the floor of the House and Senate for a vote.[58]

Group Struggle

There was predictable opposition within the executive branch to the abolition of existing programs. The Department of Labor sought to protect unemployment compensation and job training programs while the Department of Agriculture fought for Food Stamps. Housing and Urban Development wanted to preserve rent supplements. Veterans' pensions were similarly sacrosanct. Each of these bureaucratic opponents of comprehensive reform had ties to allies in Congress, while the poor were represented (as was the case in 1970–1971) primarily by welfare rights groups representing elements of the poverty population that would be harmed by the program. And, as was the case with FAP, the most persistent proponents of welfare reform were governors and mayors whose primary interest in fiscal relief could be satisfied by alternative measures short of comprehensive reform.

Corporate Power

The power of business in the 1977 policy debates was revealed less through the overt activity of business organizations than by the internationalization of business values by many, if not all, of the participants within Congress and the executive branch. This is what Lindblom termed "control without trying" (recall Chapter 5), and it is worth reiterating that he found such indirect influence to be more important than overt lobbying activities in maintaining business power in capitalistic societies.

The internalization of business values is perhaps most clearly seen in the arguments marshaled against the primary alternative to a negative income tax considered within the administration. Bureaucrats within the Department of Labor advocated a program of guaranteed public service jobs for employables, combined with a guaranteed income for unemployables. Advocates of this approach had recently lost a similar battle on the Humphrey-Hawkins bill, which began as an effort to make the federal government the employer of last resort within the U.S. economy. President Carter had supported the legislation, and signed the eventual bill, only after it had been so severely watered down as to be little more than a symbolic nod in the direction of full employment. The battle over welfare reform thus offered these interests a second chance to get a guaranteed jobs bill.

Under the Labor Department plan, employables would be offered a public service job—which would be guaranteed by the government as the employer of last resort—on a take it or leave it basis; there would be no welfare. Advocates of this approach emphasized the greater self-respect that flows out of the self-sufficiency associated with a steady job (as opposed to reliance on welfare) and pointed to the futility of creating work incentives through a negative income tax without taking strong action to move toward genuine full employment; only a major commitment to provide public service jobs could move the economy beyond a 5 to 7 percent unemployment rate in their view.

As Lindblom and Miliband would predict, bureaucratic opponents, both within HEW and the Office of Management and Budget, marshaled arguments against the plan that consistently equated business interests with the public interest. A major question centered around how much to pay workers in public service jobs. Setting wage levels at or around the minimum wage would hold down program costs while failing to lift many recipients out of poverty. However, if wages were set substantially above the minimum wage, public service jobs would be more attractive than private employment for many workers. Thus, many people would leave their current jobs to take public service jobs; as a result, the program would fail to reach the original target population. Moreover, a public service wage rate significantly above the minimum wage rate would contribute in the long run to inflationary pressures by unnaturally driving up wage rates throughout the economy. Finally, and perhaps most important, it was not at all clear that the federal government knew how to create enough jobs in the public sector to effectively serve as the employer of last resort.[59]

The Demise of Welfare Reform

Advocates of a negative income tax persuaded the president to combine welfare reform with some expansion in public service employment short of a commitment to provide jobs for all.[60] This represented a compromise acceptable to both camps. There would be a negative income tax for employables, as advocated by policy analysts at OMB and HEW. At the same time, an expansion in public service employment would appease participants from the Labor Department without committing the federal government to act as employer of last resort.

President Carter's welfare reform initiative would ultimately fail to reach the floor in either house of Congress, a casualty of the incompatibility of the objectives held by various participants and the president's ambitious domestic agenda, which included plans for comprehensive energy legislation, tax reform, national health insurance, creation of a cabinet-level Department of Education, deregulation of air and surface transportation, and civil service reform. Out of this list, tax reform, energy, health insurance, and welfare reform would all have to pass through the Ways and Means Committee in the House and the Finance Committee in the Senate. The president would have to choose among these various proposals, and he could ill afford to spend scarce political capital on an issue that was going nowhere.

With the death of welfare reform, President Carter successfully sought a major expansion in the public service jobs component of the CETA program (the Comprehensive Employment and Training Act, a block grant program for jobs and job training enacted in the Nixon years). Public service jobs created under CETA more than doubled as a result, going from 300,000 when Carter took office to 725,000 by March of 1978. In addition, various other public works and job training bills would employ or train more than 1.4 million people beyond the 2.5 million already enrolled in CETA.[61]

But there would be no commitment to act as employer of last resort, and the expansion under CETA would be short lived. Budgetary pressures brought on by a resurgence of inflation led to spending cuts for CETA in 1978, combined with a greater effort to target jobs to the hard-core disadvantaged. Ironically, as CETA became increasingly effective in targeting benefits to the poor, it lost much of its base of political support. Wilbur Cohen's objections to the negative income tax would be borne out for public jobs programs: poor people's programs invite political attack.[62]

THE LEGACY OF FAILED REFORM

There has been no attempt at comprehensive welfare reform since the failed effort of the Carter years. The Reagan administration took a very different approach to the issue. Work incentives were judged both ineffective and excessively expensive; accordingly, the administration successfully sought elimination of the work incentives provisions built into AFDC by the 1967 amendments. AFDC is once again a form of guaranteed income for qualifying mothers with children (i.e., it is a negative income tax with a 100 percent marginal tax rate on earned income).

Although various social insurance programs clearly offered a greater potential for budget savings—in the fiscal year 1981 budget, for example, the federal government spent more than $200 billion on Social Security, Medicare, and unemployment compensation, as compared with less than $70 billion for means-tested programs—the Reagan administration made repeated cuts in spending for assorted means-tested programs during President Reagan's first term, while leaving social insurance programs almost untouched.[63] These benefit cuts brought serious hardship to millions of welfare recipients, reducing benefit levels for many and ending eligibility entirely for others, without ultimately achieving the budgetary savings promised by their proponents.[64]

In the wake of the failure to enact comprehensive welfare reform, the problem of poverty continues unabated. By 1989, the poverty level for a family of four had risen with inflation to approximately $12,000 in annual income. The poverty rate for black Americans was three times as high as that for whites, at 30.7 percent, and the rate for female-headed households was almost 36 percent.[65]

Serious inequities remain in the AFDC program. In March 1984, the average monthly AFDC payment for a family of four was only $91 in Mississippi and $111 in Alabama. By contrast, the average monthly payment was $295 in Massachusetts, $431 in New York, $483 in California, and $585 in Alaska.[66] Able-bodied males remain ineligible for the program in more than half the states.

Our nation's welfare system remains both inadequate and inequitable. In the wake of the repeated failures to enact comprehensive reforms in the decade of the seventies, the question facing policy makers is whether to proceed incrementally or comprehensively. The prospects for comprehensive welfare reform will be assessed in the following chapter, which examines in some detail the conditions giving rise to nonincremental policy change.

NOTES

1. One of the key participants, Daniel P. Moynihan, explicitly characterized the proposals as a departure from the incremental model. See Daniel P. Moynihan, *The Politics of a Guaranteed Income* (New York: Random House, Vintage Books, 1973), pp. 3–16.
2. Herrell R. Rodgers, Jr., *The Cost of Human Neglect* (Armonk, N.Y.: M. E. Sharpe, 1982), Table 2-2, p. 18.
3. Martha Derthick, *The Influence of Federal Grants* (Cambridge, Mass.: Harvard University Press, 1970), p. 49.
4. The federal government will match state funds up to a maximum payment per recipient, after which the states can continue to supplement the benefit level. But there is no minimum benefit level, and the federal government is committed to match state contributions (up to the maximum) for as many recipients as a given state may have. See Derthick, pp. 35 and 43–45.
5. Sar A. Levitan, *Programs in Aid of the Poor,* 5th ed. (Baltimore: Johns Hopkins University Press, 1985), pp. 31–32. See also Tom Joe and Cheryl Rogers, *By the Few for the Few* (Lexington, Mass.: D. C. Heath, 1985), pp. 23–29.
6. Theodore R. Marmor and Martin Rein, ''Reforming 'The Welfare Mess': The Fate of the Family Assistance Plan, 1969–1972,'' in Allan P. Sindler, (ed.) *Policy and Politics in America* (Boston: Little, Brown, 1973), p. 5.
7. Levitan, p. 31.
8. Frances Fox Piven and Richard A. Cloward, *Regulating the Poor* (New York: Pantheon Books, 1971), pp. 149–161.
9. Piven and Cloward, pp. 135–139.
10. The most important factors contributing to higher welfare spending levels seem to be the degree of urbanization and industrialization, the degree of affluence (as measured by per capita income), the percentage of the population of foreign stock, and—perhaps most important—the competitiveness of the major political parties within the state. See Derthick, pp. 51–52. See also Richard E. Dawson and James A. Robinson, ''The Politics of Welfare,'' in Herbert Jacob and Kenneth N. Vines (eds.), *Politics in the American States* (Boston: Little, Brown, 1965), pp. 371–409; Thomas R. Dye, *Politics, Economics, and the Public* (Chicago: Rand McNally, 1966), pp. 124–128; and V. O. Key, Jr., *Southern Politics* (New York: Vintage Books, 1949), Chapter 14, ''Nature and Consequences of One-Party Factionalism,'' pp. 298–311.
11. Piven and Cloward, pp. 132–145.
12. Derthick, pp. 61–62.
13. Levitan, p. 34. See also Rodgers, pp. 73–74.

14. Rodgers, pp. 82–83.
15. Vincent J. and Vee Burke, *Nixon's Good Deed* (New York: Columbia University Press, 1974), pp. 24–26.
16. Frances Fox Piven and Richard Cloward provide some data on the dimensions of the problem:

> Between December 1964 and February 1969, the rolls in seventy-eight Northern urban counties exhibited a rise of 80 per cent (having already risen 53 per cent in the previous four years). In many cities, the rises were spectacular. . . . The greatest increases after 1964 occurred in the "big five" metropolitan centers where blacks had come to be concentrated; having risen 55 per cent in the early 1960's, these counties then jumped 105 per cent (the leaders, New York and Los Angeles, rose 137 and 145 per cent, respectively).

See Piven and Cloward, pp. 334–335.
17. Moynihan, p. 84.
18. See Milton Friedman, *Capitalism and Freedom* (Chicago: University of Chicago Press, 1962), pp. 177–195; and Robert J. Lampman, "Prognosis for Poverty," *Proceedings of 57th Annual Conference of the National Tax Association* (Pittsburgh: September 1964), pp. 71–81; and Lampman, "Approaches to the Reduction of Poverty," *American Economic Review, Papers and Proceedings,* 55 (May 1965), pp. 521–529. The concept of a negative income tax had been touched on by a wide variety of economists from the 1940s onward, however. See Christopher Green, *Negative Taxes and the Poverty Problem* (Washington, D.C.: Brookings Institution, 1967), pp. 57–58, especially footnote 21, p. 57.
19. All proponents of the negative income tax advocate varying payment levels according to variations in cost of living and family size.
20. Programs with efficiency benefits move an economy from a point inside its production possibility frontier to a point on that frontier, or (even better) they serve somehow to shift the whole frontier outward, making it possible to produce more goods and services with the same factor inputs.
21. Martin Anderson, *Welfare* (Stanford, Calif.: Hoover Institution Press, 1978), pp. 142–143.
22. Moynihan, pp. 58, 191–192, and 408–409; Burke and Burke, pp. 21–22. On the eventual results of the experiment, see also Martin Anderson, pp. 87–132.
23. Burke and Burke, pp. 36–39.
24. Burke and Burke, p. 41. The other members of the task force were: Marion Folsom, secretary of HEW under Eisenhower; Mitchell Ginsberg, head of the welfare program in New York City; and Wilbur Schmidt, secretary of the welfare department for the state of Wisconsin.
25. Marmor and Rein, pp. 12–16.
26. For a full account of this episode, see Nick Kotz, *Let Them Eat Promises* (Garden City, N.Y.: Anchor Books, 1971).
27. Burke and Burke, pp. 168–169.
28. Burke and Burke, pp. 160–166.
29. Burke and Burke, pp. 179 and 182. The Urban Coalition, a citizens' lobby founded in 1967 by John Gardner, a former secretary of HEW, also provided consistent lobbying support, as did the United States Catholic Conference. See Moynihan, pp. 277–284 and 298–299.
30. On the difficulties in mobilizing the poor generally, see Frances Fox Piven and Richard A. Cloward, *Poor People's Movements* (New York: Pantheon, 1977).
31. For a biography of George Wiley, the founder of NWRO, see Nick Kotz and Mary Lynn Kotz, *A Passion for Equality* (New York: Norton, 1977).

32. Burke and Burke, p. 159.
33. On NWRO's role in defeating the Family Assistance Plan, see Burke and Burke, pp. 159–164 and 172–177; and Moynihan, pp. 327–345.
34. Burke and Burke, pp. 144–146; and Moynihan, pp. 302–327.
35. Moynihan, pp. 295–302.
36. Moynihan, pp. 285–294.
37. Moynihan, p. 287.
38. Piven and Cloward, *Regulating the Poor,* p. xiii.
39. On the expansion of welfare in the 1960s, see Piven and Cloward, *Regulating the Poor,* pp. 248–284. For a critique of their thesis, see Robert B. Albritton, "Social Amelioration through Mass Insurgency? A Reexamination of the Piven and Cloward Thesis," *American Political Science Review,* 73 (December 1979), pp. 1003–1011. Piven and Cloward's response, and Albritton's reply to their response, appear in the same issue, pp. 1012–1023.
40. On this point, see John A. Young and Jan M. Newton, *Capitalism and Human Obsolescence* (Montclair, N.J.: Allanheld, Osmun, & Co., 1980). For a particularly good example of a study taking this point of view, see Janet M. Fitchen, *Poverty in Rural America* (Boulder, Colo.: Westview, 1981).
41. Stephen Kemp Bailey, *Congress Makes a Law* (New York: Random House, Vintage Books, 1964).
42. Philip Harvey, *Securing the Right to Employment* (Princeton, N.J.: Princeton University Press, 1989), pp. 99–117.
43. In this respect, the social welfare issue resembles the politics of foreign aid. On the politics of foreign aid, see Leroy N. Rieselbach, *The Roots of Isolationism* (Indianapolis: Bobbs-Merrill, 1966); and Aage R. Clausen, *How Congressmen Decide* (New York: St. Martin's, 1973), especially Chapter 8, "Presidential Pull up Capitol Hill," pp. 192–212.
44. Moynihan, p. 67.
45. Moynihan, pp. 398–438.
46. Burke and Burke, p. 147.
47. Moynihan, pp. 439–483; Burke and Burke, pp. 177–187.
48. Moynihan, pp. 439–542; Burke and Burke, pp. 152–165 and 177–187.
49. Burke and Burke, pp. 188–204.
50. Burke and Burke, pp. 184–185.
51. A. James Reichley, *Conservatives in an Age of Change* (Washington, D.C.: Brookings Institution, 1981), pp. 151–152.
52. Laurence E. Lynn, Jr. and David deF. Whitman, *The President as Policymaker* (Philadelphia: Temple University Press, 1981).
53. Jeffrey M. Berry, *Feeding Hungry People* (New Brunswick, N.J.: Rutgers University Press, 1984), pp. 184–185.
54. Joseph A. Califano, Jr., *Governing America* (New York: Simon and Schuster, 1981), p. 365.
55. Lynn and Whitman, p. 213.
56. See Lynn and Whitman, pp. 247–249, for Senator Moynihan's shocked reaction. See also Anderson, pp. 87–132, for a typical conservative's "I told you so" response.
57. Califano, pp. 322–323.
58. Califano, p. 365.
59. Lynn and Whitman, pp. 126–129.
60. Lynn and Whitman, p. 128.
61. Donald C. Baumer and Carl E. Van Horn, *The Politics of Unemployment* (Washington, D.C.: Congressional Quarterly Press, 1985), p. 91.

62. Baumer and Van Horn, pp. 125–156.
63. Timothy M. Smeeding, ''Is the Safety Net Still Intact?'' in D. Lee Bawden (ed.), *The Social Contract Revisited* (Washington, D.C.: Urban Institute Press, 1984), pp. 69–124.
64. Tom Joe and Cheryl Rogers, *By the Few For the Few* (Lexington, Mass.: Lexington Books, 1985).
65. U.S. Department of Commerce, Bureau of the Census, ''Money Income and Poverty Status of Families and Persons in the United States: 1989,'' *Current Population Reports, Consumer Income*, Series P-60, No. 168 (September 1990), pp. 56–57, 86.

CHAPTER 12

Policy Change: Constraints and Possibilities

Chapter 8 identified a series of generalizations derived from the five models reviewed in this volume. Those generalizations were confined to the agenda-setting, policy adoption, and policy implementation stages. In light of the analysis in Part II, we are now in a position to draw a number of conclusions regarding the potential for nonincremental policy change.

Nonincremental change is quite simply impossible for many issues. The analysis presented here forces us to think about policy change in a very different way than we have before. The sources of incrementalism reviewed in this volume tend to be powerful macropolitical forces largely beyond the control of policy makers in the short run. While presidential leadership or an aroused public opinion may produce a legislative breakthrough when the conditions are right, the failure of policy makers to produce nonincremental change in a given situation does not necessarily indicate a failure of leadership.

For example, there is little a determined president or legislator can do to facilitate nonincremental policy change on a given issue when the conditions for rational decision making remain unmet, as was the case throughout the 1970s on the issue of welfare reform. While the negative income tax is a perfect example of what Brown termed a rationalizing policy, it did not constitute a genuine rationalizing breakthrough, as defined in Chapter 10. In the wake of the long struggle over welfare reform, carried on through two presidential administrations, it became very clear that the negative income tax could not reconcile the conflicting objectives of the various participants. Both the Nixon and Carter initiatives qualified as incremental rationalizing policies at best. Under Reagan, rationalizing policies would take on decremental forms.

Nonincremental change is similarly precluded for what I have termed pure problems of value disagreement, like abortion or Social Security reform. Although policy outcomes will tend to be incremental in this cell, the policy process giving rise to these outcomes will be very different from what Lindblom envisioned. Consensual knowledge makes for an unusual clarity of self-interest for active groups. The redistributive consequences of proposed policies are readily apparent to all involved, with an attendant increase in the level of overt conflict. Under such circumstances, even incremental policy changes will be difficult to negotiate.

The protracted deadlock over how to meet the Gramm-Rudman budget deficit reduction targets in the fall of 1990 provided a recent example of just such an issue of "whose ox is gored." The primary conflict centered around who should bear the brunt of the various tax increases and benefit cuts necessary to meet the Gramm-Rudman targets. While workable solutions were readily available—income tax increases, gasoline tax increases, cuts in Medicare or Social Security, a value-added tax, and so on—all had immediate and highly undesirable political repercussions, which led many participants to question how much (if at all) the deficit was really harming the economy. Given the degree of conflict over objectives, both within and between the two parties, an intense political conflict followed by a compromise that goes only part way toward solving the long-term budget problem was the most one could realistically expect.

Moreover, obstacles to mobilizing the disadvantaged prevent many nonincremental proposals from being seriously considered. While most problems are brought to the agenda by affected publics, poor people lack effective lobbies and most do not vote. Welfare reform reached the agenda in 1970 because AFDC rolls were skyrocketing. The problem was defined as getting control of program costs that were rapidly becoming unacceptably high to policy makers at both the federal and state levels. While some liberals sensed an opportunity in the welfare crisis to raise benefit levels and fill in gaps in coverage, most were content to play politics with the issue, condemning the president's initiative and calling for the passage of utopian alternatives. With the leveling off of welfare rolls later in the decade, the welfare crisis lost much of its urgency for most policy makers. No one was prepared to spend much money on welfare reform, which meant that program costs would be held down by a low minimum benefit level and/or a punitive marginal tax rate.

If welfare recipients had been represented by one or more well-organized and highly legitimate beneficiary groups, as are the aged, the prospects for genuinely nonincremental change would have been much improved. Unfortunately, as we saw in Chapter 11, welfare rights groups almost inherently lack legitimacy, and the failure of significant portions of the poverty population to mobilize played a significant role in blocking even incremental reforms of welfare. The National Welfare Rights Organization represented welfare recipients in high-benefit states, who stood to lose benefits under both the Nixon and Carter proposals, while subgroups of the poor who would have gained from these initiatives remained unmobilized.

While there is no question that checks and balances at the national level contribute to incremental policy outcomes, no institutional reform can compensate for the breakdown of rational decision making or the failure of significant segments of our population to participate in politics. Our system of checks and balances works reasonably well where the conditions for rationality are approximated, and it is highly responsive to groups of all sorts that succeed in mobilizing. Similarly, the collapse of communism in Eastern Europe serves as a reminder that the grand issue of capitalism remains off the agenda within Western democracies because most of us remain satisfied with the high standard of living and considerable degree of personal freedom such a system delivers.

The most significant obstacle to nonincremental policy change stemming from our Constitution is almost surely federalism. Even where circumstances permit a major policy departure at the national level, legislative triumphs may be eroded or overturned by intergovernmental policy implementation. Given the strategic position of corporate interests at the state and local level, it would seem imperative that any coalition in favor of nonincremental policy change also include a sizeable portion of the business community. To the extent that this condition is not met for an issue, major policy changes are unlikely to endure.

While a succession of small changes can add up to a major alteration in policy, policy-making through a rapid succession of small steps does not necessarily lead to desirable policies. In principle, as Lindblom has argued in recent years, the pace of change is a function of the *number* of steps taken as well as their size: "A fast-moving sequence of small changes can more speedily accomplish a drastic alteration of the status quo than can only infrequent major policy change."[1] From Lindblom's point of view, the most serious indictment of the American political system is not that it precludes major policy departures, but rather that its emphasis on "due deliberation" may ultimately be incompatible with the effective pursuit of incrementalism.

The failure of the American system to produce policy through a rapid sequence of small steps would be more alarming if one could be assured that incremental policy-making consistently yields good results. The Vietnam War provides a classic counterexample, however, as would the more current crisis of the savings and loan industry. Both these policy failures were the product of a long series of relatively small missteps that culminated in major problems.[2] The prescriptive case for incrementalism assumes that there are no sunk costs associated with policies (e.g., that any policy can be readily reversed or replaced at any time no matter how much has been invested in it), and that small policy changes are sufficient to identify potentially undesirable consequences of policies. In reality, neither of these conditions is typically satisfied. The dangers in certain courses of action become apparent only after a whole series of incremental steps have been taken, at which time the sunk costs of governmental involvement can make policy reversal almost impossible.[3]

Welfare reform provides an excellent example of this phenomenon. We saw in Chapter 11 that the conditions for rational decision making were not satisfied in either 1969 or 1977, making some kind of incremental outcome almost inevitable. It is plausible to infer from this experience that incrementalism is, in fact, the best way to make policy. With the benefit of hindsight, President Nixon might have done better to propose the Nathan plan, which would have established for the first time a minimum benefit level to be fully funded by the federal government. While exacerbating the already existing inequity between households headed by males and females, the Nathan plan would nevertheless have brought about significant fiscal relief while at the same time improving the lives of millions of welfare recipients in low-benefit states. Alternatively, the president might have pushed for mandatory state participation in the AFDC-UF program, an incremental reform that would have ended the exclusion of male heads of households from the AFDC program without buying into the dilemmas inherent in any negative income tax scheme. The same thing could be said for President Carter in 1977.

Apart from the question of whether or not these incremental reforms would ultimately have passed (and it is by no means clear that they would have), there remains the serious question of work incentives. The marginal tax rates on earned income operating under the AFDC program even in the wake of the 1967 reforms were punitive: recipients would keep only one dollar out of every three dollars earned. To mandate state participation in AFDC-UF would be, in effect, to extend this work disincentive to able-bodied males, hardly a desirable policy or one likely to pass two houses of Congress. The Nathan plan would not have extended this misguided policy, but neither would it have reformed it.

If one could go back to 1935 and begin all over again with a blank slate—with no vested interests in the status quo—some form of negative income tax (probably along the lines of the Carter plan, which distinguished between employables and unemployables) would almost surely be preferable to the existing hodgepodge of welfare programs. But it is almost impossible to eliminate existing welfare programs, and leaving them in place makes for inevitable notch effects as individuals move up the income ladder. Moreover, a politically feasible plan would inevitably lower benefit levels for many current recipients, which is politically unacceptable to the organized representatives of the poor (who tend to be from high-benefit states) and to sympathetic legislators in control of key veto points. The proper lesson to be drawn from the negative income tax experience is not that incrementalism is a superior method of policy-making, but that sunk costs and vested interests in established policies—expanded and modified incrementally over the years—can make rational reform impossible.

Under normal circumstances, nonincremental policy change tends to occur (if at all) in two distinct stages. Issues tend to move through a predictable life cycle, and policy-making takes on a very different form when the participants have accumulated experience with an issue through a series of policy cycles. In every way, policy-making is more difficult for unfamiliar issues. New problems tend to be poorly understood and characterized by a high degree of value conflict. Moreover, new problems lack automatic agenda status as recurring issues and thus must compete for scarce space on the agenda with a whole host of other issues, including the budget, crises, and the president's program. Perhaps most important, new problems will lack well-formed policy communities. Existing policy communities will have formed in response to previous problems, will tend accordingly to misperceive new problems, and will be extremely resistant to reorganization and reform. Because new problems typically touch on the interests of a wide variety of old policy communities, the number of veto points in the legislative process will be even greater than usual. For all these reasons, unfamiliar problems tend to permit federal role breakthroughs at best.

The energy crisis of the 1970s provides an instructive example here. As noted in previous chapters, the energy issue was forced on the agenda in 1973 by the Arab oil embargo. A series of policy subsystems centering around different fuels are ill-equipped to deal with the new crisis; a familiar problem had taken on new dimensions and demanded new ways of thinking. Lacking both consensual objectives and consensual knowledge, policy makers could aspire to little more than incremental responses to the new problem. Seen in this light, President Carter's ambitious energy package stood no real chance of passage; like the negative income tax, it constituted an attempt at nonincremental change when the political circumstances of the period precluded such a change. In retrospect, the most significant action of the Carter presidency, at least for the energy issue, may well have been his successful effort to create a cabinet-level Department of Energy, thus contributing significantly to the development of a much-needed policy community.

Once the initial battle over the federal role breakthrough is finished, a process of agenda convergence often occurs, shifting the terms of the debate away from conflicts over federal objectives and toward proper means to shared ends. As the problem becomes more familiar and better understood, members of the policy community come to share a common language and a common view of how the world works. In other words, the policy area begins to move toward consensual objectives and consensual knowledge—a process that is by no means automatic, of course, and that can take more time for some policies than for others. While much policy-making on familiar issues takes the form of incremental rationalizing policies, much as Lindblom would predict, at times the members of the policy community may converge on a solution to the problem (or at least, some aspect of it), leading to what I have termed a rationalizing breakthrough.

The difficulties involved in generating and sustaining policy change should not deter us from trying to solve significant public problems. Over the past fifteen years, policy makers have been forced to confront problems growing out of experience with a wide variety of "breakthrough policies" enacted in the New Deal and Great Society periods. High expectations gave way to disappointment and disillusion in many instances; in recent years, both liberal and conservative administrations have begun to shrink from commitments made in earlier eras. In Chapter 10 we focused on three forms of decremental response to problems associated with breakthrough policies: decentralization, deregulation, and disengagement. While such strategies may be entirely appropriate for some policy areas (like airline regulation), it is hard to see how they could lead to better outcomes in the strip mining and welfare reform cases we examined in depth.

However, decrementalism is only one possible response to the complexities inherent in policy change. As noted above, nonincremental policy change is most likely to occur only for familiar problems. Federal involvement in a policy area triggers the development of a policy community. Over time, consensual objectives can develop through agenda convergence; as policy makers gain experience with a policy, consensual knowledge may follow. *To paraphrase Schattschneider, all federal role breakthroughs are an experiment in learning. Schulman's finding for the man on the moon project is thus true for social problems as well: sometimes an attempt at large change is necessary to generate the necessary knowledge base.*

While Piven and Cloward are probably right in arguing that any real welfare reform would involve a commitment to strive for full employment, attaining this goal would require a rationalizing breakthrough achieved after years of experience with public service jobs. A federal obligation to act as employer of last resort, as originally called for in the Full Employment bill of 1946 and the Humphrey-Hawkins legislation of 1976–1977, would represent a significant federal role breakthrough. While objections to such a plan in

1977 had the effect of equating business interests with the public interest, as Lindblom and Miliband would predict, HEW and OMB were probably correct in arguing that the knowledge base did not exist at that time to create anything like 1.5 million jobs, let alone to provide guaranteed jobs to as many people as might demand them.

Realistically, as Schulman also recognized, attempts at nonincremental change cannot be sustained where public support erodes. Once a focusing event has aroused a mass public, issues often lose salience in a predictable attention cycle. Where public support for governmental action remains strong over time, however, agencies may be able to withstand political attack even after an issue ceases to be salient. For example, President Reagan's attempts to weaken the Environmental Protection Agency significantly were eventually thwarted by an aroused mass public opinion, as was his attempt early in his first term to drop out of arms control negotiations with the Soviets while adding to our strategic nuclear arsenal. In terms of the concentric circles identified in Chapter 9, mass public opinion set firm, albeit broad, boundaries on policy makers on both these issues. The lesson is clear: where voters remain committed to governmental action, their leaders will follow.

Ultimately, the central theme of this book is the need for more realistic expectations regarding the potential for major policy change. As the century draws to a close, protracted budget deficits and public disillusionment with expensive policy failures severely constrain our capacity for effective action. However, realistic citizens are patient citizens, with a sustained commitment to the solution of difficult problems. Significant policy change can be attained only by a persevering public. The coming decade will reveal what kind of people we will be.

NOTES

1. Charles E. Lindblom, "Still Muddling, Not Yet Through," *Public Administration Review*, 39 (November/December 1979), p. 520.
2. On the savings and loans crisis, see Stephen Pizzo, Mary Fricker, and Paul Muolo, *Inside Job* (New York: McGraw-Hill, 1989). See also Steven V. Roberts with Gary Cohen, "Villains of the S&L Crisis," *U.S. News and World Report*, 109, no. 13, October 1, 1990, pp. 53–59.
3. Brian Hogwood and B. Guy Peters, *Policy Dynamics* (New York: St. Martin's, 1983), p. 12.

Bibliography

Abramson, Paul R.; Aldrich, John H.; and Rohde, David W. *Change and Continuity in the 1980 Elections.* Rev. ed. Washington, D.C.: Congressional Quarterly Press, 1983.

Ackerman, Bruce A., and Hassler, William T. *Clean Coal: Dirty Air.* New Haven, Conn.: Yale University Press, 1981.

Albritton, Robert B. "Social Amelioration through Mass Insurgency? A Reexamination of the Piven and Cloward Thesis." *American Political Science Review* 73 (December 1979): 1003–1011.

Allison, Graham T. *Essence of Decision: Explaining the Cuban Missile Crisis.* Boston: Little, Brown, 1971.

Almond, Gabriel. *The American People and Foreign Policy.* New York: Praeger, 1965.

Amaker, Norman C. *Civil Rights and the Reagan Administration.* Washington, D.C.: Urban Institute Press, 1988.

American Political Science Association, Committee on Political Parties. *Toward a More Responsible Party System.* New York: Holt, Rinehart, and Winston, 1950.

Anderson, James E. *Public Policy-Making.* 3d ed. New York: Holt, Rinehart, and Winston, 1984.

Anderson, Martin. *Welfare: The Political Economy of Welfare Reform in the United States.* Stanford, Calif.: Hoover Institution Press, 1978.

Appleby, Paul H. *Policy and Administration.* University: University of Alabama Press, 1949.

Arnold, Ron. *At the Eye of the Storm: James Watt and the Environmentalists.* Chicago: Regnery Gateway, 1982.

Axelrod, Regina S. "Energy Policy: Changing the Rules of the Game." In *Environmental Policy in the 1980s,* edited by Norman J. Vig and Michael E. Kraft, pp. 203–225. Washington, D.C.: Congressional Quarterly Press, 1984.

Bachrach, Peter. *The Theory of Democratic Elitism: A Critique.* Boston: Little, Brown, 1967.

Bachrach, Peter, and Baratz, Morton S. *Power and Poverty: Theory and Practice.* New York: Oxford University Press, 1970.

Bailey, Stephen Kemp. *Congress Makes a Law: The Story Behind the Employment Act of 1946.* New York: Random House, Vintage Books, 1964.

Bailey, Stephen K., and Mosher, Edith K. *ESEA: The Office of Education Administers a Law.* Syracuse, N.Y.: Syracuse University Press, 1968.

Ball, Howard; Krane, Dale; and Lauth, Thomas P. *Compromised Compliance: Implementation of the 1965 Voting Rights Act.* Westport, Conn.: Greenwood, 1982.

Baratz, Morton S. "Corporate Giants and the Power Structure." *Western Political Quarterly* 9 (June 1956): 406–415.

Bartlett, Albert A. "Forgotten Fundamentals of the Energy Crisis." *American Journal of Physics* 46 (September 1978): 876–888.

Bartlett, Robert V. "The Budgetary Process and Environmental Policy." In *Environmental Policy in the 1980s,* edited by Norman J. Vig and Michael E. Kraft, pp. 227–249. Washington, D.C.: Congressional Quarterly Press, 1984.

Bauer, Raymond A.; Pool, Ithiel de Sola; and Dexter, Lewis Anthony. *American Business and Public Policy: The Politics of Foreign Trade.* 2d ed. Chicago: Aldine-Atherton, 1972.

Baumer, Donald C., and Van Horn, Carl E. *The Politics of Unemployment.* Washington, D.C.: Congressional Quarterly Press, 1985.

Bawden, D. Lee, ed. *The Social Contract Revisited: Aims and Outcomes of President Reagan's Welfare Policy.* Washington, D.C.: Urban Institute Press, 1984.

Behrman, Bradley. "Civil Aeronautics Board." In *The Politics of Regulation,* edited by James Q. Wilson, pp. 75–120. New York: Basic Books, 1980.

Benda, Peter M., and Levine, Charles H. "Reagan and the Bureaucracy: The Bequest, the Promise, and the Legacy." In *The Reagan Legacy: Promise and Performance,* edited by Charles O. Jones, pp. 102–142. Chatham, N.J.: Chatham House, 1988.

Bentley, Arthur F. *The Process of Government: A Study of Social Pressures.* Chicago: University of Chicago Press, 1908.

Berle, Adolph A. *The 20th Century Capitalist Revolution.* New York: Harcourt, Brace, and World, 1954.

———. *Power without Property: A New Development in American Political Economy.* New York: Harcourt, Brace, and World, 1959.

Berman, Daniel M. *A Bill Becomes a Law: Congress Enacts Civil Rights Legislation.* 2d ed. rev. New York: Macmillan, 1966.

Bernstein, Marver P. *Regulating Business by Independent Commission.* Princeton, N.J.: Princeton University Press, 1955.

Berry, Jeffrey M. *Lobbying for the People: The Political Behavior of Public Interest Groups.* Princeton, N.J.: Princeton University Press, 1977.

———. *Feeding Hungry People: Rulemaking in the Food Stamp Program.* New Brunswick, N.J.: Rutgers University Press, 1984.

Birnbaum, Jeffrey H., and Murray, Alan S. *Showdown at Gucci Gulch: Lawmakers, Lobbyists, and the Unlikely Triumph of Tax Reform.* New York: Random House, 1987.

Brady, David W. *Critical Elections and Congressional Policy Making.* Stanford, Calif.: Stanford University Press, 1988.

Brady, David, and Sinclair, Barbara. "Building Majorities for Policy Change in the House of Representatives." *Journal of Politics* 46 (November 1984): 1033–1060.

Branch, Taylor. *Parting the Waters: America in the King Years, 1954–63.* New York: Simon and Schuster, 1988.

Braybrooke, David, and Lindblom, Charles E. *A Strategy of Decision: Policy Evaluation as a Social Process.* New York: Free Press of Glencoe, 1963.

Brewer, Garry D., and DeLeon, Peter. *Foundations of Policy Analysis.* Homewood, Ill.: Dorsey, 1983.

Brown, Lawrence D. *New Policies, New Politics: Government's Response to Government's Growth.* Washington, D.C.: Brookings Institution, 1983.

————. *Politics and Health Care Organization: HMOs as Federal Policy.* Washington, D.C.: Brookings Institution, 1983.

Burford, Anne M., with Greenyea, John. *Are You Tough Enough? An Insider's View of Washington Politics.* New York: McGraw-Hill, 1986.

Burke, Vincent J., and Burke, Vee. *Nixon's Good Deed: Welfare Reform.* New York: Columbia University Press, 1974.

Burns, James McGregor. *Roosevelt: Soldier of Freedom.* New York: Harcourt, Brace, Jovanovich, 1970.

Califano, Joseph A., Jr. *Governing America: An Insider's Report from the White House and the Cabinet.* New York: Simon and Schuster, 1981.

Carp, Robert A., and Rowland, C. K. *Policymaking and Politics in the Federal District Courts.* Knoxville: University of Tennessee Press, 1983.

Cater, Douglas. *Power in Washington: A Critical Look at the Struggle to Govern in the Nation's Capital.* New York: Random House, 1964.

Caudill, Harry M. *Night Comes to the Cumberlands: A Biography of a Depressed Area.* Boston: Little, Brown, 1962.

————. *My Land Is Dying.* New York: Dutton, 1971.

Chapman, Duane. *Energy Resources and Energy Corporations.* Ithaca, N.Y.: Cornell University Press, 1983.

Chubb, John E. *Interest Groups and the Bureaucracy: The Politics of Energy.* Stanford, Calif.: Stanford University Press, 1983.

Chubb, John E., and Peterson, Paul E., eds. *The New Direction in American Politics.* Washington, D.C.: Brookings Institution, 1985.

Clausen, Aage R. *How Congressmen Decide: A Policy Focus.* New York: St. Martin's, 1973.

Cobb, Roger W., and Elder, Charles W. *Participation in American Politics; Dynamics of Agenda-Building.* Baltimore: Johns Hopkins University Press, 1975.

Crandall, Robert W. *Controlling Industrial Pollution: The Economics and Politics of Clean Air.* Washington, D.C.: Brookings Institution, 1983.

Crandall, Robert W.; Gruenspecht, Howard K.; Keeler, Theodore E.; and Lave, Lester B. *Regulating the Automobile.* Washington, D.C.: Brookings Institution, 1986.

Crotty, William. *American Parties in Decline.* 2d ed. Boston: Little, Brown, 1984.

Cushman, John H., Jr. "F.A.A. Staggers Under Task of Monitoring Airline Safety." *The New York Times,* February 13, 1990, p. A1, col. 5.

Dahl, Robert A. *A Preface to Democratic Theory.* Chicago: University of Chicago Press, Phoenix Books, 1956.

————. "A Critique of the Ruling Elite Model." *American Political Science Review* 52 (June 1958): 463–469.

Davis, David Howard. *Energy Politics.* 2d ed. New York: St. Martin's, 1978.

Davies, J. Clarence. "Environmental Institutions and the Reagan Administration." In *Environmental Policy in the 1980s,* edited by Norman J. Vig and Michael E. Kraft, pp. 143–160. Washington, D.C.: Congressional Quarterly Press, 1984.

Dawson, Richard E., and Robinson, James A. "The Politics of Welfare." In *Politics in the American States,* edited by Herbert Jacob and Kenneth N. Vines, pp. 371–409. Boston: Little, Brown, 1965.

DeGrazia, Alfred. "The Myth of the President." In *Congress and the President: Allies and Adversaries,* edited by Ronald C. Moe, pp. 88–108. Pacific Palisades, Calif.: Goodyear, 1971.

Derthick, Martha. *The Influence of Federal Grants: Public Assistance in Massachusetts*. Cambridge, Mass.: Harvard University Press, 1970.

————. *Policy-Making for Social Security*. Washington, D.C.: Brookings Institution, 1979.

Derthick, Martha, and Quirk, Paul J. *The Politics of Deregulation*. Washington, D.C.: Brookings Institution, 1985.

Deutsch, Karl W. *The Nerves of Government: Models of Political Communications and Control*. New York: Free Press, 1966.

Dexter, Lewis Anthony. "Undesigned Consequences of Purposive Legislative Action: Alternatives to Implementation." *Journal of Public Policy* 1 (October 1981): 413–431.

Dommel, Paul R. *The Politics of Revenue Sharing*. Bloomington: Indiana University Press, 1974.

Downs, Anthony. *An Economic Theory of Democracy*. New York: Harper and Row, 1957.

————. *Inside Bureaucracy*. Boston: Little, Brown, 1967.

————. "Up and Down with Ecology—The Issue Attention Cycle." *The Public Interest* 28 (Summer 1972): 38–50.

Dye, Thomas R. *Politics, Economics, and the Public*. Chicago: Rand McNally, 1966.

Eads, George C., and Fix, Michael. *Relief or Reform? Reagan's Regulatory Dilemma*. Washington, D.C.: Urban Institute, 1984.

Easton, David. *A Systems Analysis of Political Life*. New York: Wiley, 1965.

Edelman, Murray. *The Symbolic Uses of Politics*. Urbana: University of Illinois Press, 1964.

Edsall, Thomas Byrne. *The New Politics of Inequality: How Political Power Shapes Economic Policy*. New York: Norton, 1984.

Eidenberg, Eugene, and Morey, Roy D. *An Act of Congress: The Legislative Process and the Making of Education Policy*. New York: Norton, 1969.

Ellsberg, Daniel. *Papers on the War*. New York: Simon and Schuster, 1972.

Engler, Robert. *The Brotherhood of Oil: Energy Policy and the Public Interest*. New York: New American Library, Mentor Books, 1977.

Epstein, Edwin M. *The Corporation in American Politics*. Englewood Cliffs, N.J.: Prentice-Hall, 1969.

Epstein, Leon D. "Electoral Decision and Policy Mandate: An Empirical Example." *Public Opinion Quarterly* 28 (Winter 1964): 564–572.

————. *Political Parties in Western Democracies*. New York: Praeger, 1967.

Finer, S. E. "The Political Power of Private Capital." Part I. *Sociological Review* 3 (December 1955): 279–294.

————. "The Political Power of Private Capital." Part II. *Sociological Review* 4 (July 1956): 5–30.

Fishel, Jeff. *Party and Opposition: Challengers in American Politics*. New York: McKay, 1973.

Fitchen, Janet M. *Poverty in Rural America: A Case Study*. Boulder, Colo.: Westview, 1981.

Freeman, J. Leiper. *The Political Process: Executive-Legislative Committee Relations*. 2d ed. New York: Random House, 1965.

Friedman, Milton. *Capitalism and Freedom*. Chicago: University of Chicago Press, 1962.

Froman, Lewis A., Jr. *The Congressional Process: Strategies, Rules, and Procedures*. Boston: Little, Brown, 1967.

Froman, Lewis A., Jr., and Ripley, Randall B. "Conditions for Party Leadership: The Case of the House Democrats." *American Political Science Review* 59 (1965): 52–63.

Gamson, William A. *Power and Discontent*. Homewood, Ill.: Dorsey, 1968.

————. *The Strategy of Social Protest*. Homewood, Ill.: Dorsey, 1975.

Garrow, David J. *Protest at Selma: Martin Luther King, Jr., and the Voting Rights Act of 1965*. New Haven, Conn.: Yale University Press, 1978.

Gelb, Joyce, and Palley, Marian Lief. *Women and Public Policies*. Revised and expanded edition. Princeton, N.J.: Princeton University Press, 1982.

Gelb, Leslie H., and Betts, Richard K. *The Irony of Vietnam: The System Worked*. Washington, D.C.: Brookings Institution, 1979.

Ginsberg, Benjamin. "Elections and Public Policy." *American Political Science Review* 70 (March 1976): 41–49.

Goodwin, Craufurd D., ed. *Energy Policy in Perspective: Today's Problems, Yesterday's Solutions*. Washington, D.C.: Brookings Institution, 1981.

Goodwin, Gilbert. *Government Policy Toward Commercial Aviation: Competition and the Regulation of Rates*. New York: King's Crown Press, 1944.

Green, Christopher. *Negative Taxes and the Poverty Problem*. Washington, D.C.: Brookings Institution, 1967.

Gross, Bertram. *The Legislative Struggle: A Study in Social Combat*. New York: McGraw-Hill, 1953.

Halperin, Morton H. *Bureaucratic Politics and Foreign Policy*. Washington, D.C.: Brookings Institution, 1974.

Harris, Richard A., and Milkis, Sidney M. *The Politics of Regulatory Change: A Tale of Two Agencies*. New York: Oxford University Press, 1989.

Harvey, Philip. *Securing the Right to Employment: Social Welfare Policy and the Unemployed in the United States*. Princeton, N.J.: Princeton University Press, 1989.

Haveman, Robert H. *The Economics of the Public Sector*. 2d ed. New York: Wiley, 1976.

Haveman, Robert H., and Margolis, Julius, eds. *Public Expenditure and Policy Analysis*. 2d ed. Chicago: Rand McNally, 1977.

Hayek, Friedrich. *The Road to Serfdom*. Chicago: University of Chicago Press, 1944.

Hayes, Michael T. "The Semi-Sovereign Pressure Groups: A Critique of Current Theory and An Alternative Typology." *Journal of Politics* 40 (February 1978): 134–161.

————. *Lobbyists and Legislators: A Theory of Political Markets*. New Brunswick, N.J.: Rutgers University Press, 1981.

————. "Interest Groups: Pluralism or Mass Society?" In *Interest Group Politics*, 1st ed., edited by Allan J. Cigler and Burdett A. Loomis, pp. 110–125. Washington, D.C.: Congressional Quarterly Press, 1983.

————. "The New Group Universe." In *Interest Group Politics*, 2d ed., edited by Allan J. Cigler and Burdett A. Loomis, pp. 133–145. Washington, D.C.: Congressional Quarterly Press, 1986.

————. "Incrementalism as Dramaturgy: The Case of the Nuclear Freeze." *Polity* 19 (Spring 1987): 443–463.

Heclo, Hugh. "Issue Networks and the Executive Establishment." In *The New American Political System*, edited by Anthony King, pp. 87–124. Washington, D.C.: American Enterprise Institute, 1978.

Hedge, David M.; Menzel, Donald C.; and Williams, George H. "Regulatory Attitudes and Behavior: The Case of Surface Mining Regulation." *Western Political Quarterly* 41 (June 1988): 323–340.

Higgs, Robert. *Crisis and Leviathan: Critical Episodes in the Growth of American Government*. New York: Oxford University Press, 1987.

Hilsman, Roger. *To Move a Nation: The Politics of Foreign Policy in the Administration of John F. Kennedy*. New York: Delta Books, 1967.

Hogwood, Brian, and Peters, B. Guy. *Policy Dynamics*. New York: St. Martin's, 1983.

Holden, Matthew, Jr. " 'Imperialism' in Bureaucracy." *American Political Science Review* 60 (December 1966): 943–951.

Horowitz, David L. *The Courts and Social Policy*. Washington, D.C.: Brookings Institution, 1977.

Hubbert, M. King. *Energy Resources*. A Report to the Committee on Natural Resources of the National Academy of Sciences and National Research Council. Washington, D.C.: National Academy of Sciences Publication 1000-D, 1962.

———. "Industrial Energy Resources." In *Nuclear Power and the Public*, edited by Harry Foreman, pp. 244–279. Garden City, N.Y.: Anchor Books, 1972.

Ingram, Helen. "Policy Implementation Through Bargaining: The Case of Federal Grants-in-Aid." *Public Policy* 25 (Fall 1977): 499–526.

Joe, Tom, and Rogers, Cheryl. *By the Few for the Few: The Reagan Welfare Legacy*. Lexington, Mass.: Lexington Books, 1985.

Jones, Charles O. "Speculative Augmentation in Federal Air Pollution Policy-Making." *Journal of Politics* 36 (May 1974): 438–464.

———. *Clean Air: The Policies and Politics of Pollution Control*. Pittsburgh: University of Pittsburgh Press, 1975.

———. *An Introduction to the Study of Public Policy*. 3d ed. Monterey, Calif.: Brooks, Cole, 1984.

———, ed. *The Reagan Legacy: Promise and Performance*. Chatham, N.J.: Chatham House, 1988.

Kalt, Joseph P. "The Costs and Benefits of Federal Regulation of Coal Strip Mining." *Natural Resources Journal* 23 (October 1983): 899–906.

Kash, Don E., and Rycroft, Robert W. "Energy Policy: How Failure Was Snatched from the Jaws of Success." Paper delivered at the 1983 annual meeting of the American Political Science Association, Chicago, Illinois, September 1–4, 1983.

Keefe, William J. *Parties, Politics, and Public Policy in America*. 4th ed. New York: Holt, Rinehart, and Winston, 1984.

Kendall, Willmoore, and Carey, George W. "The 'Intensity' Problem and Democratic Theory." *American Political Science Review* 62 (March 1968): 5–24.

Kenski, Henry C., and Kenski, Margaret Corgan. "Congress Against the President: The Struggle Over the Environment." In *Environmental Policy in the 1980s*, edited by Norman J. Vig and Michael E. Kraft, pp. 97–120. Washington, D.C.: Congressional Quarterly Press, 1984.

Key, V. O., Jr. *Southern Politics in State and Nation*. New York: Vintage Books, 1949.

Kingdon, John W. *Congressmen's Voting Decisions*. New York: Harper and Row, 1973.

———. *Agendas, Alternatives, and Public Policy*. Boston: Little, Brown, 1984.

Kotz, Nick. *Let Them Eat Promises: The Politics of Hunger in America*. Garden City, N.Y.: Anchor Books, 1971.

Kotz, Nick, and Kotz, Mary Lynn. *A Passion for Equality: George Wiley and the Movement*. New York: Norton, 1977.

Krasnow, Erwin G.; Longley, Lawrence D.; and Terry, Herbert A. *The Politics of Broadcast Regulation*. 3d ed. New York: St. Martin's, 1982.

Kuhn, Thomas S. *The Structure of Scientific Revolutions*. 2d ed. enlarged. Chicago: University of Chicago Press, 1970.

Lamb, Charles M. "Equal Housing Opportunity." In *Implementation of Civil Rights Policy*, edited by Charles S. Bullock III and Charles M. Lamb, pp. 148–183. Monterey, Calif.: Brooks/Cole, 1984.

Lampman, Robert J. "Prognosis for Poverty." *Proceedings of the 57th Annual Conference of the National Tax Association*, pp. 71–81. Pittsburgh, Pa., September 1964.

———. "Approaches to the Reduction of Poverty." *American Economic Review, Papers and Proceedings* 55 (May 1965): 521–529.

Latham, Earl. *The Group Basis of Politics: A Study of Basing-Point Legislation.* Ithaca, N.Y.: Cornell University Press, 1952.

————. "The Group Basis of Politics: Notes for a Theory." *American Political Science Review* 46 (June 1952): 376–397.

————. *The Politics of Railroad Coordination, 1933–1936.* Cambridge, Mass.: Harvard University Press, 1959.

Lave, Lester B., and Omenn, Gilbert S. *Clearing the Air: Reforming the Clean Air Act.* Washington, D.C.: Brookings Institution, 1981.

"Leadership Survey." *Washington Post,* Special Edition, July 20, 1979.

Levitan, Sar A. *The President's Agenda: Domestic Policy Choice from Kennedy to Carter.* Baltimore: Johns Hopkins University Press, 1982.

————. *Programs in Aid of the Poor.* 5th ed. Baltimore: Johns Hopkins University Press, 1985.

Light, Paul C. *Artful Work: The Politics of Social Security Reform.* New York: Random House, 1985.

Lindblom, Charles E. "The Science of 'Muddling Through.'" *Public Administration Review* 19 (Spring 1959): 79–88.

————. *The Intelligence of Democracy: Decision-Making Through Mutual Adjustment.* New York: Free Press, 1965.

————. *Politics and Markets: The World's Political-Economic Systems.* New York: Basic Books, 1977.

————. "Still Muddling, Not Yet Through." *Public Administration Review* 39 (November/December 1979): 520.

————. *The Policy-Making Process.* 2d ed. Englewood Cliffs, N.J.: Prentice-Hall, 1980.

————. "The Market as Prison." *Journal of Politics* 44 (May 1982): 324–336.

————. *Democracy and Market Systems.* Oslo: Norwegian University Press, 1988.

Lipsky, Michael. *Protest in City Politics: Rent Strikes, Housing, and the Power of the Poor.* Chicago: Rand McNally, 1970.

Lowi, Theodore J. "American Business, Public Policy, Case Studies, and Political Theory." *World Politics* 16 (July 1964): 677–715.

————. "Machine Politics—Old and New." *The Public Interest* 9 (Fall 1967): 83–92.

————. *The End of Liberalism: Ideology, Policy, and the Crisis of Public Authority.* New York: Norton, 1969.

Lustik, Ian. "Explaining the Variable Utility of Disjointed Incrementalism: Four Propositions." *American Political Science Review* 74 (June 1980): 342–353.

Lynn, Laurence E., Jr., and Whitman, David deF. *The President as Policymaker: Jimmy Carter and Welfare Reform.* Philadelphia: Temple University Press, 1981.

Marmor, Theodore R. *The Politics of Medicare.* Chicago: Aldine, 1973.

Marmor, Theodore R., and Rein, Martin. "Reforming 'The Welfare Mess': The Fate of the Family Assistance Plan, 1969–1972." In *Policy and Politics in America: Six Case Studies,* edited by Allan P. Sindler, pp. 3–28. Boston: Little, Brown, 1973.

Marx, Wesley. "Can Strip Mining Clean Up Its Act?" *Readers Digest,* March 1987, pp. 121–125.

Mayhew, David R. *Congress: The Electoral Connection.* New Haven, Conn.: Yale University Press, 1974.

McConnell, Grant. *Private Power and American Democracy.* New York: Knopf, 1966.

McFarland, Andrew S. "Recent Social Movements and Theories of Power in America." Paper delivered at the 1979 annual meeting of the American Political Science Association, Washington, D.C., August 31, 1979.

Means, Gardiner C. *The Corporate Revolution in America: Economic Reality vs. Economic Theory.* New York: Collier Books, 1964.

Melnick, R. Shep. *Regulation and the Courts: The Case of the Clean Air Act.* Washington, D.C.: Brookings Institution, 1983.

Menzel, Donald C. "Implementation of the Federal Surface Mining Control and Reclamation Act of 1977." *Public Administration Review* 41 (March/April 1981): 212–219.

———. "Redirecting the Implementation of a Law: The Reagan Administration and Coal Surface Mining Regulation." *Public Administration Review* 43 (September/October 1983): 411–420.

Merelman, Richard M. "On the Neo-Elitist Critique of Community Power." *American Political Science Review* 62 (June 1968): 451–461.

Merton, Robert K. "The Unanticipated Consequences of Purposive Social Action." *American Sociological Review* 1 (1936): 894–904.

Miliband, Ralph. *The State in Capitalist Society.* New York: Basic Books/Harper Colophon Books, 1969.

Mitchell, Robert Cameron. "Public Opinion and Environmental Politics in the 1970s and 1980s." In *Environmental Policy in the 1980s,* edited by Norman J. Vig and Michael E. Kraft, pp. 51–74. Washington, D.C.: Congressional Quarterly Press, 1984.

Moe, Terry M. *The Organization of Interests: Incentives and the Internal Dynamics of Political Interest Groups.* Chicago: University of Chicago Press, 1980.

Mosher, Frederick C. *Democracy and the Public Service.* New York: Oxford University Press, 1968.

Moynihan, Daniel P. *The Politics of a Guaranteed Income: The Nixon Administration and the Family Assistance Plan.* New York: Random House, Vintage Books, 1973.

Murphy, Jerome T. "The Education Bureaucracies Implement Novel Policy: The Politics of Title I of ESEA: 1965–1972." In *Policy and Politics in America: Six Case Studies,* edited by Allan P. Sindler, pp. 160–198. Boston: Little, Brown, 1973.

Nachmias, David, ed. *The Practice of Policy Evaluation.* New York: St. Martin's, 1980.

Nakamura, Robert T., and Smallwood, Frank. *The Politics of Policy Implementation.* New York: St. Martin's, 1980.

Nathan, Richard P. *The Administrative Presidency.* New York: Wiley, 1983.

Navarro, Peter. "The Politics of Air Pollution." *The Public Interest* 59 (Spring 1980): 36–44.

Neustadt, Richard E. *Presidential Power: The Politics of Leadership from FDR to Carter.* Rev. ed. New York: Wiley, 1980.

Noble, Kenneth R. "After 40 Years, the Silence Is Broken on a Troubled Nuclear Arms Industry." *The New York Times,* Sunday, October 16, 1988, p. E4, col. 1.

Noll, Roger G., and Owen, Bruce M. *The Political Economy of Deregulation: Interest Groups and the Regulatory Process.* Washington, D.C.: American Enterprise Institute, 1983.

Olson, Mancur, Jr. *The Logic of Collective Action: Public Goods and the Theory of Groups.* New York: Schocken Books, 1970.

———. *The Rise and Decline of Nations: Economic Growth, Stagflation, and Social Rigidities.* New Haven, Conn.: Yale University Press, 1982.

Oppenheimer, Bruce I. *Oil and the Congressional Process: The Limits of Symbolic Politics.* Lexington, Mass.: Lexington Books, 1974.

———. "Policy Effects of U.S. House Reforms: Decentralization and the Capacity to Resolve Energy Issues." In *Cases in Public Policy-Making,* 2d ed., edited by James E. Anderson, pp. 116–138. New York: Holt, Rinehart, and Winston, 1982.

Ornstein, Norman J. "The Democrats Reform Power in the House of Representatives, 1969–75." In *America in the Seventies: Problems, Policies, and Politics,* edited by Allan P. Sindler, pp. 2–48. Boston: Little, Brown, 1977.

Orren, Karen. "Standing to Sue: Interest Group Conflict in the Federal Courts." *American Political Science Review* 70 (September 1976): 723–741.

Ostrom, Vincent. *The Political Theory of a Compound Republic: A Reconstruction of the Logical Foundations of American Democracy as Presented in the Federalist.* Blacksburg, Va.: Center for the Study of Public Choice, Virginia Polytechnic Institute and State University, 1971.

Page, Benjamin, and Brody, Richard. "Policy Voting and the Electoral Process: The Vietnam War Issue." *American Political Science Review* 66 (September 1972): 979–995.

Palmer, John L., and Sawhill, Elizabeth V. *The Reagan Experiment: An Examination of the Economic and Social Policies under the Reagan Administration.* Washington, D.C.: Urban Institute, 1982.

"Partisanship in Congress Up Sharply in 1985." *Congressional Quarterly Weekly Report,* January 11, 1986, pp. 86–88.

Peltason, Jack W. *Federal Courts in the Political Process.* New York: Random House, 1954.

———. *Fifty-Eight Lonely Men: Southern Federal Judges and School Desegregation.* Urbana: University of Illinois Press, Illini Books ed., 1971.

Peterson, H. Craig. *Business and Government.* 2d ed. New York: Harper and Row, 1985.

Piven, Frances Fox, and Cloward, Richard A. *Regulating the Poor: The Functions of Public Welfare.* New York: Pantheon, 1971.

———. *Poor People's Movements: Why They Succeed, How They Fail.* New York: Pantheon, 1977.

Pizzo, Stephen; Fricker, Mary; and Muolo, Paul. *Inside Job: The Looting of America's Savings and Loans.* New York: McGraw-Hill, 1989.

Polsby, Nelson W. *Policy Innovation in America: The Politics of Policy Initiation.* New Haven, Conn.: Yale University Press, 1984.

Pomper, Gerald M. "From Confusion to Clarity: Issues and American Voters, 1956–1968." *American Political Science Review* 66 (June 1972): 415–428.

———. *Voter's Choice: Varieties of American Electoral Behavior.* New York: Dodd, Mead, 1975.

Portney, Paul R., ed. *Public Policies for Environmental Protection.* Washington, D.C.: Resources for the Future, 1990.

Pratt, Henry J. *The Gray Lobby.* Chicago: University of Chicago Press, 1976.

Quade, E. S. *Analysis for Public Decisions.* New York: American Elsevier, 1975.

Rae, Nicol C. *The Decline and Fall of the Liberal Republicans: From 1952 to the Present.* New York: Oxford University Press, 1989.

Ranney, Austin. *The Doctrine of Responsible Party Government: Its Origins and Present State.* Urbana: University of Illinois Press, 1954.

———. *Curing the Mischiefs of Faction: Party Reform in America.* Berkeley: University of California Press, 1975.

Ranney, Austin, and Kendall, Willmoore. *Democracy and the American Party System.* New York: Harcourt, Brace, 1956.

Rasnic, Carol D. "Federally Required Restoration of Surface-Mined Property: Impasse Between the Coal Industry and the Environmentally Concerned." *Natural Resources Journal* 23 (April 1983): 335–349.

Reagan, Michael D. *Regulation: The Politics of Policy.* Boston: Little, Brown, 1987.

Reagan, Michael D., and Sanzone, John G. *The New Federalism.* 2d ed. rev. New York: Oxford University Press, 1981.

Reichley, A. James. *Conservatives in an Age of Change: The Nixon and Ford Administrations.* Washington, D.C.: Brookings Institution, 1981.

———. "The Rise of National Parties." In *The New Direction in American Politics,* edited by John E. Chubb and Paul E. Peterson, pp. 175–200. Washington, D.C.: Brookings Institution, 1985.

RePass, David E. "Issue Salience and Party Choice." *American Political Science Review* 65 (June 1971): 389–400.

Richardson, Richard J., and Vines, Kenneth N. *The Politics of Federal Courts: Lower Courts in the United States.* Boston: Little, Brown, 1970.

Rieselbach, Leroy N. *The Roots of Isolationism: Congressional Voting and Presidential Leadership in Foreign Policy.* Indianapolis: Bobbs-Merrill, 1966.

———. *Congressional Reform in the Seventies.* Morristown, N.J.: General Learning Press, 1977.

Ripley, Randall B. *Majority Party Leadership in Congress.* Boston: Little, Brown, 1969.

Ripley, Randall B., and Franklin, Grace A. *Congress, the Bureaucracy, and Public Policy.* 2d ed. rev. Homewood, Ill.: Dorsey, 1976.

Roberts, Steven B., with Cohen, Gary. "Villains of the S&L Crisis." *U.S. News and World Report,* October 1, 1990, pp. 53–59.

Robertson, David B., and Judd, Dennis R. *The Development of American Public Policy: The Structure of Policy Restraint.* Glenview, Ill.: Scott, Foresman, 1989.

Rockman, Bert A. "The Style and Organization of the Reagan Presidency." In *The Reagan Legacy,* edited by Charles O. Jones, pp. 3–29. Chatham, N.J.: Chatham House, 1988.

Rodgers, Herrell R., Jr. *The Cost of Human Neglect: America's Welfare Failure.* Armonk, N.Y.: M. E. Sharpe, 1982.

Rosenbaum, Walter A. *Energy, Politics, and Public Policy.* 1st ed. Washington, D.C.: Congressional Quarterly Press, 1981.

———. *Environmental Politics and Policy.* Washington, D.C.: Congressional Quarterly Press, 1985.

———. *Energy, Politics, and Public Policy.* 2d ed. Washington, D.C.: Congressional Quarterly Press, 1987.

Ross, Robert L. "Dimensions and Patterns of Relations among Interest Groups at the Congressional Level of Government." Ph.D. dissertation, Michigan State University, 1962.

———. "Relations among National Interest Groups." *Journal of Politics* 32 (February 1970): 96–114.

Rossiter, Clinton, ed. *The Federalist Papers.* New York: New American Library, Mentor Books, 1961.

Rothstein, Robert L. "Consensual Knowledge and International Collaboration: Some Lessons from the Commodity Negotiations." *International Organization* 38 (Autumn 1984): 733–762.

Rowland, C. K., and Marz, Roger. "Gresham's Law: The Regulatory Analogy." *Policy Studies Review* 1 (February 1982): 572–580.

Russell, Louise B. *Medicare's New Hospital Payment System: Is It Working?* Washington, D.C.: Brookings Institution, 1989.

Sabato, Larry J. *PAC Power: Inside the World of Political Action Committees.* New York: Norton, 1984.

Salamon, Lester M., and Lund, Michael S., eds. *The Reagan Presidency and the Governing of America.* Washington, D.C.: Urban Institute, 1984.

Salisbury, Robert H. "An Exchange Theory of Interest Groups." *Midwest Journal of Political Science* 8 (February 1969): 1–32.

———. "Are Interest Groups Morbific Forces?" *Political Science Paper No. 56.* St. Louis, Mo.: Washington University, 1980.

———. "Interest Representation and the Dominance of Institutions." *American Political Science Review* 78 (March 1984): 64–77.

Sampson, Anthony. *The Seven Sisters: The Great Oil Companies and the World They Shaped.* New York: Viking, 1975.

Schattschneider, E. E. *Party Government.* New York: Rinehart, 1942.

————. *The Semi-Sovereign People: A Realist's View of Democracy in America.* New York: Holt, Rinehart, and Winston, 1960.

————. *Two Hundred Million Americans in Search of a Government.* New York: Holt, Rinehart, and Winston, 1969.

Scher, Richard, and Button, James. "Voting Rights Act: Implementation and Impact." In *Implementation of Civil Rights Policy,* edited by Charles S. Bullock III and Charles M. Lamb, pp. 20–54. Monterey, Calif.: Brooks/Cole, 1984.

Schlozman, Kay Lehman, and Tierney, John T. *Organized Interests and American Democracy.* New York: Harper and Row, 1986.

Schneider, Keith. "Defects in Arms Industry Minimized in Early Reagan Years." *The New York Times,* November 7, 1988, p. A1, col. 1.

Schulman, Paul R. "Nonincremental Policy-Making: Notes Toward an Alternative Paradigm." *American Political Science Review* 69 (December 1975): 1354–1370.

Shaffer, William R. *Party and Ideology in the United States Congress.* Lanham, Md.: University Press of America, 1980.

Sharkansky, Ira. *The Routines of Politics.* New York: Van Nostrand Reinhold, 1970.

Sherrill, Robert. *The Oil Follies of 1970–1980: How the Petroleum Industry Stole the Show and Much More Besides.* Garden City, N.Y.: Anchor Press/Doubleday, 1983.

Shils, Randy. *And the Band Played On: Politics, People, and the AIDS Epidemic.* New York: St. Martin's, 1987.

Shover, Neil; Clelland, Donald A.; and Lynxwiler, John. *Enforcement or Negotiation? Constructing a Regulatory Bureaucracy.* Albany: State University of New York Press, 1986.

Simon, Herbert A. *Models of Man, Social and Rational: Mathematical Essays on Rational Human Behavior in a Social Setting.* New York: Wiley, 1957.

Sinclair, Barbara Deckard. "Party Realignment and the Transformation of the Political Agenda: The House of Representatives, 1925–1938." *American Political Science Review* 71 (September 1977): 940–953.

Smeeding, Timothy. "Is the Safety Net Still Intact?" In *The Social Contract Revisited,* edited by D. Lee Bawden, pp. 69–124. Washington, D.C.: Urban Institute Press, 1984.

Steinbruner, John D. *The Cybernetic Theory of Decision: New Dimensions of Political Analysis.* Princeton, N.J.: Princeton University Press, 1974.

Steiner, Gilbert Y. *Social Insecurity: The Politics of Welfare.* Chicago: Rand McNally, 1966.

————. *The State of Welfare.* Washington, D.C.: Brookings Institution, 1971.

Stern, Philip M. *The Best Congress Money Can Buy.* New York: Pantheon, 1988.

Stigler, George J. "The Theory of Economic Regulation." *Bell Journal of Economics and Management Science* 2 (Spring 1971): 359–365.

Stiglitz, Joseph E. *Economics of the Public Sector.* New York: Norton, 1986.

Stobaugh, Robert, and Yergin, Daniel, eds. *Energy Future: Report of the Energy Project at the Harvard Business School.* 3d ed. rev. New York: Random House, Vintage Books, 1983.

Stockman, David A. *The Triumph of Politics: The Inside Story of the Reagan Revolution.* New York: Avon, 1987.

Stokes, Donald E. "Some Dynamic Elements of Contests for the Presidency." *American Political Science Review* 60 (March 1966): 19–28.

Sullivan, John L., and O'Connor, Robert E. "Electoral Choice and Popular Control of Public Policy: The Case of the 1966 House Elections." *American Political Science Review* 66 (December 1972): 1256–1268.

Sundquist, James L. "Needed: A Political Theory for the New Era of Coalition Government in the United States." *Political Science Quarterly* 103 (Winter 1988–1989): 613–635.

Tobin, Richard J. "Revising the Clean Air Act: Legislative Failure and Administrative Success."

In *Environmental Policy in the 1980s,* edited by Norman J. Vig and Michael E. Kraft, pp. 227–249. Washington, D.C.: Congressional Quarterly Press, 1984.

Truman, David B. *The Government Process: Political Interests and Public Opinion.* New York: Knopf, 1951.

Tugwell, Franklin. *The Energy Crisis and the American Political Economy: Politics and Markets in the Management of Natural Resources.* Stanford, Calif.: Stanford University Press, 1988.

Turner, Julius, and Schneier, Edward V., Jr. *Party and Constituency: Pressures on Congress.* Baltimore: Johns Hopkins University Press, 1970.

U.S. Congress, House of Representatives, Committee on Government Operations. "Surface Mining Law: A Promise Yet to Be Fulfilled." Eleventh Report, 100th Congress, 1st Session, 1987. House Report 100-183.

U.S. Department of Commerce, Bureau of the Census. "Money Income and Poverty Status of Families and Persons in the United States: 1989." *Current Population Reports, Consumer Income,* Series P-60, No. 168, September 1990.

U.S. Department of Energy, Energy Information Administration. *Historical Plant Cost and Annual Production Expenses for Selected Electric Plants, 1982.* Washington, D.C.: U.S. Government Printing Office, August 1984.

Van Horn, Carl E. "The Congressional Response to a Decade of Change." *Journal of Politics* 39 (August 1977): 624–666.

———. *Policy Implementation in the Federal System: National Goals and Local Implementors.* Lexington, Mass.: Lexington Books, 1979.

Vietor, Richard H. K. *Environmental Politics and the Coal Coalition.* College Station: Texas A & M University Press, 1980.

Vig, Norman J. "The President and the Environment: Revolution or Retreat?" In *Environmental Policy in the 1980s,* edited by Norman J. Vig and Michael K. Kraft, pp. 77–95. Washington, D.C.: Congressional Quarterly Press, 1984.

Vig, Norman J., and Kraft, Michael E. *Environmental Policy in the 1980s.* Washington, D.C.: Congressional Quarterly Press, 1984.

———, eds. *Environmental Policy in the 1990s.* Washington, D.C.: Congressional Quarterly Press, 1990.

Vogel, David. "The Power of Business in America: A Reappraisal." *British Journal of Political Science* 13 (January 1983): 19–43.

———. *Fluctuating Fortunes: The Political Power of Business in America.* New York: Basic Books, 1989.

Walker, Jack L. "Protest and Negotiation: A Case Study of Negro Leadership in Atlanta, Georgia." *Midwest Journal of Political Science* 7 (May 1963): 99–124.

———. "Setting the Agenda in the U.S. Senate: A Theory of Problem Selection." *British Journal of Political Science* 7 (October 1977): 423–445.

———. "The Origins and Maintenance of Interest Groups in America." *American Political Science Review* 77 (June 1983): 390–406.

Wattenberg, Martin P. *The Decline of American Political Parties, 1952–1980.* Cambridge, Mass.: Harvard University Press, 1984.

Weber, Max. "Essay on Bureaucracy." In *Bureaucratic Power in National Politics,* 3d ed., edited by Francis E. Rourke, pp. 85–96. Boston: Little, Brown, 1978.

Weidenbaum, Murray L. *Business, Government, and the Public.* Englewood Cliffs, N.J.: Prentice-Hall, 1977.

———. *The Future of Business Regulation: Private Action and Public Demand.* New York: American Management Association, 1979.

Weimer, David L., and Vining, Aidan R. *Policy Analysis: Concepts and Practice.* Englewood Cliffs, N.J.: Prentice-Hall, 1989.

Wengert, Norman. *Natural Resources and the Political Struggle.* Garden City, N.Y.: Doubleday, 1955.

Wenner, Lettie M. *The Environmental Decade in Court.* Bloomington: Indiana University Press, 1982.

Whalen, Charles, and Whalen, Barbara. *The Longest Debate: A Legislative History of the 1964 Civil Rights Act.* New York: New American Library, Mentor Books, 1985.

Wildavsky, Aaron B. *The Politics of the Budgetary Process.* 4th ed. Boston: Little, Brown, 1984.

Wilson, Graham K. *Business and Politics: A Comparative Introduction.* Chatham, N.J.: Chatham House, 1985.

Wilson, James Q. *Political Organizations.* New York: Basic Books, 1973.

————. "The Politics of Regulation." In *The Politics of Regulation,* edited by James Q. Wilson, pp. 357–394. New York: Basic Books, 1980.

————. *The Politics of Regulation.* New York: Basic Books, 1980.

Wilson, Woodrow. "The Study of Administration." *Political Science Quarterly* 2 (June 1887): 197–222.

Woll, Peter. *Public Policy.* Washington, D.C.: University Press of America, 1974.

Young, John A., and Newton, Jan M. *Capitalism and Human Obsolescence: Corporate Control versus Individual Survival in Rural America.* Montclair, N.J.: Allanheld, Osmun, 1980.

Zeigler, L. Harmon, and Peak, G. Wayne. *Interest Groups and American Society.* 2d ed. Englewood Cliffs, N.J.: Prentice-Hall, 1972.

Index

Abandoned Mine Land Fund, 103, 113–114
Abortion, 19, 51, 140
Acid rain, 15, 98
Adjustment of objectives to policies, 18–19, 179
Agenda-setting, 2–3; in classical model, 31–33; in corporate power model, 67–71; and focusing events, 32; in group struggle model, 50–51; in incremental model, 17–18; and political inequality, 119–120; and ready-made solutions, 32–33; and receptivity to nonincremental policy proposals, 32, 39; in responsible parties model, 81; on surface mining issue, 99–101, 118–120
Aid to Families with Dependent Children (AFDC): and AFDC-UF, 171, 178, 197–198; changing composition of beneficiaries, 170, 171, 172; consolidated with Food Stamps and SSI under Carter proposal, 188; cross-state variations, 170–171, 173, 190–191; disincentives to work, 171–172, 173; as form of negative income tax, 176, 180, 190; incentives for family breakup, 171, 173; inequities ameliorated by Food Stamps, 186; and New Federalism proposals of President Reagan, 43; sharp rise in welfare rolls in 1960s, 172,

192n; work incentive reforms of 1967, 149, 171–172, 176, 198
Air pollution: as example of conflict over problem definition, 15, 51; as example of focusing event, 32; as example of incrementalism, 5; as example of issue network, 93
Air Quality Act of 1967, 150, 152, 157
Airline deregulation: and decrementalism, 161, 167n; and diffusion of consensual knowledge, 143–144n, 145n; as exception to incremental model, 22; prospects for reregulation, 39; as pure problem of knowledge base, 142; unanticipated policy consequences, 16
Andrus, Cecil, 106
Appleby, Paul H., 42n
Attentive public, 134, 155. *See also* Policy communities

Bachrach, Peter, 68
Baratz, Morton S., 68
Bauer, Raymond A., 52
Bentley, Arthur F., 44, 46
Block grants, 38
Breakthrough policies, 147; federal role breakthroughs distinguished from rationalizing breakthroughs, 149–151